DEFINING POWER

Influence and Force
in the Contemporary
International System

DEFINING POWER

Influence and Force
in the Contemporary
International System

John M. Rothgeb, Jr.

St. Martin's Press   New York

Senior editor: Don Reisman
Managing editor: Patricia Mansfield-Phelan
Project editor: Talvi Laev
Production supervisor: Alan Fischer
Art director: Sheree Goodman
Maps: Maryland CartoGraphics, Inc.
Cover design: Jeannette Jacobs Design

76543
fedcba
For information, write: St. Martin's Press, Inc., 175 Fifth Avenue, New York, NY 10010.
ISBN: 0-312-06105-6 (paperback)
         0-312-08682-2 (clothbound)

Library of Congress Cataloging-in-Publication Data

Rothgeb, John M.
    Defining power : influence and force in the contemporary
international system / John M. Rothgeb, Jr.
         p.   cm.
    Includes bibliographical references.
    ISBN 0-312-08682-2 (clothbound), 0-312-06105-6 (paperback)
    1. International relations.   2. Balance of power.   I. Title.
JX1391.R587   1992
327—dc20   92-50035
                                                                                CIP

Published and distributed
outside North America by
THE MACMILLAN PRESS LTD
Houndmills, Basingstoke, Hampshire RG21 2XS
and London
Companies and representatives
throughout the world

ISBN 0-333-58894-0

A catalogue record for this book is available from the British Library.

Preface

Defining Power examines the use of influence and force in international politics. In doing so, it deals with power, one of the most basic concepts in political analysis. For centuries, scholars and political leaders have attempted to determine the fundamental nature of power, the resources that may be employed when wielding power, the limits associated with the use of these resources, and the appropriate standards for judging and comparing the varying approaches that differing international actors take when seeking to influence others. They have also wrestled with questions of how the exercise of power has changed over time. These are the topics that this book addresses.

This project was motivated by the need to investigate how the international system has evolved since the end of the Second World War and how the relationships among international actors have changed. As it is today, the international system is very different from the one that existed when the fighting stopped in 1945. Indeed, it can be argued that the world of 1945 can more easily be compared with the world of 1800, or perhaps even earlier eras, than with the world of the 1990s. While the international systems of each of these earlier periods share some characteristics, the alterations since 1945 have been profound. As a result, the world of the future is likely to be less and less similar to the world of the past. International values have changed, and so has the nature of international actors and the issues they dispute. When these features of the system shift, then so too does the structure of attempts to gain influence. Hence, it is necessary to examine what power is and how it may be exercised.

In this book, two types of comparisons are made wherever possible. The first is across time, with the specific focus on variations between the patterns of behavior found in past international systems and those of the post–World War II period. The second is between differing actors in the contemporary world; here the contrast is between the behavior of the members of the Western world and that of less privileged international actors. The purpose of the first type is to illustrate the nature and depth of international change, whereas the goal of the second is to show that approaches to power and conceptions of it vary greatly, depending on the actors one considers. In addition, this book discusses the complications associated with the ever-increasing role of nonstate actors.

This project is an outgrowth of the courses on international politics that I teach at Miami University. All my students and colleagues at that institution have encouraged me over the years. My chairman, Steven M. DeLue, arranged for the reduced teaching load that allowed me to write the bulk of this book, and Ryan Barilleaux assisted with the timing. Diego Abente, Walter Arnold, and Gus Jones all were kind enough to listen as I outlined my arguments, and they provided me with useful feedback. Two graduate assistants also helped: Jeff Piek was efficient in checking many of my references, and Dlynn Armstrong did an excellent job of locating the maps.

I owe debts to many others as well. Mickey East has been a model mentor and friend, and Frank Zagare was, as always, a fountain of good advice. Larry Fuell and Bret Billet discussed many of the points in this book with me on several occasions, and I benefited from their comments. Several reviewers read the manuscript and made excellent suggestions: Mark Amen, University of South Florida; Larry Elowitz, Georgia College; Vicki L. Golich, Pennsylvania State University; Jeffrey A. Hart, Indiana University; Neil S. Lewis, University of Wisconsin at Stevens Point; J. Philip Rogers, George Washington University; Philip A. Schrodt, University of Kansas; and Michael P. Sullivan, University of Arizona. Don Reisman of St. Martin's Press has been a superb editor. And last, but certainly not least, are the members of my family, who more than anyone else have helped me to understand the true nature of power.

John M. Rothgeb, Jr.

Contents

Maps

Tables

Maps

Tables

DEFINING POWER

Influence and Force
in the Contemporary
International System

1

Introduction

MILITARY DOMINANCE IN INTERNATIONAL POLITICS

In September 1945, the United States, the Union of Soviet Socialist Republics, and the United Kingdom stood at the pinnacle of international politics. They attained this lofty position because, with the assistance of the other members of the coalition that President Franklin D. Roosevelt referred to as the United Nations, they had just completed a war in which they totally defeated three of the mightiest military machines the world had ever known: Nazi Germany, fascist Italy, and militarist Japan. The struggle against these three aggressor nations was the bloodiest and costliest in world history. It brought to new heights the apparent value of military capabilities as a means of providing for national security and achieving national goals. More than anything, this war appeared to demonstrate that military strength was an essential component in the foreign policy of all countries, particularly those that aspired to play an important role in international affairs.

During the war, each of the major belligerents had placed its primary emphasis on accumulating the resources needed to fight to the finish. Whole economies were devoted to the war effort, and national armed strength reached heights never before imagined. New military tactics and weapons systems made previous systems of planning and of destruction pale by comparison. In the air, a new dimension of combat was introduced and nearly perfected as sustained aerial bombardment destroyed or crippled one city after another. At sea, ships supported by aircraft could project strength over previously unheard-of distances, and submarines could almost silently stalk and destroy enemy vessels, thereby threatening total ruin for those countries that depended on the high seas as a commercial highway.

It was in the land battles, however, that some of the most spectacular changes in warfare occurred. Combined air and armored thrusts allowed an attacking force to demoralize opponents and to sweep to breathtaking triumphs that made the spectacular achievements possible only a few years before seem primitive in comparison. The conquests of Alexander, Caesar, Napoleon, and even the Germans in 1870 and again in 1914 were dwarfed by the rapid victories of the Second World War. Given favorable developments, a country's armed forces could seize hundreds of square kilometers in a day, and could gobble up whole nations in a week. The Germans demonstrated this lightning action in their invasions of France and the Low Countries in 1940 and during action in the Soviet Union in 1941 and 1942. The Soviet and Anglo-American

1

armies displayed the same ability for speedy movement in 1944 and 1945 as they drove the Germans out of the Soviet Union and Eastern and Western Europe.

The value of military strength extended far beyond its mere application on the battlefield. Spurred by the dictates of total war and backstopped by their vast military capabilities, the major combatants unhesitatingly cajoled and even forced smaller states to conform to the political and military imperatives of the worldwide conflict. Indeed, such behavior began even before the war as one smaller country after another found its fate determined by the great powers' maneuvering for position among themselves. The spring of 1938 saw Austria absorbed by Germany while the other militarily dominant countries in Europe merely watched. Czechoslovakian territorial integrity was cruelly sacrificed at Munich in the fall of 1938 as the United Kingdom and France appeased Germany, seeking to place a diplomatic cover over their lack of military preparedness. Less than a year later, the Soviet Union and Germany brazenly divided Poland between themselves and consigned the Baltic states of Estonia, Latvia, and Lithuania to Soviet domination. At the same time, the Germans prepared the alliance framework that would give them a free hand to fight a war in Western Europe against France and Great Britain, and the Soviets sought desperately to avoid being dragged into a war against Hitler's Third Reich.

Thus did the military and security problems confronting the great powers in Europe lead them to engage in uncaring and even brutal behavior toward six much smaller countries. At the same time, the victims' lack of military capabilities left them with little choice but to yield to the strong.

This pattern of great-power behavior continued during the war years and was applied to regions as diverse as Latin America, the Middle East, and Europe. In Latin America, the United States pressured several countries to sever diplomatic relations, suspend trade, and declare war on the Axis coalition. The United States also organized an effort to isolate Argentina, labeled the "Bad Neighbor" by Secretary of State Cordell Hull, when it refused to agree to U.S. demands.[1] In the Middle East, the British seized portions of Iraq in order to ensure both their communications with India and their access to Iraqi oil.[2] Shortly after the Nazi attack on the Soviet Union in June 1941, Iran found itself occupied by the Soviets and the British as these countries tried to ensure an unfettered overland supply route for American lend-lease deliveries.[3] For its part, Saudi Arabia became the subject of intense Anglo-American negotiations regarding access to its oil fields. Interestingly, the British and the Americans tended to treat the Saudis as spectators who needed only to be informed of the decisions reached by the Western giants.[4]

It was once again in Europe, however, that great-power military might had the greatest effect. After the war, the combination of its cosmopolitan ideology and military capabilities allowed the Soviet Union to mold Eastern Europe in its own image. In the waning months of the hostilities, it imposed the Communist-dominated Lublin committee on Poland, and soon after the war ended, it sponsored Communist governments in Czechoslovakia, Hungary, Romania, Bulgaria, and East Germany. As a result, the Soviets created a security zone of subservient states that would help guard against a future resur-

Map 1. The Middle East

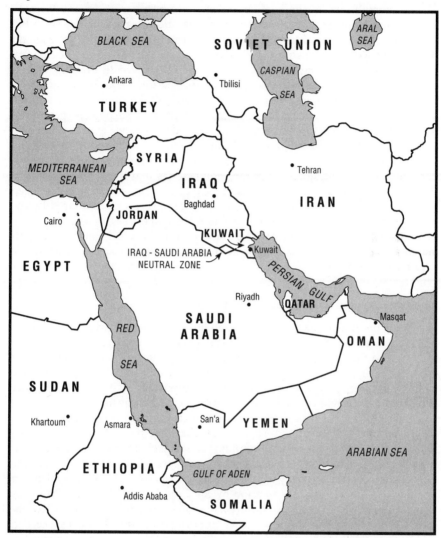

gence of the German military machine. Soviet military muscle was used to guarantee both the compliance of the new Eastern European governments with Soviet political and economic demands and the noninterference of its erstwhile allies, the United States and Great Britain, with Soviet plans.

British and American military success had similar effects in Western Europe: liberal democracies with economic systems based on free enterprise sprang up wherever Western arms were predominant. The same was true in the Far East, where U.S. military achievements resulted in the destruction of the militarist Japanese government and the installation of an American-inspired constitutional democracy.

These military dispositions would structure the post–World War II world for over forty years, as the Eastern and Western partners of the anti-German alliance became suspicious of one another's intentions; each regarded the other as insensitive to its needs to maintain its security in a potentially hostile and threatening world.[5] The result was a cold war struggle in which the military balance between the respective competitors was believed to be fundamental both to national security and to each side's international political standing.

Fueled by mutual antagonism and competition, the United States and the Soviet Union, former allies in the struggle against the Axis powers, proceeded to build the most fearsome military engines of destruction the world had ever seen. Indeed, the armed strength of the United States and the Soviet Union grew so disproportionately large when compared either with any historical counterparts or with potential contemporary competitors that the term *superpower* was coined to describe the two countries. Great as their armed forces had been at the conclusion of the Second World War, they were soon outpaced by the massive firepower that the superpowers assembled in the years of "peace" after the war. By the mid-1960s, each of these two military behemoths was estimated to have the capacity to destroy its rival totally, and quite possibly the whole world as well.

Postwar Limits to Military Strength

With these awesome military capabilities, the superpowers should have been like elephants trampling through the grass formed by the smaller countries around the globe, experiencing little difficulty in swaying the behavior of others to their own purposes.[6] But this was not always the case. Starting early in the cold war, it was hinted that the superpowers' ability to bend other countries to their will through sheer military might had its limits.

As early as 1948, just three years after their moment of supreme triumph, the Soviets were stymied by a Yugoslavian challenge to their hegemonic position within the international Communist movement. Despite Stalin's alleged remark that "I shall shake my little finger and there will be no more Tito," the Yugoslavian leader not only survived but also thrived as the symbol of an alternative to monolithic domination by the Communist leviathan.[7] Problems also developed in the 1950s, as the large, but militarily inferior, People's Republic of China refused to submit to Soviet authority. Even tiny Albania succeeded in divorcing itself from participation in the Soviet orbit of submissive satellite states.

The United States experienced similar difficulties during this period. Among other problems, it confronted situations both in Korea and during the Geneva negotiations on Indochina in which its clear military superiority was insufficient to force smaller and weaker adversaries into submitting to American terms.

These problems confronted by the superpowers were seen by many as anomalies—unusual events in a world in which military strength still played a major and, indeed, a predominant role. Thus, the United States and the Soviet Union continued to build their military prowess at a blistering pace. All the while, they adhered to the belief that such capabilities would not only ensure their security vis-à-vis one another, but would also give them political influence and guarantee their ability to affect decisively the behavior of smaller countries around the world. Starting in the 1960s and continuing into the 1980s, the superpowers more than doubled their capacity to attack any point in the world with a frightening array of nuclear weapons. During the same period, increasingly sophisticated conventional weapons were also included in their arsenals for use in such smaller brushfire wars as might break out in more remote parts of the world.

As time went on, however, it became increasingly evident that military capabilities did not provide the same degree of strength and influence that they had during the Second World War. In the mid-1960s, the United States found itself mired in a large-scale war in Southeast Asia against North Vietnam, whose population was only one tenth the size of the American population. Over a half million American troops, billions of dollars in military and economic aid, and substantial air and naval commitments were made in an attempt to save South Vietnam, the United States' ally. The violence, especially the aerial bombardment, inflicted on both North Vietnam and the National Liberation Front insurgents in South Vietnam in many ways exceeded the nonnuclear force used against the more militarily formidable Japanese during World War II.[8] But in the end, the American effort was futile, and the world's mightiest military machine was unable to defeat a militarily insignificant opponent.

Six years after the American fiasco in Vietnam ended in 1973, the Soviet Union found itself caught in a similar trap in Afghanistan. Once again, a superpower placed its prestige on the line and poured troops, money, and sophisticated weapons technology into a war against a much smaller opponent.[9] And once again, the world watched as an apparently ragtag band of guerrillas humbled the superpower. After a contest lasting nearly as long as the American debacle in Vietnam, the Soviets withdrew ignominiously from Afghanistan.

Events of the 1970s dramatically illustrated the new limits to authority derived from military muscle. Oil prices increased rapidly after the Arab members of OPEC (Organization of Petroleum Exporting Countries) imposed an oil embargo during the October War of 1973. As a result, the United States and its advanced industrialized allies in Western Europe and Japan—all of which depended heavily on oil to fuel their economies—found themselves being virtually blackmailed by a group of smaller and militarily weaker countries. Without oil, the industrialized countries faced disorder that could lead to disaster. When oil prices rose by approximately 400 percent in about three months, there was severe economic dislocation in these nations.[10]

In late 1979, Iranian revolutionaries challenged American prestige by seizing the U.S. Embassy in Tehran. Many of the occupants were held hostage for over a year as the revolutionaries sought to demonstrate their hatred for the United States.

Curiously enough, in each of these crises, the substantial military superiority of the United States and its Western allies provided virtually no advantage. In fact, many analysts judged any attempts to use the military as counterproductive in that they would only further damage Western interests.[11] One should remember that two of the most important Arab members of OPEC, Saudi Arabia and Iraq, were among the countries that the United Kingdom and the

United States had so little trouble coercing just thirty years earlier during the Second World War. One also might recall that Iran was easily forced to toe the line during the same period. Now, three decades later, far stronger American military forces could only stand by impotently while their country was humiliated and the health of its economy was threatened.[12]

Other, more commonplace, trends have also been at work. An increase in the volume of international commerce has created interdependent relationships, particularly among Western nations, that closely tie their economic and political systems to one another. As a result, new foreign policy orientations and goals have begun to emerge, and new forms of competition and conflict have appeared, that are not especially amenable to solutions from the barrels of guns or through other forms of international violence. For what might be the first time in history, most leaders of the Western advanced industrialized countries recognize that military-based threats might actually be counterproductive as a diplomatic technique.

POWER IN A CHANGING INTERNATIONAL ARENA

As we have just seen, international politics has changed over the past five decades. Until the postwar era, many scholars regarded the international system as stable because its basic nature involved a game of competition played out by interacting independent entities. Within this framework, each actor had to safeguard its own interests and usually was suspicious of any arrangement that would possibly infringe on its pursuit of an autonomously determined set of foreign and domestic goals. For centuries, this was the basic structure of international politics, and most analysts regarded it as very unlikely to change. As Robert Gilpin puts it:

> The fundamental nature of international relations has not changed over the millenia. International relations continue to be a recurring struggle for wealth and power among independent actors living in a state of anarchy. The classic history of Thucydides is as meaningful a guide to the behavior of states today as when it was written in the fifth century B.C.[13]

Given the competitive and anarchic nature of international politics, a country's ability to bend others to its will—that is, to exercise power—was always essential to its self-preservation and to the attainment of its international objectives. Thus, because countries frequently pursued clashing interests, conflict among them resulted. This conflict constituted the essence of international politics, and the relative power relationships among international actors were treated as the focal point for the study of international relations. In fact, the late Hans Morgenthau, one of the most respected scholars in the field of international relations, argues that "international politics is of necessity power politics."[14] This view has been echoed by another author, who said more recently that "there is really only one approach which enables students to appreciate the essence of the field [of international politics]. The approach, for want of better terminology, is power politics."[15]

Power has been a central concern for a wide range of international theorists. These include theorists who regard international politics as a struggle among nations that seek to dominate one another, idealists who seek to influence others to aid in the construction of a new world order based on a firm moral foundation, and analysts who conceptualize the commercial relations among states as the true stuff of international relations.[16] In each case, an important part of getting what one wants involves manipulating the behavior of others, which is what the exercise of power is all about.

The Role of the Military

In investigating the function of power in international politics, the comparative military capability of differing nations traditionally has been an important area for study. This is due to the special role that war has all too frequently played in the international arena. Joseph Nye recognizes this role when he notes that for most analysts "war has been the ultimate indicator of national military strength."[17] Harold and Margaret Sprout agree that "power . . . has been seen historically in military terms and most specifically as a state's 'war-making ability',"[18] and E. H. Carr says that "potential war being thus a dominant factor in international politics, military strength becomes a recognized standard of political values."[19]

In this kind of international climate, when two or more countries had incompatible goals about which their governments and people felt strongly, the military resources of the contenders would often determine the winner and loser. While actual fighting usually did not occur, the threat to fight or the fact that a state possessed a particular array of military strength figured prominently in international negotiations. In international politics, "the power to hurt—the sheer unacquisitive, unproductive power to destroy things that somebody treasures, to inflict pain and grief—is a kind of bargaining power."[20] A country's military capabilities, combined with the perception that it was willing to use them, was a vital backstop to the various diplomatic, political, economic, and other techniques that it might employ in conducting its foreign relations.

As one scholar notes, "historically, military power has tended to be superior . . . to other forms of power. Ever since the world became politically organized in terms of independent states, each claiming military sovereignty, force has been regarded as the ultimate arbiter in the settlement of conflicts."[21] Another analyst makes the same point when he writes that "the supreme importance of the military instrument lies in the fact that the ultima ratio of power in international relations is war. Every act of the state, in its power aspect, is directed to war, not as a desirable weapon, but as a weapon which it may require in the last resort to use."[22] In fact, so dominant has been the role assigned to military power that many scholars have treated other national characteristics—such as population, political organization, geographical position and topography, endowment of natural resources, and economic capacity—almost solely in terms of how they contribute to the state's ability to wage war successfully.[23]

Diplomats and world leaders also saw the importance of the military. Shortly after Hitler came to power in Germany in 1933, Winston Churchill proclaimed, "Thank God for the French Army," before the House of Commons. Churchill believed that that army would be the final guarantee of British and European safety in the face of the steadily growing German menace.[24] Cordell Hull, former United States secretary of state, expressed his appreciation of the value of the military to diplomacy by noting:

> When I came to the State Department I thought for a time, when talking to Axis diplomats, that they were looking me in the eye; but I soon discovered that they were looking over my shoulder at our armed forces and appraising our strength. Here, I came to feel, was the controlling factor in their acts and utterances toward us.[25]

From antiquity until the middle of the twentieth century, international politics could accurately be described as being dominated by the great military powers.[26] Such nations set the rules for the international political game; they determined the nature of international political discourse; they defined the structure of the international arena; they had the capacity to settle disputes with and among smaller states on terms the larger states found acceptable; and they controlled the resolution of all questions pertaining to distributing international resources, especially those resources that they defined as important. Relative military capability also defined the pecking order among the largest countries and was an important means for resolving major disputes, as the bloody history of international wars indicates. In fact, "recognition as a great power [was] normally the reward of fighting a large-scale war."[27] And "any symptom of military inefficiency or unpreparedness in a great power [was] promptly reflected in its political status."[28]

The Changing Nature of Power Resources

As has been indicated, trends at work for over four decades have increasingly forced serious analysts to examine the traditional predominance assigned to military capabilities in international politics. In addition, the rise to international prominence of such nonmilitary powers as Japan and Germany, the collapse of the Soviet Union as a superpower, the liberation of Eastern Europe, the unification movement in the European Community, and the growing strength of the newly industrializing countries in the Pacific Basin all call the value of the military into question. Many other developments could also be cited to show that rapid change is afoot. Indeed, in recent years, the pace of events has so quickened that some analysts have speculated that an international revolution may be under way. They see the rules of the international political game shifting so suddenly and dramatically that they believe that the basic stability of the international arena that Gilpin described may be a thing of the past.[29]

Essentially, such analysts contend that wars are so dysfunctional that they have become obsolete and that military strength no longer has much applicability in the international arena.[30] Analysts adopting this viewpoint usually cite as evidence the absence of warfare since 1945 and the increased economic interdependence among the advanced industrialized countries.[31]

These beliefs, which are far from universally accepted, are challenged on several grounds. For one thing, as Kenneth Waltz notes, "the structure of international politics has not been transformed; it remains anarchic in form."[32] That is, no international political community has emerged to provide a form of supranational organization to replace the nation-state. Foreign policy and international politics still are conducted within the same basic decentralized international framework that has existed for centuries. In addition, as Michael Sullivan points out, international wars have been fought no less frequently since 1945 than during other eras.[33] Finally, many argue that the military remains an essential instrument of power in international relations because it both provides the much needed security shield behind which international commerce can be conducted with confidence and serves as the ultimate guarantee of a nation's safety.[34]

The basic thesis advanced herein is a synthesis of these divergent views regarding international changes. It will be argued that, although the international system remains anarchic and is dominated by the interactions of independent states, the degrees and types of conflicts among nations, the types of issues that structure relations among states, the goals that states pursue, and the resources used to pursue those goals and to exercise power in international politics all have changed or are in the process of changing. This thesis fundamentally agrees with Geoffrey Blainey's contention that it is "unwise to regard international relations since 1945 as an old game obeying completely new rules. It is a slightly different game obeying the same rules."[35] In other words, the structure of the game remains the same, but the interactions, the nature of the competition, and the reasons for conflict within the game have all shifted.

As will be illustrated later, the sum of the effects of these changes may now appear revolutionary, but the changes themselves have been evolving since the end of the Second World War. Until recently, these shifts have been obscured in part by the military and political competition between the superpowers that formed the basis of the cold war. The end of that conflict, however, is at long last permitting analysts to devote their full attention to the new international circumstances and their implications for the conduct of international politics as the world moves toward the twenty-first century.

It will be argued here that (1) international politics remains highly competitive and conflictual and that (2) international actors will continue to pursue divergent international objectives and will seek to protect their interests by trying to manipulate the behavior of others. That is, the exercise of power will remain important. In fact, it is maintained here that understanding power and how it is exercised is vital to comprehending international politics and to analyzing it properly. However, two key changes relating directly to power have occurred. One concerns how countries define their goals and vital interests, and the other, how resources are most appropriately used to exercise power. There is a third important change: parallel international universes have evolved which interact with one another, but appear to operate according to different rules and involve very different casts of characters.

Goals and Issues.   With regard to the first development—the goals countries are interested in and the issues they deem vital—many scholars have noted that nations have traditionally focused their foreign policies on achieving military and territorial security.[36] A variety of new goals and issues that have emerged, however, lead to new definitions of what security means. It is no longer accurate to depict nonmilitary issues in the following terms: "When states cooperate with one another to maintain postal or transport services, or to prevent the spread of epidemics or suppress the traffic in drugs, these activities are described as 'non-political' or 'technical.' "[37] While such a description may have been accurate when it was written in 1939, it is no longer applicable to the international scene. Forty years ago, epidemics and drug trafficking, no matter how tragic, may have been seen as nonpolitical, and consequently as not involving the exercise of power when negotiations between nations took place. Today matters are quite different. In recent years, public opinion polls have consistently indicated that the American public (for one) regards such things as the AIDS epidemic and drug trafficking as major issues, both domestically and internationally. In fact, by the late 1980s Americans were more concerned with economic threats to the United States' international prestige than they were with military challenges.[38]

The emergence of new issues does not mean that power no longer plays the role it once did, for it does. Whatever the issue, states still need to obtain the cooperation of others if they are to get what they want. But, instead of constantly going head to head over military-security matters, they compete vigorously with one another in different arenas, seeking to manipulate one another in an attempt to obtain concessions that will prove beneficial.[39] Countries have not suddenly become altruistic as the world has changed, nor are they likely to fade away or to lose their dominant role in the international arena. They remain much as they were. The most important difference is what they argue over—and why. And power remains basic to the understanding of the international system precisely because one can expect international conflict to continue, whatever the issue in dispute may be.

Resources.   This brings us to the question of resources. When issues change, then so too must the means for attacking problems. A definition of national interests that centered on protecting and controlling territory, people, and natural resources meant that the military was absolutely important to the exercise of power. As attention has shifted, so has the focus on resources for exercising power and influence. When a country wishes to induce another to change its economic policy in order to secure greater access to markets or to obtain more investment, economic instruments are more appropriate than military force. The same is true for fighting pollution, epidemics, and drugs. And, as mentioned previously, these very issues increasingly count in international politics. Thus, the military has been consigned to an ever-smaller role in the contemporary world.

This does not mean, however, that the military no longer has any role at all, or that war is a thing of the past, as some would have it. The Persian Gulf War illustrates the continuing necessity of military forces. While the role for the military is getting smaller and the role for economics and politics in modern diplomacy larger, the military remains vital. For one thing, there are simply too many heavily armed countries in this world to do away with the protection that the military affords. Accidents and miscalculations are still possible. For another, wars do continue to occur in some parts of the world, and military establishments are vital to national security, both for those states that are directly

This examination copy of

Defining Power
Influence and Force in the Contemporary International System
by JOHN M. ROTHGEB, JR.

is sent to you with the compliments of
your St. Martin's Press representative.

Your comments on our books help us estimate printing requirements, assist us in preparing revisions, and guide us in shaping future books to your needs. Will you please take a moment to fill out and return this postpaid card?

☐ you may quote me for advertising purposes
☐ I have adopted this book for _____ semester, 19 _____ .
☐ I am seriously considering it.

Date _____

Comments

Name _____ Department _____
School _____ Phone Number ( ) _____
City _____ State _____ Zip _____

Course Title _____ Enrollment _____
Present Text _____
Do you plan to change texts this year? Yes ☐   No ☐   When is your decision due? _____
Is your text decision   individual ☐   committee ☐   department ☐
If committee or department, please list others involved _____

BUSINESS REPLY MAIL

FIRST CLASS   PERMIT NO. 1147   NEW YORK, NY

POSTAGE WILL BE PAID BY

College Department
ST. MARTIN'S PRESS, INC.
175 FIFTH AVENUE
NEW YORK, N.Y. 10010

involved and for those that rely on the belligerents. Beyond this, one should never discount the important international traditions surrounding the armed forces as symbols of national unity and purpose. For these reasons, the military will continue to figure in international calculations. But a time may be coming, if it has not already arrived, when military resources will play almost no part in defining the relations between selected members of the international system.

Parallel International Universes. When we speak of international change, we must do more than talk about shifting issues and resources. By nature, change is almost always uneven, affecting some actors one way, others another way, and still others almost not at all. Thus, it is important to specify who is affected by change and how. This brings us to the third point mentioned earlier, the evolution of parallel international universes in which differing countries have very different patterns and qualities of interactions with one another. As Nye states, "the games of world politics are being played by different actors with different piles of chips at different card tables."[40]

Describing the world as groupings of different types of countries is not new. Until recently, many authors have discussed the post–World War II international system as being composed of three or more "worlds," with a state's level of economic development, ideological predispositions, and political and military alliance orientations serving as the key characteristics for differentiating one world from another.[41] This scheme was popularized by the cold war conflict between the East and the West, which created two "natural" political-military groupings of countries and a third noninvolved, or nonaligned, group. The concurrent differences between developed and developing states reinforced these distinctions by drawing attention to the vast variations that existed in such factors as levels of wealth and industrialization, types of cultural and religious practices, and histories of international imperialism and domination. The present concept of parallel international universes draws on and extends these earlier discussions. As just noted, the previous treatments of differing "worlds" focused on a state's development, ideology, and political-military alignments. The current discussion, however, is concerned with the basic conduct found within and between groups of states.

The decreased importance of the military as a determinant of the relations between some countries is a good place to start the discussion of these differences in conduct. Within the current international system has emerged a grouping of states that have become exceptionally reliant on one another and that at the same time no longer pose any military-security threat to each other. It is interesting that this situation exists among countries that generally are regarded, both individually and collectively, as the most powerful in the world, in both an economic and a military sense. In the past, militarily powerful states perceived one another as threats, thus producing considerable tension and even occasional outbreaks of war. At present, however, it is inconceivable that the advanced industrialized countries in Europe, North America, and East Asia would ever turn to military force, or that they would even hint at the use of such force, in order to settle any disputes among themselves. The very countries that fought to the finish in a total war just fifty years ago have now set the military aside, probably forever, as an instrument of statecraft.

The absence of mutual security threats and military conflicts with one another is not the only thing that sets these countries apart. They also possess the world's most advanced economies, and as a group they have the world's highest standards of living. In addition, they have deeply committed themselves to international commerce, and to this end they have created and currently manage the primary international economic and commercial organizations. Beyond this, their societies and their economies are extensively tied to one another through various transnational linkages, and their governments engage in substantial collaborative efforts to coordinate policy. Of course, this does not mean that these countries do not have conflicts with one another, for they do. However, while they do engage in competition, their relations with each other are of a different order of magnitude from those that they have with other countries or that other countries have among themselves.

In addition to this category of immensely privileged states, we have a second category that is far more amorphous and diverse. The members of this collection of societies include (1) the very poorest countries of the world, (2) newly industrializing middle-income countries, (3) nations made wealthy because they are blessed by natural resources that are in great demand internationally, and (4) Communist and ex-Communist states.

One characteristic of these countries is the degree to which they continue, both internally and externally, to exhibit militarily based violence. Domestically, the use of force is found in military coups d'état undertaken to change governments and in insurgency movements designed to promote revolutions. Internationally, one finds that the only wars fought in the last four decades have involved these countries.[42] It is interesting that the advanced industrialized countries that comprise the first group of nations apparently have forsaken war among themselves but continue to engage in combat against opponents from the second category.

Another characteristic of these countries is the degree to which so many of them were dominated by stronger states in the past and, in some cases, continue to be dominated at present. In the past, control by others was a result of the predominantly military supremacy of the European imperialist powers in Latin America, Africa, and Asia, and of the Soviet Union in Eastern Europe. At present, domination comes in the form of the ability of outside forces to control, at least in part, the access of these states to key international economic resources and to control as well some of the most important economic management functions within these states.

Yet another characteristic of these countries is their pattern of international interactions. For the most part, these nations have far fewer diplomatic, political, and economic contacts with one another than with the advanced industrialized states. As a result, this has profoundly affected their ability to solve some of their most pressing problems on their own.[43]

The changing nature of the resources used by at least some actors in the international arena and the emergence of new issues and radically different categories of countries have implications for the operation of the international system. These developments may be expected to have important and even profound effects on how power is conceptualized and exercised in international politics.

ORGANIZATION OF THE BOOK

In this work the guiding principle for analyzing the ongoing changes in the contemporary international system revolves around an examination of the concept of power. Power serves as the primary focus because a great number of analysts have long regarded it as fundamentally important in international politics. Given its presumed central role in interactions among nations and in management of the international arena, it might well serve as one of the best starting places for inquiring into the evolution of change in international politics.

In examining power, the discussion considers several points. The first is how international political theorists define power. This subject is tackled in Chapter 2. As will be seen, while opinions vary among scholars as to what power is, there is a substantial consensus that regards power in behavioral and relational terms and links it to conflict. Power does not exist in a vacuum; rather, it requires both interaction among countries and a degree of conflict. Power also is sometimes viewed as a form of international political currency that nations use to acquire outcomes and to achieve their foreign policy goals. These subjects, together with several other definitional questions, are explored in some depth in this chapter.

In Chapter 3, attention turns to the context in which power is exercised— the international system. The chapter begins with a discussion of the structural characteristics that scholars typically attribute to the international arena. The nature of anarchy and of politics within an anarchic framework are discussed, as are the security and other problems that states confront. Historic examples illustrate these points. The chapter then turns its attention to the world since 1945 to consider how parallel international universes evolved and how they operate differently from one another at the present time. Data pertaining to the levels of trade, the incidence of involvement in international wars, the frequency of civil wars, and the use of economic sanctions demonstrate the wide variations found in the contemporary international arena between the behavior of advanced industrialized countries and that of other actors. A key assumption in this chapter is that one cannot understand power in international politics unless one understands the international social system in which it is exercised.

Chapter 4 examines the exercise of power and the resources it requires. Historically, the resources used to exercise power have been grouped into two categories—those that rely on coercion and those that are based on some form of persuasion. More recently, analysts have discussed the use of exchange-based techniques involving a payoff of some type as a third method for gaining influence in the international system. Each of these approaches to wielding power is examined in this chapter. Next, attention turns to the relative efficacy of each approach and to the criteria that may be used for investigating their effectiveness, their relative applicability in the parallel international systems found in the contemporary world, the conditions under which they are best employed, and the inherent problems associated with their use. Among other examples, the differing roles of the United States and the Soviet Union in post– World War II Europe and the recent reactions to these roles will serve as illustrations.

Chapter 5 takes a closer look at the most often discussed method of exercising power in the international arena—coercion. While this technique is described in some theoretical detail in Chapter 4, the analysis in this chapter focuses on the specific tactics that international actors typically use when seeking to coerce one another and on how effective these tactics are. Both military and economic coercion are examined. In investigating the use of force, three general tactics—defense, compellence, and deterrence—are considered. Each tactic is defined and examined to determine its effectiveness in accomplishing a nation's purposes in the contemporary world. Attention centers on both military and economic resources and on how they might be employed when using these tactics. The chapter also addresses the question of what specific circumstances must be present in order for each tactic to have the desired effect and how likely it is that these conditions will be present in any given international configuration. In addition, the discussion deals with the tendency for these tactics to boomerang, thereby hurting the initiator as well as the target of the coercion attempt. The applicability of each of these instruments of coercion in the parallel international systems described in Chapter 3 is considered throughout this chapter.

The final chapter summarizes the basic points made in the book and considers what we can say about the exercise of power in international politics as we approach the next century. A key part of this chapter, and of earlier chapters as well, is to draw historical comparisons between power in the contemporary world and in worlds of the past. Only through such comparisons can we appreciate the essence of what is currently happening in the international system.

Notes

1. Cordell Hull, *The Memoirs of Cordell Hull*, vol. 2 (New York: Macmillan, 1948), chap. 99.

2. Peter Calvocoressi and Guy Wint, *Total War* (New York: Penguin Books, 1979), 162.

3. Winston S. Churchill, *The Grand Alliance*, vol. 3 of *The Second World War* (New York: Bantam Books, 1977), 402–22; Calvocoressi and Wint, 164.

4. Hull, *Memoirs*, chap. 110.

5. For discussions of the origins of the cold war, one should consult A. W. DePorte, *Europe between the Super-Powers* (New Haven, Conn.: Yale University Press, 1979); John Lewis Gaddis, *The United States and the Origins of the Cold War, 1941–1947* (New York: Columbia University Press, 1972); Louis J. Halle, *The Cold War as History* (New York: Harper and Row, 1967); and Vojtech Mastny, *Russia's Road to the Cold War: Diplomacy, Warfare, and the Politics of Communism, 1941–1945* (New York: Columbia University Press, 1979).

6. This analogy is taken from Cecil Crabb, *The Elephants and the Grass* (New York: Praeger, 1965).

7. This quote is found in Nikita Khrushchev, *Khrushchev Remembers* (New York: Bantam Books, 1971), 411. The validity of the quote is questioned in Adam B. Ulam, *Expansion and Coexistence: Soviet Foreign Policy, 1917–73* (New York: Praeger, 1974), 469.

8. Lloyd C. Gardner, "Old Wine in New Bottles: How the Cold War Became the Long Peace," in *The Long Postwar Peace: Contending Explanations and Projections*, ed. Charles W. Kegley, Jr. (New York: HarperCollins, 1991), 144.

9. At 13 million people in 1979, Afghanistan's population was only 5 percent of the Soviet

population of 262 million. To fully grasp the disparity in strength, one must realize that the Soviets fought against guerrillas that represented only a portion of the Afghanistani people.

10. This figure is based on data from David H. Blake and Robert S. Walters, *The Politics of Global Economic Relations* (Englewood Cliffs, N.J.: Prentice-Hall, 1987), 182; and from Joan Edelman Spero, *The Politics of International Economic Relations* (New York: St. Martin's, 1981), 257.

11. For a discussion of the problems associated with the possible use of force during the oil embargo, see Henry Kissinger, *Years of Upheaval* (Boston: Little, Brown, 1982), 877–80. The potential difficulties relating to employing force during the hostage crisis are discussed in Jimmy Carter, *Keeping Faith: Memoirs of a President* (New York: Bantam Books, 1982), 459.

12. Even the Gulf War in 1990–91 between the United Nations coalition and Iraq shows how ineffective military threats have become, for the Iraqis failed to shrink before the threat of war, though it came from a collection of countries with an overwhelming preponderance of military capabilities.

13. Robert Gilpin, *War and Change in World Politics* (New York: Cambridge University Press, 1981), 7.

14. Hans J. Morgenthau, *Politics among Nations: The Struggle for Power and Peace* (New York: Alfred A. Knopf, 1948), 33.

15. Colin S. Gray, *The Geopolitics of the Nuclear Era: Heartland, Rimlands, and the Technological Revolution* (New York: Crane, Russak, 1977), 2.

16. These varying theoretical viewpoints have been analyzed by a number of scholars. One of the earliest of these efforts is the distinction E. H. Carr makes between realists and idealists in his *The Twenty Years Crisis, 1919–1939* (New York: St. Martin's, 1939). Another is found in Hedley Bull, *The Anarchical Society* (New York: Columbia University Press, 1977). Finally, Joseph M. Grieco has produced an excellent comparison between what he refers to as realist and neoliberal theorists in *Cooperation among Nations: Europe, America, and Non-Tariff Barriers to Trade* (Ithaca, N.Y.: Cornell University Press, 1990).

17. Joseph S. Nye, Jr., *Bound to Lead: The Changing Nature of American Power* (New York: Basic Books, 1990), 78.

18. Harold Sprout and Margaret Sprout, *Toward a Politics of the Planet Earth* (New York: D. Van Nostrand, 1971), 165.

19. Carr, *The Twenty Years Crisis,* 109.

20. Thomas C. Schelling, *Arms and Influence* (New Haven, Conn.: Yale University Press, 1966), v.

21. Klaus Knorr, *The Power of Nations: The Political Economy of International Relations* (New York: Basic Books, 1975), 19.

22. Carr, *The Twenty Years Crisis,* 109.

23. One of the earliest of these discussions is found in Frederick L. Schuman, *International Politics: The Western State System in Transition* (New York: McGraw-Hill, 1941), 291–95. Others include Morgenthau, *Politics among Nations,* chap. 9; Vernon Van Dyke, *International Politics* (New York: Appleton-Century-Crofts, 1966), chap. 11; A. F. K. Organski, *World Politics* (New York: Alfred A. Knopf, 1968), chaps. 7 and 8; and John Spanier, *Games Nations Play* (Washington, D.C.: Congressional Quarterly Press, 1987), chap. 7.

24. Winston S. Churchill, *The Gathering Storm,* vol. 1 of *The Second World War* (Boston: Houghton Mifflin, 1948), 68.

25. Hull, *Memoirs,* 457.

26. Even those who have studied the foreign policy of smaller states have recognized the degree to which great powers have controlled the international scene. One example is Maurice A. East, "Size and Foreign Policy Behavior: A Test of Two Models," *World Politics* 25, no. 4 (July 1973): 556–76. Another is Robert Rothstein, *Alliances and Small Powers* (New York: Columbia University Press, 1968).

27. Carr, *The Twenty Years Crisis,* 109.

28. Carr, *The Twenty Years Crisis,* 110.

29. Examples of authors who discuss such rapid change are Carl Kaysen, "Is War Obsolete? A Review Essay," *International Security* 14, no. 4 (Spring 1990): 42–64; John Mueller, *Retreat from Doomsday: The Obsolescence of Major War* (New York: Basic Books, 1989); James Lee Ray, "The Abolition of Slavery and the End of International War," *International Organization* 43, no. 3 (Summer 1989): 405–39; and Richard Rosecrance, *The Rise of the Trading State: Commerce and Conquest in the Modern World* (New York: Basic Books, 1986).

30. See Mueller, *Retreat from Doomsday,* for a particularly compelling discussion of this subject.

31. See Mueller, *Retreat from Doomsday.* An excellent source describing the incidence of international war since 1945 is found in J. David Singer, "Peace in the Global System: Displacement, Interregnum, or Transformation?" in *The Long Postwar Peace: Contending Explanations and Projections,* ed. Charles W. Kegley, Jr. (New York: HarperCollins, 1991), 56–84.

32. Kenneth N. Waltz, "The Origins of War in Neorealist Theory," *Journal of Interdisciplinary History* 18, no. 4 (Spring 1988): 615–28.

33. Michael P. Sullivan, *Power in Contemporary International Politics* (Columbia: University of South Carolina Press, 1990), 52–53.

34. See Robert Gilpin, *U.S. Power and the Multinational Corporation* (New York: Basic Books, 1975); and Nye, *Bound to Lead,* 31.

35. Geoffrey Blainey, *The Causes of War* (New York: Free Press, 1988), 121.

36. For example, see Wolfram F. Hanrieder, "Dissolving International Politics: Reflections on the Nation-State," *American Political Science Review* 72, no. 4 (December 1978): 1276–87; and Rosecrance, *Rise of the Trading State.*

37. Carr, *The Twenty Years Crisis,* 102.

38. Nye, *Bound to Lead,* 141.

39. The degree to which trade negotiations reflect conflict and competition as states seek to protect their interests is described in Joseph M. Grieco, *Cooperation among Nations.*

40. Nye, *Bound to Lead,* 182.

41. One of the earliest discussions of the notion that the international arena was divided into three "worlds" is found in Irving Louis Horowitz, *The Three Worlds of Development: The Theory and Practice of International Stratification* (New York: Oxford University Press, 1966). Another is presented in Lawrence W. Martin, ed., *Neutralism and Nonalignment* (New York: Praeger, 1962).

42. Singer, "Peace in the Global System," 60–75.

43. The diplomatic, political, and economic interactions of the states in this category are described in Herb Addo, "The Structural Basis of International Communication," *Papers of the Peace Science Society* 23 (1974): 81–100; and in Johan Galtung, "A Structural Theory of Imperialism," *Journal of Peace Research* 8, no. 2 (1971): 81–117.

2

Defining Power

This chapter elaborates on the defining characteristics of power in international politics. It begins with a consideration of what power is and how it is related to politics. Attention centers on the extent to which power may be defined (1) as a goal of foreign policy, (2) as the control of physical and/or political resources, or (3) as the ability to control others and/or to manipulate one's environment as well as the outcomes associated with the events occurring within that environment. Consideration is given to the advantages and disadvantages of using each of these conceptions of power, and to why most analysts employ a control-oriented definition.

The next section takes a look at the nature of the actors in the international arena. When power is defined as controlling others, it is important to consider who and what is controlled. Both sovereign and nonsovereign actors are discussed.

Next, the discussion turns to some of the basic implications of defining power as the ability to control others. As we will see, power is found only when members of the international system interact with one another. Accordingly, power involves conflict and is intimately related to how international actors perceive one another. Why power is often surrounded by such a high degree of controversy is also discussed.

The next section considers the context within which power is exercised. Context is a key to limiting power. All power is exercised within a particular social setting; therefore, when the setting changes, so does the exercise of power. This social setting may be defined by answering the question, "who is trying to get whom to do what?"[1] That is, the identity of the countries involved in the power relationship and the issues they are arguing about are vital to a comprehension of what is going on and to the outcome one can expect. Finally, the efficacy of the resources employed in any attempt to wield power is tied closely to the context in which the attempt is made. Power resources are not infinitely fungible, which "means that specifying the context is increasingly important in estimating the actual power that can be derived from power resources."[2]

In examining each of these issues, consideration is given to the costs and uncertainty associated with exercising power. Costs and uncertainty come in several forms. One is derived from the absence of a capacity to predict success with confidence. Another is associated with the reactions of one's opponent(s) to any attempt to exert influence. A third is a product of the inability to gauge fully the degree to which one may have to consume one's own resources, both

17

physical and political, in order to succeed in the exercise of power. Finally, one can never be sure about how other members of the international system may react to one's attempt to use power.

Before proceeding with the chapter, it may be useful to clarify some basic terminology. In the discussion that follows, an *actor* is defined as the entity (usually a nation-state) that seeks to exercise power, and a *target* is the entity (again, usually a nation-state) that is the object of the attempt to exercise power. In addition, throughout this work the terms *power, control,* and *influence* are used interchangeably.[3] Some analysts, such as Arnold Wolfers, disagree with this approach:

> It is appropriate . . . to distinguish between power and influence, the first to mean the ability to move others by the threat or infliction of deprivations, the latter to mean the ability to do so through promises or grants of benefits.[4]

As we will see here and in later chapters, the key to power resides in the ability to control others and to manipulate one's environment. The resources used to accomplish this control should not in any way be regarded as determining when power has or has not been exercised. Moreover, using threats and deprivation generally is associated with employing military force, which, as Chapter 1 discussed, is found less and less often in the interactions between at least some members of the contemporary international arena. Thus, tying one's use of the term *power* to such a restriction would potentially render the concept ever less applicable to the current international arena. As a result, the reader should realize from the beginning that the conception of power used in this book does not necessarily require the employment of force.

DEFINITIONAL AMBIGUITY

As we noted in Chapter 1, many scholars and world leaders consider power to be one of the central concepts in the analysis of international politics. Indeed, Harold Lasswell and Abraham Kaplan go one step further, maintaining that "the concept of power is perhaps the most fundamental in the whole of political science."[5] E. H. Carr agrees, noting that "power is an indispensable instrument of government."[6] With regard to the indispensability of power to governments and to political analysis, David Baldwin argues that an intimate relationship exists between a government's strength and its policy options, whether domestic or international.[7] Klaus Knorr sums up the essence of Baldwin's point by stating that "only the strong can hope to 'muddle through'."[8]

The perceived centrality and importance of power to the study of international phenomena is also demonstrated by the frequency with which the term is found in the literature on world politics. International actors are commonly referred to as superpowers, great powers, major powers, middle powers, small powers, and even micropowers. Systemic configurations are described as involving such things as balances of power, power vacuums, power configurations, and power arrangements. Even foreign policies are sometimes classified according to how they respond to, or fail to respond to, the dictates of power. Balance of power policies generally are regarded as those that recognize the

"realities" of how power must be manipulated and/or augmented to guarantee a nation's security.[9] The policy that once was called appeasement and that now stands discredited as a result of the events of the late 1930s is seen as one that failed to place a sufficient emphasis on the importance of power, particularly militarily based power, in international politics.[10]

Power as Resources, a Goal, or Control

Even though the term *power* is used with great frequency and figures prominently in international analysis, it has been subject to considerable definitional confusion. An important reason for this conceptual fog has to do with the differing ways authors use the term. We find that power variously refers to a nation's total resources, to a specific foreign policy goal, and to the means used to attain goals.[11] Robert Gilpin, for instance, defines power in terms of resources, saying that the term relates "simply to the military, economic, and technological capabilities of states."[12] Hans Morgenthau treats power as a goal, stating in an oft-quoted passage that "international politics, like all politics, is a struggle for power. Whatever the ultimate aims of international politics, power is always the immediate aim."[13] Jeffrey Hart notes that studying power as a means to an end may lead to two further types of definition: it may be seen as the ability either to control targets or to control one's environment and the events occurring within that environment. Each type of control may be useful for achieving certain international objectives. Both types of definitions are found in the literature; Joseph Nye says that "power means an ability to do things and control others,"[14] and Karl Deutsch observes that it "is a symbol of the ability to change the distribution of results."[15]

Further muddying the conceptual waters are those analysts who provide more than one definition for the concept. An example is Morgenthau, who, as was just noted, defines power first as a goal and then proceeds to define it as the ability to control others when he states that "when we speak of power, we mean man's control over the minds and actions of other men."[16]

Power as Resources.   Each of these approaches to defining power has its strengths and weaknesses. Viewing power as the total sum of a nation's resources is in some ways a product of viewing the international system as involving a balance of power. When we think in terms of a balance, the tendency is to regard strength as a commodity that can be measured and weighed, much as we can do with physical resources.[17] A resource-based definition usually relies on examining such factors as the size of a country's military forces, its level of defense expenditures, the size of its economy, the amount of territory it controls, and the number of people found within its borders.[18] The chief advantage of this definition is its concreteness, for it is relatively easy to measure such characteristics.

The difficulties associated with a resource approach, however, can be formidable. Two important problems involve the types of resources appropriate for determining that an actor is strong and an actor's ability to convert these resources into something that results in influence.[19] Among the many examples we can cite are contests such as those between the Germans and the French-British alliance in 1940 and between the Israelis and the Arab states in 1967.

In the case of the German confrontation with the Allies in 1940, a virtual deadlock should have emerged inasmuch as the combatants had nearly equal resources. The countries on the Allied side had a total population of 80–85 million compared to Germany's population of about 75 million. With regard to military resources, the French-British coalition fielded a total of around 3,000 tanks, 11,000 artillery pieces, and 136 divisions of troops. The comparable German figures were about 2,400 tanks, 7,700 artillery pieces, and 136 divisions of troops.[20] Thus, as the moment for a showdown approached in May 1940, the resources of the two sides were nearly equal, although the Allies actually had more resources in certain categories. Based on these statistics, most military analysts, world leaders, and scholars of international relations who studied the situation at the time expected a stalemate.[21]

The actual course of events was quite different. When the Germans struck on May 10, they shattered the Allied lines quickly. Within a week, France's leading political and military leaders realized that the situation confronting them was desperate, and by mid-June the French were compelled to surrender.[22] The equality of the resources available to the combatants turned out to be a poor predictor of the results of the actual test of strength.

The Arab-Israeli conflict presents another kind of anomaly. In this case, the distribution of resources clearly favored one side over the other. The Arab coalition in 1967 included Egypt, Jordan, and Syria, with a combined population that was more than ten times the size of Israel's. The armed forces of the two sides reflected a similar disparity in numerical strength. And yet, when hostilities commenced on June 5, 1967, the Israelis quickly decimated their opponents' armed forces and seized substantial amounts of territory. Once again, the resource picture had little to do with the outcome, for the ostensibly weaker side had almost no trouble defeating an antagonist that ostensibly had superior capabilities.

Odd results such as these two examples represent are not confined to the military realm. In the field of economics, we may ask how it is that a relatively small nation contained in a series of islands, such as Japan, had much greater economic influence than the former Soviet Union, which included over fifty-eight times as much territory within its borders and had approximately twice as many people. The same is true in political relations: Brazil, for example, has traditionally packed a far less impressive punch than the United Kingdom, despite the fact that its expanse of territory and its population are far larger.

When we consider the problems associated with matching a nation's resources with its ability to influence others and to get what it wants on the international scene, we see that the resource-based definition of power is problematic.[23] As a result, analysts tend to refer to resources as putative power,[24] as a power base,[25] or as power potential,[26] as distinct from actual power.

Power as a Goal.   Analyzing power as a goal also leads to difficulties, for it actually says little about what power *is*. When power is a foreign policy goal, exactly what do actors pursue? For the most part, we find that the discussion of goals generally turns to something far more specific. For example, Kenneth Waltz argues that "the ultimate concern of states is not for power, but for security."[27] Robert Keohane agrees that foreign policy behavior is oriented toward the specific objectives that decision makers believe will benefit their countries and that discussing power itself as a goal is not especially illuminat-ing.[28] Deutsch reinforces this point by noting that "power cannot accomplish more than a succession of random impacts on the environment unless there is some relatively fixed goal or purpose . . . by which the application of power can be guided or directed."[29] In other words, unless a country knows what it wants, it has little chance of getting it. Simply regarding the accumulation of power as a goal without specifying what a country may wish to obtain leads nowhere. Moreover, such a conception of power shades quickly into the ap-proach just discussed, for there is a tendency to equate the pursuit of power as an end in itself with the building up of resources and capabilities, which, of course, leads back to a resource-based definition.

Power as the Ability to Control.   In recent years, the shortcomings of the resource-based and goal-oriented interpretations of power have led more and more analysts to turn to definitions based on the conception of power as an ability either to control others or to control the environment. Such definitions go to the heart of what many see as the true stuff of power: getting your way when you truly want to and being able to act in any way you wish.[30] Control-ling other actors is a central theme in the definitions offered by a number of scholars. For instance, Lasswell and Kaplan say that "the exercise of influ-ence . . . consists in affecting policies of others than the self."[31] Bruce Russett and Harvey Starr provide a variation on this refrain when they state that "power means getting one's way . . . in its most general form, influence means getting others to do the things you want them to do."[32] Keohane and Nye offer what may be the most popular version of this genre when they observe that "power can be thought of as the ability of an actor to get others to do some-thing they otherwise would not do."[33] Simon, Dahl, Singer, Baldwin, and Nye offer virtually identical definitions.[34] Deutsch also views power in these terms when he claims that it is "the ability to command and be obeyed, in competi-tion with rival commands by other contenders, and in competition with the autonomous desires of the audience."[35]

Definitions that are based on the ability to control other members of the international system have two key features. First, the actor who wishes to exercise power must have a clear idea of the behavior expected of the target. As stated earlier, you cannot expect to get someone to do something unless you know what you want them to do. Second, the target must be reluctant to perform the required task; that is, the target must resist. It can hardly be said that an actor is exercising power if the target was about to do what was desired as a result of motivations independent of the actor's demands. One cannot claim to be exercising power when one tells a sleeping dog to lie down. Thus, in order to determine that power has been exercised, the preferences of the target must be known at least in part.[36]

Control-oriented definitions also come in another form: some analysts see power as the ability to induce or to resist certain types of change in the interna-tional environment. Deutsch provides the best definitions in this category. He notes first that "power . . . is the ability to prevail in conflict and to overcome obstacles."[37] He elaborates on this meaning in another place when he explains that "to have power means not to have to give in, and to force the environment or the other person to do so . . . in a sense, it is the ability to afford not to learn [from the environment]."[38] Basically, the powerful can require that the international system conform to their rules. In a sense, powerful actors ultimately mold the international arena and set the rules by which others must play the international game. Of course, over time stagnation and perhaps the eventual evaporation of their strength may be the result if actors fail to remain in contact with the overall course of international events.[39]

These two conceptions of power as control are related and overlap somewhat, but they are also distinct. They are similar in the sense that for any nation an important part of the international environment consists of the other countries found around the world. When the behavior of these countries can be controlled, then it becomes possible to control an essential feature of the environment. In addition, manipulating the behavior of other countries is frequently useful for attaining one's objectives. For example, during the Falkland Islands War against Argentina in 1982, the British ability to secure American cooperation in providing intelligence proved very helpful for the successful prosecution of the war. As a result, the British eventually achieved the outcome they desired—return of the Falkland Islands to the United Kingdom. Securing the United States' cooperation eased the United Kingdom's manipulation of the international environment.

Controlling actors and controlling the environment also can be two different operations. While others constitute an important part of the environment, they are not the only element actors must contend with. The United States and its Group of Five partners (the United States as well as France, Germany, Great Britain, and Japan) learned this in 1985 when their negotiations to regulate international currency exchange rates met with only modest success.[40] The European great powers found themselves confronting a similar situation in July of 1914 as they plunged toward a war that no one wanted.[41] In each case, international interactions and events appeared to take on a life of their own that no one seemed to have any power to stop. Efforts to control the behavior of other actors may actually have rendered the control of the environment more unlikely.

Most often, however, controlling the behavior of other actors goes a very long way toward manipulating the environment. After all, in most situations, the environmental changes that an actor desires are best achieved by securing a change in the behavior of other actors. In addition, while they are conceptually distinct, the actor-based and the environment-based definitions share a view of power that rests on the actor's ability to exert control and to get its way. Thus, the definition used in this book will "fudge" the difference between controlling actors and controlling the environment, and will focus more generally on the actor's simple ability to control and to obtain what it wants.

INTERNATIONAL ACTORS

Defining power as based on an actor's ability to control other members of the international system creates the need to consider what international actors are. In the current international arena, many analysts have judged a number of different entities, both political and nonpolitical, to qualify as actors in international politics. Some of these actors are nearly as old as international politics itself, and others are of relatively recent origin. A brief overview of a few of them may help us distinguish some of the basic characteristics of an international actor and to determine what the definition of power outlined in the preceding section applies to.

The State

When we think about actors, it is useful to differentiate between those that are sovereign and those that are nonsovereign. Sovereignty is an international legal concept that applies to determining the location of supreme authority in the international system.[42] Only one international actor, the state, has supreme authority. Sovereignty confers on the state the right to control a given expanse of territory and the people living on it, and in the process the right to make and enforce such rules, or laws, as are deemed necessary. The state also has the right to interact with other states and to seek to protect its interests in the international arena.

Thus, the sovereign state is a political and territorial entity that controls the people and other organizations and groups associated with that territory. The state has two types of rights under international law. The first is the supreme authority to make and enforce laws for the territory and the people within its jurisdiction. No political or legal entity has the right to supersede these laws. Within its allotted physical space, the state's laws and authority know no limits, except those that are self-imposed. This right to make and enforce laws is referred to as *internal sovereignty*.[43]

Moreover, states do not have the right to interfere in one another's internal affairs.[44] No matter how repugnant a government's conduct toward its own territory and people, the doctrine of sovereignty denies other governments the right to intervene to force the malefactor to change its behavior. At the same time, the right to intervention is also denied those who would do mischief and create disorder in other countries.

Noninterference is therefore a two-edged sword, for it protects everyone. On the one hand, sovereignty provided no international aid to those whom Idi Amin butchered in Uganda in the early and mid-1970s; it offered no succor to Emperor Bokassa's victims in the Central African Republic during the same time period; and it contained no remedy for the internal opponents that Saddam Hussein gassed to death during the 1980s. In none of these cases did other states have the international legal right to interfere to put a stop to reprehensible behavior by a government toward the people it ruled. On the other hand, sovereignty denies legal standing to attempts to intervene in the functioning of duly constituted states through such means as terrorism or guerrilla warfare.

A second aspect of sovereignty, labeled *external sovereignty,* has to do with the international, or foreign policy–oriented, obligations of states toward one another. Morgenthau sums these obligations up as the three principles of sovereignty: independence, equality, and unanimity.[45] *Independence* means that states have the right to formulate and to conduct their policies, both foreign and domestic, without clearing their decisions with other political entities. All the state's decisions are made by its duly constituted decision makers. *Equality* means that all states have the same formal standing under international law and according to international custom. No state is legally regarded as superior to any other. *Unanimity* means that a state is bound by international rules and procedures only if it agrees to be so bound. That is, treaties and international conventions apply to a state only if it agrees to let them apply. When a state does enter into such agreements, however, it is expected to comply with their terms. Therefore, international law is a product of coordinating the behavior of states, and not of subordinating their behavior to a higher authority, as is the case with domestic law.[46]

As a territorial entity, the state enjoys great advantages over other actors in the international arena inasmuch as the globe is presently divided among states. There is virtually no territory that is not controlled by one state or another, and the state is supreme within its assigned area. Thus, all other actors are by necessity forced to exist within a framework in which one or another state (and sometimes several) has the right to create rules to regulate their behavior. This advantage has made the state "the dominant organizational form of contemporary world politics."[47] Indeed, many scholars have long taken "it for granted that states were 'the actors' of world politics."[48]

The Nation

The state is a historical creation of the European system, emerging only in the sixteenth century after the Treaty of Westphalia was negotiated to end the Thirty Years' War. When imperialism led to the expansion of the European system to other parts of the world, the state as an organizational form was transplanted. The nation, a second important contemporary actor, is also usually regarded as a product of the European system. The emergence of nations as international actors is generally considered a product of more recent trends, dating from the nineteenth century and blossoming into full flower in the twentieth century.[49]

Although the terms *nation* and *state* are often used interchangeably, the two are actually distinct. The state is a sovereign entity recognized as having certain specific rights under international law, whereas the nation is a more amorphous creation that may be characterized as a product of emotion rather than of the mutual recognition that is the basis for state authority. A nation usually is defined as existing when a group of people have a strong mutual identification with one another that expresses itself in the desire for self-rule.[50] In other words, a nation exists when a people feel they form a political community that is different from all other political communities in terms of history, culture, traditions, and so forth. As a result, they seek incorporation as a self-ruling political entity recognized by other such entities as independent and equal. To put it more briefly, nations are political communities that usually have a powerful desire to form a state of their own and believe they have a right to do so.

In the current international arena, many nations, including France, Denmark, Norway, Sweden, and Japan, have become organized as separate states. These entities may be referred to as nation-states because the state and the nation coincide almost perfectly with one another. In addition, many nations are incorporated into larger political entities and do not currently have, or have not in the recent past had, the right of self-rule. The Armenians, Azerbaijanis, Georgians, and Ukrainians in the former Soviet Union are examples. The Slovenians, Croatians, and Serbians in what was Yugoslavia are others. The Ibos and Yorubas in Nigeria[51] and the Tamils and Sinhalese in Sri Lanka are still others. These are (or, in some cases, were) examples of multinational states.

Nations are generally considered to become international actors when they organize to challenge the authority of the state. Specifically, they attempt to conduct relations and policies of their own without working through whatever state has jurisdiction over the territory within which they reside. In the traditional state-dominated international system, *only* states had the right to formulate policy and conduct international relations. All other individuals, organizations, and groups of whatever kind within the state were expected to use the good offices of the state to pursue any international interests they had. In the current international arena, many nations refuse to do this. Part of the reason is that their leaders believe that the government of the state in which they are located will not look out for their interests in an acceptable way. Another part is that they believe they have a right to self-rule and that conducting a foreign policy of their own is one clear indicator of their claim to this status.

As a result of this attitude, some nations that have not yet been incorporated as states (and perhaps never will be) engage in diplomatic and political discourse, conduct economic and business negotiations, and organize for international violence. Croatia, Slovenia, and Lithuania all conducted their own diplomacy before being recognized as independent, and the Palestine Liberation Organization continues to do so in its search for independence. Prior to independence, some of these nations also engaged in numerous attempts at economic bargaining with other members of the international system. Finally, the Tigers of Tamil Elam and the Palestine Liberation Organization are the military arms of their respective nations. In each case, a nonstate actor plays a substantial role in world politics, conducts a "foreign policy" of its own choosing, refuses to regard any state as having the right to dominate it, and must be considered by other actors (both state and nonstate) in formulating their own policies.[52]

International and Transnational Organizations

A third category of contemporary nonsovereign actors consists of a mixed grouping that includes international and transnational organizations. International organizations are created by sovereign states in order to handle certain types of problems that recur in international politics and that individual states have trouble dealing with in any but a collective manner. Such problems include maintaining international security, managing international trade, transferring capital to less developed countries to aid them in developing, and coordinating the economic policies of some of the more dominant industrial states. In an attempt to manage these problems, the United Nations, the International

Monetary Fund, the World Bank, and the Organization for Economic Cooperation and Development were set up. Each of these organizations is a product of
state design and has states as its members. At the same time, each has a
permanent organizational structure, a bureaucracy and employees of its own,
and policies and procedures that are distinct from those followed by the members either collectively or individually.

Transnational organizations, unlike international organizations, are not
formed by states, their membership is not composed of states, and they are not
designed exclusively to take care of the problems that states cannot take care of
themselves. Instead, these organizations generally are a product of private
interests that seek to conduct business or other relationships across international borders. Such organizations may collaborate with states in an effort to
attain their objectives, but they set their goals autonomously and they rarely
hesitate to take action on their own in pursuit of these goals when states are
unable or unwilling to assist them. These organizations may be political, as is
Amnesty International; economic, as are international banks and multinational
corporations; or humanitarian, as is the International Red Cross.

In the contemporary world, one of the strongest transnational organizations is the multinational corporation. Raymond Vernon defines the multinational corporation as a cluster of businesses joined together by bonds of common
ownership and able to exploit a common pool of resources.[53] Such corporations
have a headquarters in one country, known as the home state, and subsidiaries
that do business in other countries, known as host states. These corporations
often have immense amounts of capital, technology, and entrepreneurial talent.
Each of these resources is considered vital to the development, growth, and
management of modern economic and social structures, and multinational corporations are regarded by many as important possible contributors in each of
these areas.[54] Indeed, in some states the need for these resources is so great that
their governments court the corporations in an attempt to convince them to
locate within their borders.

Multinational corporations can set their own policy priorities as to where
to locate their facilities, and they can maintain subsidiaries in more than one
state. As a result, they have a degree of independence that few transnational
actors can match; this also makes them a complicated target for states to
control. For example, as mentioned earlier, the Group of Five experienced
considerable difficulty when they sought to manipulate international currency
exchange rates in 1985. These states found it quite difficult to modify currency
values largely because of the behavior of multinational corporations and other
transnational actors, including banks and international investment firms.
These actors move such large volumes of capital across international borders
on a daily basis that it has become very difficult for governments to fine-tune
exchange rates.

Another example of the independent policy roles of these corporations is
found in the European natural gas pipeline controversy that erupted in the
early years of the Reagan administration. This dispute revolved around a proposed agreement between the Soviet Union and several Western European
governments to construct a pipeline that would transport natural gas from the
Soviet Union to Western Europe, where it would be marketed. From the Euro-

pean and Soviet standpoints, the deal was excellent. The Soviets would obtain income from the sale of the gas, and the Europeans would gain access to a much-needed source of energy.

The United States objected, however, for it feared that, by becoming dependent on Soviet gas, the Europeans might be subject at some future date to Soviet economic pressures. The upshot could be political and security-related problems for the Europeans. As a result, the Reagan administration sought to block the deal by ordering the American-headquartered firms that would provide equipment essential to constructing the pipeline not to sell their wares to the interested parties. One of these firms was Dresser Industries, with headquarters in Dallas, Texas, and a subsidiary in France. In conformity with the Reagan administration ruling, Dresser's American plant did not ship equipment to the Soviets. But its French facility was not within the jurisdiction of the U.S. government and therefore was free to carry on business. This it did.[55] Thus, the U.S. attempt to halt the deal failed in part because it could not regulate the actions of a multinational corporation that fell within the jurisdiction of another country.

As these two examples show, the current international scene is peopled with a complex array of actors, each with its own goals and policy-making capabilities, and each determined to conduct international business in an attempt to further its own interests. In fact, it might be argued that policy-making capabilities and a determination to conduct international business are the basic features that distinguish an international actor.

Despite its confrontations with many newcomers that now challenge its dominance, the state remains the preeminent actor in international politics. Accordingly, the primary (though not exclusive) focus in this book will be on how states behave when exercising power.

SOME IMPLICATIONS OF DEFINING POWER AS CONTROL

Having completed our brief digression into the discussion of actors in international relations, we can now consider some of the implications of a control-oriented definition of power. This section examines the relational, comparative, and conflictual nature of power, the role of perception, and why the exercise of power invariably leads to controversy and, on occasion, fear.

The Relational Nature of Power

When we define power as the ability of an actor to control the behavior of a target, by implication we are speaking of a situation in which an interactive relationship exists. If one country seeks to control the behavior of another, then at a minimum it must have some degree of contact with the entity it wishes to control, for "there is no meaningful way to characterize a state's power in a . . . vacuum."[56] Power is exercised only in a social context. In a world in which states and other actors lived in complete isolation from one another, power would become a meaningless concept.[57] Without contact there can be no control.

We can illustrate the importance of this contact with a familiar contemporary example: the difficulty governments have experienced in combating terrorism. Governments have failed to stop international terrorism not because they are unable to marshal their resources for the task, but because it is nearly impossible to locate most of the terrorists, who belong to clandestine organizations. For the most part, in those rare instances when governments have been able to find terrorist organizations, they have been able to deal with them effectively. But those who cannot be found cannot be subjected to control; thus, establishing contact becomes the key to the exercise of power.

In addition, when there is no contact between two entities, the desire to control is usually absent. Not only must the actor and the target interact with each other, but the two must be interdependent, or mutually reliant. The interdependence must be so great that the actor believes that achieving a desired goal or avoiding an undesired set of circumstances will be possible only if it can affect the behavior of the target.[58] In the absence of such a situation, the target will fall outside the actor's locus of interest, and the actor will have little reason to want to control the target's behavior. Except in unusual circumstances, then, the exercise of power may be viewed in utilitarian terms: actors will seek to exercise influence over targets only when they believe they will receive some benefits from doing so. Otherwise they will not bother, for the wielding of power always costs the actor something, whether it be money, lives, the opportunity to pursue an alternative course of action, or something else.[59]

An example of these points is found in the American isolationist period of the 1920s and 1930s. During this era, the U.S. government concluded that a European-oriented policy would entail substantial costs in at least three areas. It might entail (1) extending considerable economic assistance to European states; (2) maintaining a larger military establishment in the United States than desired; and (3) being drawn into any future European military conflicts. During this period, most Americans felt that these costs and risks were too great to counterbalance any gains the United States might receive from more extensive involvement in Europe. Hence, the United States pursued a policy of minimal entanglement in Europe and avoided using its considerable resources for purposes of manipulating the behavior of European states.[60] The United States preserved its contacts and interactions with Europe, but in many ways the continent now fell outside of the American locus of interest.

During the same period, the attitude of the United States to Central America and the Caribbean was very different. The United States believed that it had special economic, moral, and security concerns in this part of the world. Economically, many American firms conducted business and invested in the region; morally, Americans felt it was their duty to shepherd their neighbors to the south down the path to good government; and, of course, since Central America and the Caribbean lie on the southern borders of the United States, the establishment of an unfriendly strong state there would constitute a serious security hazard. Another consideration that encouraged the United States' involvement in the Americas was the apparently lower cost of this involvement compared to involvement in Europe. In addition, any activities conducted in Central America presented a very low risk of world war, which was not the case with Europe. Therefore, the United States pursued a policy of manipulation in the Latin American region; prolonged American interventions in Nicaragua and Cuba are but two examples.[61]

Power and Perception

As noted earlier, the existence of a relationship between actor and target is essential to the exercise of power; however, interactions alone are not sufficient. The actor must also believe that controlling the target will bring benefits and that these benefits will outweigh any potential costs the actor may pay for the influence attempt.[62]

In this way, the actors' perception becomes important to the exercise of power, for actors pursue a particular course only when they *perceive* it is useful to do so. There is no guarantee, however, that the actors will correctly calculate these benefits and costs. In fact, J. David Singer observes that the actor's emotions will often lead to a miscalculation of benefits and costs.[63] One example is the United States' commitment to Vietnam in the 1960s and 1970s. The United States' strong desire to contain communism clouded the ability of American decision makers to assess both the costs and the geopolitical advantages of American involvement. As a result, they consistently underestimated the costs and overestimated the advantages.[64]

Perception is vital to the exercise of power in yet another way, namely, in how the target views both the actor and the influence attempt. As Klaus Knorr states, "power is what people think it is."[65] That is, targets respond to their impression of the actor and comply with an actor's demands when they think they have no real choice in the matter.

Perception and Resources. A target may perceive that an actor is strong, first, because of the actor's resource base and, second, because of the actor's reputation. A large resource base, as was discussed earlier, is quite distinct from the actual possession of power. The two are related, however, when the target of the influence attempt believes that the actor's resources are so substantial that it has no option but to follow the actor's dictates.[66]

Such a situation occurred during the Suez crisis in 1956 when the Soviet Union demanded that the United Kingdom stop its invasion of Egypt and withdraw. This demand was effective because the Soviets had larger military capabilities than the British and because the United States refused to guarantee that it would assist the British in the event of Soviet action. What is more, the U.S. government informed the British that it would exert financial pressures on the United Kingdom if it failed to halt its attack. The British felt they had no choice but to halt the invasion because the demands came from two countries with far superior resources, both military and economic. In effect, Soviet and American resources played an important part in the exercise of power because the British felt that resistance would be futile.[67]

Resources played an important role in an earlier crisis too: the Munich crisis in the fall of 1938. At the close of the Munich conference between Neville Chamberlain of the United Kingdom, Edouard Daladier of France, and Adolf Hitler of Germany, it was agreed that the Sudeten region of Czechoslovakia would be ceded to Germany. Conforming to such an agreement was anathema to the Czechs, but fighting meant that they would be forced to take on the full

Map 2. Europe in 1938

weight of the superior German armed forces, with no help from either the British or the French. Thus, the Czechs perceived that the discrepancy in the resources available to the two countries left them with no choice but to abide by the terms of the Munich agreement.[68]

For a more contemporary example, we can consider the case in Poland in the early 1980s, when the rising tide of the Solidarity trade union movement threatened the stability of the Soviet-backed Communist government. In order to prevent the Polish government's collapse, the Soviet Union ordered the regime of General Wojciech Jaruzelski to outlaw Solidarity and put its leaders under arrest. Once again, the clear capacity of Soviet resources to dominate Polish resources forced the Polish government to conform to Soviet dictates.[69]

A slightly different situation is found in French-British-Italian relations in 1935. Here we have a case of two countries, France and Britain, that hesitated to follow world opinion demanding the imposition of harsh economic sanctions against Italy after the Italians' unprovoked invasion of Ethiopia. The French and British hesitated because of their desires to bring Italy, together with its apparently significant military resources, into a coalition against Hitler's Germany. The French and British believed that imposing crushing economic sanctions would so alienate the Italians that forming an alliance would become impossible. Hence, they partially conformed to the Italian demand that the sanctions be muted.[70]

Perception and Reputation.   A clear superiority in resources does not always guarantee a country's domination in a situation: the actor's reputation also enters into the target's calculations.[71] A country's reputation refers to the degree to which its past behavior affects expectations regarding its present and future behavior. A government's or leader's reputation for making difficult decisions and taking tough action in the past may well convince targets that they should comply. In contrast, governments that shy away from hard choices or that often fail in their attempts to alter the behavior of others will find themselves confronting recalcitrant targets.

A prominent example today of a tough reputation is that held by successive Israeli governments. Israel has so great a reputation for hard-nosed behavior that would-be challengers hesitate to take any action that might invoke an Israeli response. Examples of an ineffective reputation are found in the United Kingdom's inability in the summer of 1914 to convince Germany that it would go to war if Germany invaded Belgium and in the Soviet Union's lack of success in verbally coercing the Finns into granting the Soviet Union territorial concessions in November 1939. The United Kingdom failed in part because in the past it had always shown leeriness of military involvement on the Continent. The Soviet Union failed because its military capabilities were suspect: it had experienced military failures in Poland a decade earlier, and the Red Army of the 1930s was poorly organized and led.[72]

Realizing the importance of reputation in the exercise of power often serves as a guidepost to a government's foreign policy behavior. The desire to foster a resolute image was one of the primary factors that motivated President John F. Kennedy during the Cuban missile crisis. Together with many of his advisers, Kennedy concluded early on that the United States had no choice but to react vigorously to the Soviet attempt to place medium- and intermediate-range ballistic missiles in Cuba in October of 1962. It was reasoned that doing otherwise would be a sign of faintheartedness in the Kennedy administration and would give it a reputation for softness that would in turn encourage the Soviet Union to embark on further assaults on the United States' position in other parts of the world.[73]

In the early 1970s the Nixon administration's desire for a carefully phased and orderly wind-down of the United States' role in Vietnam shows us again that a government's concern with its image and reputation often serves to direct its foreign policy. As Nixon's special assistant for national security affairs, Henry Kissinger, wrote in *The White House Years:*

> The Nixon Administration entered office determined to end our involvement in Vietnam . . . [but] for nearly a generation the security and progress of free peoples . . . depended on confidence in America. We could not simply walk away from an enterprise involving two administrations, five allied countries, and thirty-one thousand dead as if we were switching a television channel. . . . As the leader of democratic alliances we had to remember that scores of countries and millions of people relied for their security on our willingness to stand by allies. . . . No serious policymaker could allow himself to succumb to the fashionable debunking of "prestige" or "honor" or "credibility."[74]

A final example of a different sort is the general consternation that was voiced upon the revelation in 1987 that the Reagan administration had been dealing with the Iranian government in an effort to secure the release of hostages held in Lebanon by terrorists sympathetic to Iran. The administration's motive was understandable enough, for it desired to do all it could to relieve the suffering of both the hostages and their families. The problem with the policy was that many felt it showed that the American government had no stomach for standing firm, which in the end would lead the terrorists to seize more hostages in the hope of obtaining still further concessions from the United States. Thus, one would merely trade the freedom of some for the imprisonment of others.

Power and Conflict

Another key aspect of power has to do with conflict. The reader may recall the observation that a power relationship exists only when there is conflict and that power is, after all, the ability to control the behavior of someone else. The actor does not exercise power if the target was already doing what the actor wanted. In such cases, the target and not the actor would control the target's behavior.

In assessing the element of conflict in a power relationship, it is necessary first to consider (1) the preferences of both the actor and the target, and whether they are at odds with one another; (2) whether the actor communicates those preferences to the target; (3) whether the target understands the preferences of the actor, realizes that those preferences are at odds with the target's own preferences, and chooses to alter its behavior in response to this information; and (4) the degree of behavior modification that takes place.

Preferences.   Preferences indicate what the actor and target want. Do their goals or objectives conflict with one another, or are their values essentially similar? A situation in which the target actually agrees with the actor and therefore does just about what the actor wants, which does not involve the use of power, is often mistaken for one in which an exercise of power actually occurs.

Two examples immediately come to mind. The first was the conflict between Britain and Germany in the summer of 1940. At that time, the Germans were supremely triumphant on the European Continent, having just inflicted a crushing defeat on France. Britain was all that stood between Germany and the mastery of all of Western Europe. The British were in dire straits, with much of their armed forces' equipment lost during a hasty retreat from the Continent back to their islands. A quick German assault appeared all that was needed to finish them off. Thus, Hitler ordered the preparation of Operation Sea Lion, which called for the invasion of Britain. In order to implement the plan, however, the Germans had to defeat Britain's Royal Air Force. In one of the most important turning points in history, the German operation failed, and Britain was not invaded.[75]

The second example concerns the American use of nuclear weapons over the last four decades as a preventative measure against a Soviet attack on the United States. The essential point of the U.S. policy was that the threat of a massive strike using nuclear weapons against the Soviet Union would guarantee American security because the possible Soviet gains from attacking the United States would be far outstripped by the losses that would occur as a result of the American counterattack. As everyone knows, there was no Soviet attack on the United States, and so, many analysts have presumed that the nuclear-based American strategy was successful. The threat of nuclear retaliation had supposedly kept the peace.

The problem with this assessment is that there is no solid evidence that the Soviets ever wanted to attack the United States. In the British-German example, the Germans clearly seemed bent on crossing the English Channel to conquer the United Kingdom. After all, they were at war with Britain, British intelligence learned of Operation Sea Lion, and the German Luftwaffe began a furious air assault on Britain in what apparently was preparation for an actual invasion. The case for possible Soviet designs on the United States is far weaker. Indeed, many scholars assert that nuclear weapons actually had little effect on Soviet policy as far as a physical assault on the United States was concerned.[76] As K. J. Holsti puts it, the case for the American exercise of power "could be inferred only if we knew the Soviet Union had strong intentions of launching an attack, but was dissuaded by threats of American retaliation."[77] Since the evidence suggesting that the Soviets had designs is dubious, we cannot definitely label U.S. nuclear policy as the successful employment of power.

Communications.   Without some sort of communication, the target cannot be expected to respond to the actor. Therefore, any conformity between the wishes of the actor and the behavior of the target becomes merely coincidental and not a product of design that one has in mind when one refers to the use of power. Taken together, the second and third components—communication of preferences and understanding of those preferences and acting on them—also imply a degree of timing, for the exercise of power requires that the actor's preferences must be communicated before the target's behavior occurs.[78] Otherwise, the one cannot be said to be the product of the other.

John Lewis Gaddis's description of Soviet-American relations in the waning months of the Second World War illustrates the importance of communication. Early in 1945, as European territories occupied by the Nazis were liberated by the United States, the United Kingdom, and the Soviet Union, dissension developed between the Western allies and the Soviet Union over the disposition of the liberated areas in Eastern Europe. The Western allies felt that the Soviets were denying them a voice in determining the type of government to be established in these areas. At about the same time, the Soviets requested a large postwar loan from the United States to aid in the reconstruction of the Soviet economy. Averell Harriman, the American ambassador to the Soviet Union, urged that the U.S. government tie the loan to Soviet behavior in Eastern Europe as a means of obtaining greater Soviet compliance with American wishes. Apparently, even though the idea appealed to many in Washington, the loan negotiations and Soviet behavior never were explicitly linked. That is, the United States never communicated its intentions to the Soviet Union. Thus, the loan never was used as a means for obtaining leverage over the Soviets.[79] Without communication, it was not possible to obtain the change in behavior that the United States wanted because the Soviets never were made aware of the linkage.

Another example of the importance of communication is found in the Korean War. Prior to the outbreak of hostilities in June 1950, the U.S. government failed to communicate its commitment to defend South Korea. In fact, on several occasions representatives of the U.S. government stated very explicitly that the United States did *not* feel any special commitment. As a result, North Korean and Soviet policymakers planning an attack on South Korea could not take an American defense of Korea into account in their preparations for an assault. The United States could not affect the actions of others when it stated that it would not take a particular course of action. Once again, the actor's failure to communicate its actual preferences to its opponent eliminated the possibility of exerting influence.[80]

The Korean War also illustrates the problems surrounding the inability to understand communications. Alexander George and Richard Smoke point out that the intervention of the Communist Chinese armed forces into the war in the fall of 1950 was preceded by several Chinese attempts to alert the United States that they might indeed intervene. These attempts began in the late summer of 1950, as Chinese Foreign Ministry officials issued warnings both through diplomatic channels and by radio. Communications continued in November as Chinese troops massed along the Chinese-Korean border and even crossed into Korea to fight U.S. forces for a brief period. In each case, the Chinese government sought to signal the United States that it would object strenuously if American troops invaded North Korea. However, U.S. decision makers either ignored, discounted, or failed to understand the Chinese communications. Therefore, the United States did not become completely aware of Chinese preferences, could not see the degree to which Chinese and American preferences were at odds with one another, and thus was unable to alter its behavior to reflect the Chinese desires. Interestingly, few U.S. policymakers desired a war with China. A full comprehension of Chinese preferences would very likely have led American officials to reconsider a move into North Korea to unify it with South Korea.[81]

Behavior Modification.   The final element to consider when we examine conflict and power is the degree to which behavior modification takes place. In thinking about this factor, we should realize that the exercise of power need not be considered absolute. That is, the actor may alter the target's behavior only in part, or it may simply increase the probability that the target will engage in a particular form of behavior.[82] Indeed, such behavioral alterations probably should be treated as more common in international relations than absolute or total modifications of behavior. Alternatively, the actor may simply reinforce behavior that the target already is displaying but may be inclined to abandon at some point in the future unless the actor does something to prevent it. This kind of partial behavioral control is especially prevalent in diplomatic negotiations and similar bargaining. In such negotiations, each side seeks to affect the behavior of the other, with the end result being the target's partial compliance with the actor's desires, leading to a compromise.[83]

An example of only partial behavior modification is the British-French-Italian relationship after the invasion of Ethiopia in 1935. As noted earlier, in this case, the British and French faced the need to place strong, airtight economic sanctions against Italy. When Italy objected, Britain and France, responding to Italian pressures, decided on only moderate economic penalties. While the Italians did not get all of what they wanted (which was no sanctions at all), they got some of it. Instead of strong, airtight sanctions, Italy faced only a watered-down version. Italy did not fail to exercise power with regard to Great Britain and France just because some sanctions were put in place. British and French behavior, after all, was modified by their views of Italian preferences.[84]

A second example of partial compliance also illustrates the reciprocal exercise of power. Reciprocal power exists when two international actors seek to control one another's behavior, with the end result that each exerts some control over the other. As alluded to earlier, bargaining situations involving give-and-take by both parties may lead to reciprocal relationships. The SALT II (Strategic Arms Limitation Talks) negotiations provide a good illustration. From the Soviet point of view, the American deployment of cruise missiles was a major issue in these negotiations. Such missiles are similar to pilotless aircraft that fly very low to avoid radar detection. While slow, they are inexpensive to produce (when compared with other weapons systems), have considerable accuracy, and are difficult to defend against. These characteristics made them particularly frightening to the Soviets, who demanded strict limitations on the weapons. The Americans resisted such limits. For their part, the Americans worried about a new Soviet bomber, dubbed the Backfire, which could, with refueling, attack targets in the United States. The United States demanded the inclusion of the Backfire in the terms of any SALT II agreement. The Soviets refused.

In the end, after hard bargaining, each side gave in somewhat to the other. The Americans agreed to a short-term quantitative limit to cruise missiles and to the demand that their range be limited to 375 miles. The Soviets agreed they would limit production of the Backfire and would not station it in the northern part of the Soviet Union where it would pose the greatest threat to the United States.[85] Each side got only part of what it wanted, and each side affected the behavior of the other. In the absence of the U.S. and Soviet attempts to exert influence, the behavior of the other side clearly would have been different. That is, the United States would have produced more cruise missiles of longer range, and the Soviets would have produced more Backfires and stationed them in the north. Power was exercised, and it was done reciprocally.

For an example of behavior reinforcement, we might consider the United States and the Soviet Union in 1962 at the time of the Cuban missile crisis. In the spring of 1961, the United States had sponsored an attempt to invade Cuba and overthrow the Castro regime. After this plan, the so-called Bay of Pigs fiasco, failed abysmally, the Kennedy administration foreswore a similar future attempt.[86] It was not clear, however, that no further operations would ever occur under a future administration. At the end of the Cuban missile crisis, the United States agreed as part of the formula for resolving the crisis that it would never seek to invade Cuba.[87] Thus, the Soviet requirement that the United States commit itself to a live-and-let-live policy with regard to Cuba reinforced behavior that the United States already was displaying and that the Soviets preferred. It also increased the probability that the United States would continue to display the preferred behavior in the future. In this case, the display of power related to ensuring that a particular type of action would not be abandoned by one's adversary and that it would continue in the future.

These examples might lead the reader to conclude that when partial changes in behavior and reinforcement occur, the actor has exercised less power over the target than when the change in the target's behavior is more complete. This is not entirely correct, for the degree to which power has been exercised is largely determined by the target's level of commitment to the behavior that is affected. Even partially modifying the behavior of a target that is highly committed to a course of action may prove far more difficult than securing a complete change of behavior when the target is not particularly concerned with continuing down the path in question. The reason is that with commitment comes the willingness to accept more pain and greater costs. Arnold Wolfers notes that, in exercising power, "much depends on the value that nations attach to the goals they seek to attain . . . the higher this value, the greater the incentive to bear higher costs."[88]

Thus, the commitment of a target to its goals is an important consideration when we are evaluating the successful use of power. Actors concerned only with affecting behavior of marginal interest to a target may therefore experience so much success that they appear formidable. By comparison, actors that are more ambitious or have an interest only in altering behavior that the target is very committed to may seem much less capable, even when they obtain partial concessions that the target loathed making.[89]

The SALT I agreement between the United States and the Soviet Union illustrates the first of these situations. The five-year interim agreement that was associated with the treaty stated that the United States was permitted to deploy 1,054 intercontinental ballistic missiles and 710 submarine-launched ballistic missiles. The Soviets were allowed 1,618 and 950, respectively. Many critics of the SALT process complained that these unequal numbers indicated that the Soviets had cleverly outmaneuvered the American negotiators and that it represented a substantial U.S. concession to Soviet demands. That is, the Soviets were seen as having very successfully exercised power by forcing the United States to accept a ceiling for their missiles that was far lower than the Soviet level. Such an interpretation, however, overlooked the fact that at the time of the negotiations the United States had no immediate plans to construct more missiles in either category. Thus, the supposedly great display of Soviet power resulted more from the United States' lack of commitment to the goal of building more missiles than from Soviet demands and preferences.[90]

The Uruguay Round of GATT (General Agreement on Tariffs and Trade) negotiations illustrates how achieving a partial concession may be a significant display of power. A key issue during these negotiations was the degree to which the European Community would be allowed to pay European farmers a subsidy for the agricultural goods they produced. The United States firmly opposed the European subsidy program because it promoted agricultural output in Europe. The result would be reduced European imports of food and more exports, which in turn would drive down the price of certain agricultural goods on world markets. In order to create more competitive international agricultural markets, during the Uruguay Round the United States demanded that the Europeans cut their subsidies for domestic output by 75 percent. Because agricultural subsidies were a major political issue in the European Community, the European negotiators adamantly refused. After lengthy bargaining, the Europeans finally agreed to a 30 percent cut. While this went only partway toward meeting the American terms, it still represented a considerable concession to American demands, given the Europeans' strong commitment to subsidies.[91]

Power and Controversy

This brings us to the controversial nature of power and the emotional response many people have to it. Controversy and emotion are often associated with the exercise of power because of its very nature. As has been discussed, power involves a situation in which an actor and a target are at cross-purposes, with the two wishing to pursue courses of action that are incompatible with one another. Power comes into play when the actor uses some of the resources at its disposal to convince, cajole, or compel the target to change its behavior, either totally or in part, to conform to the actor's wishes. In such a situation, the target must at least to some degree give up the pursuit of its own interests and move according to the actor's directions. Under these circumstances, controversy is virtually automatic because the target must accept the loss of some of its autonomy. As noted previously, all international actors value autonomy and the ability to control their own policy selections. This is especially true of actors that possess sovereignty, a principle that enshrines as vital the freedom to determine one's own policies.

Two other considerations often magnify this controversy. The first is uncertainty. The exercise of power means that a target must give up some of its policy preferences for those of the actor. One can never be sure where the actor's preferences will lead and what the consequences may be for the target. Such uncertainty naturally creates anxiety. Moreover, when a target becomes subject to the wishes of another entity, it can never be sure of the limits to the control it experiences. Giving in to control by another is unsettling in itself, but this tension is magnified by the difficulties in not knowing whether the concessions are simply a prelude to more.

Another consideration that heightens the controversy surrounding power relates to the emotional satisfaction some people derive from controlling others. Baldwin points out that for some people power is not only instrumental (i.e., it is used to attain a goal), but it is emotionally pleasing as well (i.e., it leads to the opportunity to bully others).[92] Knorr also notes that controlling others may lead to emotional responses when he states that "possession of great power easily induces in leaders the dangerous development of hubris and what has been called the 'arrogance of power'."[93] That is, power may create the impression that one is all-knowing.

When these emotions are combined with the uncertainty that is always present when power relationships exist, one has the formula for extreme controversy and a situation in which emotions may operate at full force. The gravity of the situation may be exacerbated when an actor is unable to distinguish between power and what Singer refers to as "fate control."[94] While power involves modifying a target's behavior to suit the actor's preferences, fate control is deciding what will happen to the target—whether its people will be enslaved, its land laid waste, its resources looted, and so on.

Such considerations lead to trouble, for those who are afflicted with the "arrogance of power," who enjoy bullying, or who mistake fate control for power, tend to engage in excesses that can lead to extreme tragedy. History is replete with examples of genocidal acts ranging from the horrendous abuses associated with Hitler's New Order for Europe to the outrages of the Khmer Rouge in Cambodia in the 1970s. We should recall, however, that it is not power itself that leads to these untoward occurrences. Instead, it is character flaws in those who are given the opportunity to control the behavior of others and in those who follow them, and it is the shortcomings found in the societies that produce such unacceptable behavior.

POWER AND CONTEXT

Factors that specify the limits to power may be labeled contextual. As Lasswell and Kaplan remind us, all social relationships exist within a particular set of circumstances. If the circumstances change, then the relationship also changes.[95] The same students who revere a professor as wise when teaching classes may deride him for incompetence when he competes against them in a sporting event. Thus, different circumstances can produce a very different relationship.

Power operates in much the same way. In some contexts, a particular international actor may appear capable of doing almost anything, while in others it may seem a helpless giant, leading us to wonder at what Baldwin refers to as the "paradox of unrealized power."[96] For example, we can compare the strength displayed by the United States when it forced the mighty Soviet Union to back down during the Cuban missile crisis with the pitiful sight just six years later when U.S. forces were unable to handle the ostensibly far weaker forces of North Vietnam.

The analytical scheme presented in this section may be used to examine the contextual factors that determine the limits of power. Although this scheme does not explain conclusively why power is limited, it will be useful for defining context and helping to provide some understanding of where limits come from.

In investigating context, we may begin with Baldwin's proposal that "the international political analyst start with the assumption that power resources are situationally specific."[97] A number of scholars have proposed that the social context for wielding power be examined in terms of four interrelated variables: weight, domain, range, and scope.[98] *Weight* is defined as the actor's ability to affect the likelihood that something will happen or that a target will behave in a particular way. *Domain* refers to the set of targets that an actor controls. *Range* is resource oriented, having to do with the types of rewards and punishments an actor can bestow or inflict on a target when seeking to exercise power. Finally, *scope* relates to the types of behavior by the target that the actor controls. Taken together, these four factors go a long way toward determining the strength of an actor and the limits to its influence. Let us examine each in its turn.

Weight

Weight is the actor's ability to affect the probability that a target will do something. Of special importance in determining an actor's weight are its degree of organization,[99] the specificity of its goals,[100] the target's perception of the actor, and the quality of communications between actor and target. Since the last two factors have already been discussed, attention here will center on the first two.

Organization and specificity of goals are keys to weight because they help determine how well the actor is able to set its objectives and how much is demanded of the target. Organization is a vital component in the actor's ability to determine what it hopes to achieve and to setting priorities among these aspirations. As was noted earlier, when actors are uncertain or do not know what they want, then they cannot effectively manipulate a target's behavior. Organization is also a key to consistency in the actor and to the transmission of clear and easily understood signals.

An example of the problems associated with lack of organization, uncertainty as to goal, and inconsistent signals is found in the Reagan administration's policy toward terrorism. Publicly, from its earliest days in office this administration sent a series of tough messages to international terrorist organizations, particularly those operating out of the Middle East. Libya, Syria, Iran, and, on occasion, Iraq all were branded as sponsors of terrorism and received special attention as the United States sought to isolate them. In addition, firm action was taken: President Reagan permitted U.S. naval forces to bombard suspected terrorist hideouts in Lebanon, he authorized an air raid against Libya in 1986, and he ordered the interception of a flight carrying terrorists who had seized a cruise ship in the Mediterranean and murdered American passengers. Thus, the United States appeared set on a tough no-compromise stance with regard to terrorists.

At a level that was hidden from public view, however, the same Reagan administration sent very different signals. It bargained with the Iranian government, offering Iran much needed military equipment in exchange for the release of certain hostages. It also tilted toward Iraq in its war with Iran. Both acts sent signals to two of the terrorist-sponsoring states that were far different from those that were being sent publicly. Apparently, the Reagan administration had a very difficult time determining whether it wanted to combat terrorists or buy them off. In part, this inability was a product of a lack of organization within the administration. The result was a dissipated United States' effort that sapped its weight. Fighting terrorists is never easy; it is made all the more difficult when the effort is disorganized and the policy formulated is inconsistent.

The degree to which very specific or more general goals are pursued can also affect weight. Deutsch argues that it is far more difficult to achieve extremely specific goals than more general objectives.[101] The reason has to do with the definition of failure associated with a specific goal. When an actor is extremely specific, then even a slight deviation from its wishes means failure. When an actor is more general, then the toleration for variation is greater.

We can illustrate this point by considering the United States' goals vis-à-vis Korea since 1954: to protect South Korea and to unify North and South Korea under a democratic form of government. Protection is the more general of the two goals; all it requires is that North Korean military forces not do something—invade South Korea. Unification is far more specific, for it requires a particular type of government and implies a distinct type of economic system (free enterprise) and certain kinds of social institutions (a free press, for one). Thus, although the United States has enjoyed considerable success in protecting South Korea, it has not gone very far toward the version of unification it prefers. In the case of the first goal, American weight has been fairly great; in the case of the second, it has been negligible.

Domain

The domain of power is the number and types of targets an actor is able to control. In the past, domain was usually defined in territorial terms; the targets most easily controlled were those that were physically closest. Usually, then, if an actor could control anyone it would be a bordering country, and as the actor moved further away from its borders, its domain would shrink. The transportation and communications revolutions of the nineteenth and twentieth centuries changed this pattern somewhat. Still, geographical distance was seen as a key to domain.[102]

On the contemporary international scene, at least three factors have a strong effect on domain: the actor's ability to locate the target it seeks to influence; whether other actors are prepared to cooperate with and to try to protect the target; and the target's willingness to accept control.

Location is important because it is impossible to control those you cannot find or those you have no contact with. As the reader may recall, a basic part of the power equation calls for interaction between actor and target. The inability to locate means that no interaction can be established. Protection essentially means that either the target to be influenced is provided with an alliance (meaning that the actor must take on additional targets when it seeks to exert influence, thereby increasing the potential risk of failure), or else the target is given some kind of shelter.

Location and protection are of particular relevance when we examine nonsovereign actors. By their very nature, states are easily located because they are territorial. Nationalist groups, international terrorists, and multinational corporations are not territorial entities, and therefore are not always so easily found. Or, if located, they may obtain offers of succor from other actors and therefore may be difficult to deal with.

International terrorism and guerrilla warfare offer examples of the problem of location. Terrorism and guerrilla warfare are tactics used by the weak. They use these tactics because they realize that their opponents have far more resources and thus that a head-to-head confrontation could spell disaster. An important component of both terrorist and guerrilla tactics is the ability of the terrorist to blend with the rest of the population, thereby making the terrorist hard to find. Thus, the opponent's greater resources are in part neutralized because the opponent is not able to determine who the resources should be directed against. The absolutely vital aspect of such tactics is the ability to mix in with others, which in turn requires at least the marginal acceptance of the terrorists or guerrillas by some portion of the population as a whole. The United States confronted precisely this problem in Vietnam. U.S. forces had sufficient firepower to destroy those it could locate, but the problem was locating the enemy's guerrilla forces. The inability to locate them consistently and effectively limited the domain of American power.

As an example of protection, let us again look at the case of Dresser Industries and the European natural gas pipeline from the Soviet Union. The Reagan administration was stymied in its effort to regulate Dresser because vital parts of Dresser's operations were located outside the United States and came under the jurisdiction and protection of the French government. Thus, the American ability to control Dresser was limited by the fact that Dresser found an ally that was willing to help out. Dresser's location in France placed the corporation beyond the American domain.

The third factor affecting domain, the target's willingness to accept the actor's demands, is closely related to the severity of those demands and to the tactics the actor uses to obtain compliance. The tactics for getting compliance are discussed in a later chapter. For the moment, it should be sufficient to recall that when demands are extreme enough that they appear to limit the target's autonomy and independence of action, they are most likely to be resisted. More moderate demands that leave targets free to maneuver and to set their own policy are much less likely to create resentment. When all other things are equal, severity may be treated as restricting an actor's domain.

Range

Range refers to the types of rewards and punishments an actor can mete out to a target. As such, it is closely associated with the resources available to the actor. An actor's range of resources is affected by its total size, the efficiency with which it uses resources, and its ability to set goals and priorities and to obtain political support for these goals and priorities.

Size may be defined as the total pool of resources under the actor's control. They may be human, financial, or territorial (which includes natural resources). Obviously, larger total resources increase an actor's ability to offer a target inducements or to move against it with some form of punishment. An offer of assistance from the United States is more enticing than the same offer from Cuba because the United States has a much larger resource base than Cuba.

Size may also translate into a greater variety of resources, allowing the actor to tailor the resource used in the influence attempt to the type of demand being made. Baldwin notes the importance of variety when he refers to the "mistaken belief that power resources useful in one policy-contingency framework will be equally useful in a different one."[103] The effective exercise of power in several types of circumstances requires that one have resources appropriate to those situations.[104] Thus, the political, military, and economic resources available to the United States owing to its large size provide it with the capacity to operate with some effectiveness in more areas than can Japan, which has important economic resources but is deficient in other areas.

The effects of efficiency are similar to those of size. The actor that uses resources efficiently obtains more per unit of resource than can the less efficient actor. This augments both the actor's pool and its variety of resources. A clear example of the value of efficiency is found in the comparison of the United States and the Soviet Union in the post–World War II years. The Soviet Union was over twice the physical size of the United States and had a larger population. Yet, the United States consistently had the larger pool of resources for use in supporting its foreign policy, and it also had a greater variety of resources. The basic reason for the difference was the efficiency of the United States as compared with the Soviet Union, where wasted resources were almost a way of life.

Setting goals and priorities has been described as important to an actor's weight. They affect range as well, in that poor policy coordination dissipates resources as decision makers work at cross-purposes with one another and expend financial and other resources pursuing contradictory policies. Marshaling political support for policy is also important, for when people contribute freely to a cause they care for, the effect is to increase the pool of resources. At the same time, it also avoids the waste of resources associated with enforced compliance with policy decisions.

Once again, a comparison of the United States and the Soviet Union is illustrative. With separatist movements in Lithuania, Latvia, Estonia, Georgia, the Ukraine, Armenia, and Azerbaijan, the Soviets had trouble obtaining foreign policy support and were forced to spend resources enforcing the will of the central government. With the exception of protests against certain specific policies, such problems have been rare in the United States. This was a key contributing factor to the smaller Soviet resource range.

Scope

Scope is the type of behavior exhibited by the target that the actor controls. When thinking about scope, we must understand that international actors display many types of behavior and that they generally resist external attempts to control their behavior. As we have noted previously, this resistance is often quite strenuous when it involves external moves to restrict autonomy and freedom of action. Energetic resistance can also be expected when outsiders seek to regulate the target's way of life, its culture, or its system of beliefs. The British willingness in 1940 to fight to the bitter end against the Nazis to safeguard their democratic system; the opposition of nationalist groups around the world to incorporation into sovereign states controlled by representatives from other nations; and the many religious struggles throughout the globe all attest to the degree to which international actors resent threats to their way of life, culture, and beliefs.

Thus, striving to obtain total control over a target can be very difficult and can require that the actor make huge expenditures of resources. Indeed, the resource requirements involved in the pursuit of total control and the target's resistance render bids in this direction largely futile. Still, attempts have been made. One of the most infamous was the German effort during World War II to establish a New Order for Europe that would obliterate the cultures of the subject peoples and seize their resources for use by Germans. These plans failed because of the resistance by those the Germans sought to subjugate and because of the exertions of other countries that feared they might be next on the German "hit list."

Total control may also be counterproductive for the actor. For one thing, it may require an output of resources that far exceeds any benefits the actor can hope to receive in return. For another, it is usually unnecessary because the actor often is concerned with only one or a few aspects of the target's behavior. For example, an actor concerned with the military security threat posed by a target may wish to control the target's armed forces in one way or another and may be prepared to expend resources to that end. Such an actor has no need to regulate the target's postal system, its administration of justice, or its methods of education. Putting resources into managing such activities would be wasteful. For the most part, simple prudence inclines international actors toward the desire to regulate only a small part of the target's scope of activities.

Even seeking to dominate only one or a few of the behavior patterns of the target may present problems. As mentioned elsewhere in this chapter, actors must carefully set goals for themselves regarding the type of behavior they wish to regulate and must factor in the target's tendency to resist. With regard to these factors, let us repeat the point that an actor cannot expect to obtain something from a target unless the actor knows what it wants, and that an actor usually meets the least resistance when the behavior it wishes to regulate is marginally related to the target's existence.[105]

When an actor seeks to influence the behavior of others, it should conceptualize resources as issue-specific. That is, each type of behavior that one wishes to affect should be treated as requiring a different type of resource. Holsti makes this point when he says:

> Nuclear weapons would be irrelevant in negotiations on cultural exchanges, just as [an] Arab country's vast oil resources could not be effectively mobilized to influence the outcome of international negotiations on satellite communications. Influence is always specific to a particular issue, and resources must be relevant to that issue.[106]

Thus, no single resource should be regarded as useful for all attempts to wield power. No "ultimate" resource exists that will allow an actor to do whatever it wants.[107]

The French made precisely this discovery in 1923 when they invaded the Ruhr region of Germany to secure prompt German reparations payments.

Although the French army could occupy German territory, it could not make German laborers work. In the absence of the willingness to work, reparations could not be paid, and the French found that their efforts produced nothing but international scorn.

The Soviets confronted much the same problem in the post–World War II era, finding that their incredible military strength gave them the ability to affect only a restricted scope of behavior. For forty-five years, from 1945 to 1990, the Soviet occupation of Eastern Europe allowed it to control the military and political affairs of those countries. But it could not force those countries to be efficient and creative in the economic realm.

Therefore, as a general rule, we might propose that when we think of scope, we must begin with the premise that control is never complete. In addition, it is important to regard all international resources as best used in a limited way to modify only some types of behavior. As a result, no actor should ever be seen as omnipotent when dealing with any other actor, no matter how great the apparent disparity between the two may be.

CHAPTER SUMMARY

Three approaches to defining power were discussed. The first treats power as an actor's total resources. While this leads to an easily measured definition, it raises fundamental problems relating to which resources best confer power on an actor and to the conversion process by which resources lead to the ability to have one's way. The second approach defines power as a goal that actors pursue. The basic difficulty with using this definition is that a discussion of goals must be more specific. Merely asserting that power is a goal tells us little about what an actor wants. In addition, goal-oriented discussions often result in regarding power as the accumulation of resources. The third definition centers on viewing power as the ability to control other actors and/or the international environment. This definition is widely used in the scholarly community and conforms to many people's general understanding of the concept— that it is the ability of an actor to get what it wants.

When power is conceptualized in control-oriented terms, it is important to outline the nature of the international actors that may be regulated. International actors were found to be organized entities that formulate goals and policies of their own and that pursue their international interests without relying on the good offices of a higher authority that they recognize as having jurisdiction over their behavior.

One distinction that can be made among international actors is between those that are sovereign and those that are not. The recognized government of a duly constituted state is the only sovereign international entity. States are territorial by nature and have the right to make the ultimate decisions about the people and groups residing within their physical area. Governments also are the only international actors that have traditionally been allotted rights and privileges under international law.

Three types of nonsovereign actors were discussed. The first is the nation.

Nations are political communities with members who regard themselves as so distinct from other political communities that they believe they should be granted the right of self-rule. In the current international arena, many nations have achieved this goal and have created their own nation-states. Many other nations, however, have not attained self-rule, but try to conduct their own international or foreign policies as they seek independence.

A second nonsovereign actor is the international organization. Such entities are created by states to handle important ongoing international problems and are composed of governments. Transnational organizations constitute a third type of nonsovereign actor. These organizations are not formed by states, and their membership is not made up of states. Instead, they are set up by nongovernmental interests to pursue international solutions to problems that these entities regard as vital. Multinational corporations are one example of this type of international actor.

Defining power as the ability to control others has several implications. First, the actor and the target must interact with one another and must be interdependent. Second, perception will inherently play an important part in the exercise of power in several ways. One is that actors must believe they will benefit from manipulating a target or the environment. Another pertains to how a target views the actor's resource base and its reputation. In addition, the actor's policies may be guided by the desire to appear resolute. Third, exercising power also means that the actor and the target must be in conflict with one another. In assessing conflict, it is useful to consider the preferences of the actor and the target, the communications between the two, the degree to which the target understands the actor's preferences and acts to conform to them, and how much of a change in the target's behavior takes place. Finally, power was described as controversial because it involves external control over the target, it includes a degree of uncertainty as to the actor's intentions, and some actors find it emotionally satisfying to manipulate and bully others.

The final section of this chapter examined the limits to power. Limits were posited as being a product of the context in which power is exercised. Four key variables were discussed as defining context: weight, domain, range, and scope. Weight pertains to the probability that a target will do what the actor wants. The actor's organization, the types of goals it pursues, and its ability to communicate with the target are factors affecting weight. Domain relates to the number and types of international targets the actor controls. In the contemporary world, the ability to locate the target, the degree to which other international actors cooperate with the target, and the target's willingness to accept control are all important considerations when investigating domain. Range is defined as the types of rewards and punishments the actor has at its disposal. The important elements for determining an actor's range are its size, its efficiency in using resources, and its ability to set goals and rally political support for those goals. Finally, scope is the type of behavior by the target that the actor controls. Absolute control over most targets is very difficult, requires a high resource expenditure, and usually is both unnecessary and counterproductive.

Having set forth a definition of power, the analysis next considers the basic characteristics of the international system in which power is exercised.

Notes

1. David Baldwin, "Power Analysis and World Politics: New Trends vs. Old Tendencies," *World Politics* 31, no. 2 (January 1979): 181. E. H. Carr agrees with Baldwin, stating that "in order to understand a political issue, it is not enough . . . to know what the point at issue is. It is necessary also to know between whom it has arisen." See E. H. Carr, *The Twenty Years Crisis, 1919–1939* (New York: St. Martin's, 1939), 102.

2. Joseph S. Nye, Jr., *Bound to Lead: The Changing Nature of American Power* (New York: Basic Books, 1990), 189.

3. Robert Dahl takes the approach that it is appropriate to substitute these terms freely for one another in his classic essay "The Concept of Power," *Behavioral Science* (July 1957): 202.

4. Arnold Wolfers, *Discord and Collaboration* (Baltimore: Johns Hopkins University Press, 1962), 103. Harold and Margaret Sprout take a similar view, defining power as "those interactions in which physical force, active or latent, is deemed to be the determining factor." See Harold Sprout and Margaret Sprout, *Toward a Politics of the Planet Earth* (New York: D. Van Nostrand, 1971), 168. Klaus Knorr and Harold Lasswell and Abraham Kaplan take a slightly different approach and regard power as appropriate only to situations involving conflict. When cooperation is found, even in conjunction with conflict, then these authors prefer to use the term *influence*. See Klaus Knorr, *The Power of Nations: The Political Economy of International Relations* (New York: Basic Books, 1975), 3; and Harold D. Lasswell and Abraham Kaplan, *Power and Society* (New Haven, Conn.: Yale University Press, 1950), 76.

5. Lasswell and Kaplan, *Power and Society*, 75.

6. E. H. Carr, *The Twenty Years Crisis*, 107.

7. David A. Baldwin, "The Costs of Power," *Journal of Conflict Resolution* 15, no. 2 (1971): 149.

8. Knorr, *The Power of Nations*, 23.

9. Inis Claude discusses the connection between foreign policy and the balance of power in *Power and International Relations* (New York: Random House, 1962).

10. See Hans Morgenthau, *Politics among Nations: The Struggle for Power and Peace* (New York: Alfred A. Knopf, 1948), 65; and Geoffrey Blainey, *The Causes of War* (New York: Free Press, 1988), 28.

11. See Jeffrey Hart, "Three Approaches to the Measurement of Power in International Relations," *International Organization* 30, no. 2 (Spring 1976): 289–305; and Wolfers, *Discord and Collaboration*, 105–6.

12. Robert Gilpin, *War and Change in World Politics* (New York: Cambridge University Press, 1981), 13.

13. Morgenthau, *Politics among Nations*, 27.

14. Nye, *Bound to Lead*, 154.

15. Karl W. Deutsch, *The Analysis of International Relations* (Englewood Cliffs, N.J.: Prentice-Hall, 1978), 45.

16. Morgenthau, *Politics among Nations*, 28.

17. Sprout and Sprout, *Toward a Politics of the Planet Earth*, 164.

18. One example of this sort of definition is provided in J. David Singer, Stuart Bremer, and John Stuckey, "Capability Distribution, Uncertainty, and Major Power War, 1820–1965," in *Peace, War, and Numbers*, ed. Bruce M. Russett (Beverly Hills, Calif.: Sage, 1972), 19–48.

19. See Hart, "Three Approaches to the Measurement of Power," 290, for a description of these problems.

20. The figures regarding the comparative strength of the Allied and German forces are from Alistair Horne, *To Lose a Battle: France 1940* (New York: Penguin Books, 1979), 217–21.

21. See Peter Calvocoressi and Guy Wint, *Total War: Causes and Courses of the Second World War* (New York: Penguin Books, 1979), chaps. 4–6.

22. The chaos among French governmental figures is described vividly in Winston S. Chur-

chill, *Their Finest Hour,* vol. 2 of *The Second World War* (New York: Houghton Mifflin, 1949), chap. 2.

23. Michael Sullivan says that such discrepancies between resources and influence are rare and that a resource-based definition actually captures much of what scholars and world leaders typically mean when they use the term *power.* See Michael P. Sullivan, *Power in Contemporary International Politics* (Columbia: University of South Carolina Press, 1990), 105–7.

24. Knorr, *The Power of Nations,* 9.

25. Dahl, "The Concept of Power," 203.

26. See Deutsch, *The Analysis of International Relations,* chap. 2; Sprout and Sprout, *Toward a Politics of the Planet Earth,* 172–73; and Robert Keohane and Joseph S. Nye, Jr., *Power and Interdependence* (Boston: Little, Brown, 1977), 11.

27. Kenneth N. Waltz, "The Origins of War in Neorealist Theory," *Journal of Interdisciplinary History* 18, no. 4 (Spring 1988): 616.

28. Robert O. Keohane, *After Hegemony: Cooperation and Discord in the World Political Economy* (Princeton: Princeton University Press, 1984), 22.

29. Karl Deutsch, *The Nerves of Government* (New York: Free Press, 1966), 110.

30. Deutsch, *Nerves of Government,* 247.

31. Lasswell and Kaplan, *Power and Society,* 71.

32. Bruce Russett and Harvey Starr, *World Politics: The Menu for Choice* (New York: W. H. Freeman, 1989), 127.

33. Keohane and Nye, *Power and Interdependence,* 11.

34. See Herbert A. Simon, "Notes on the Observation and Measurement of Political Power," *Journal of Politics* 15, no. 4 (November 1953): 504; Dahl, "The Concept of Power," 202–3; J. David Singer, "Inter-Nation Influence: A Formal Model," in *International Politics and Foreign Policy,* ed. James N. Rosenau (New York: Free Press, 1969), 380; Baldwin, "Power Analysis and World Politics," 162–63; and Nye, *Bound to Lead,* 25–26.

35. Deutsch, *The Analysis of International Relations,* 51.

36. Nye, *Bound to Lead,* 25–26. It should be noted that determining preferences is not easy; thus for all practical purposes, if a country generally gets what it wants there is an inclination to label it as powerful.

37. Deutsch, *The Analysis of International Relations,* 23.

38. Deutsch, *Nerves of Government,* 111.

39. Deutsch, *Nerves of Government,* 247–48.

40. Yoichi Funabashi describes these negotiations in his *Managing the Dollar: From the Plaza to the Louvre* (Washington, D.C.: Institute for International Economics, 1989).

41. Richard Ned Lebow provides a superb portrait of the slide to war in his *Between Peace and War: The Nature of International Crisis* (Baltimore: Johns Hopkins University Press, 1981), chap. 5. Barbara Tuchman also describes how the interactions among the European great powers took on a virtual life of their own and became almost uncontrollable, in *The Guns of August* (New York: Macmillan, 1962).

42. Theodore A. Couloumbis and James H. Wolfe, *Introduction to International Relations: Power and Justice* (Englewood Cliffs, N.J.: Prentice-Hall, 1982), 54.

43. See Hedley Bull, *The Anarchical Society* (New York: Columbia University Press, 1977), 8; Russett and Starr, *World Politics,* 58; and John Spanier, *Games Nations Play* (Washington, D.C.: Congressional Quarterly Press, 1987), 55–56.

44. K. J. Holsti, *International Politics: A Framework for Analysis* (Englewood Cliffs, N.J.: Prentice-Hall, 1983), 84.

45. Morgenthau, *Politics among Nations,* 309–11.

46. Morgenthau, *Politics among Nations,* 310. The implications of coordinated law are discussed in the next chapter of this book.

47. George Modelski, *Principles of World Politics* (New York: Free Press, 1972), 80.

48. Modelski, *Principles of World Politics,* 76.

49. For a discussion of the historical development of nations and nationalism, see Alfred Cobban, *The Nation State and National Self-Determination* (New York: Thomas Y. Crowell, 1969).

50. See Gale Stokes, "The Underdeveloped Theory of Nationalism," *World Politics* 31, no. 1 (October 1978): 150–60; and Arthur N. Waldron, "Theories of Nationalism and Historical Explanation," *World Politics* 38, no. 3 (April 1985): 416–33.

51. It should be noted that the word *nation* is a European term. In a non-European context other terms, such as *tribe*, typically are used to refer to the same basic phenomenon. Thus, in Africa, the Ibos and Yorubas in Nigeria are labeled tribes, even though they are more populous than many European nations.

52. One recent illustration of how a nation may affect the course of affairs within a state in a very telling way is the assassination of the Indian leader Rajiv Gandhi, who was killed in May of 1991 by a member of a militant Tamil group. Another more historical example is found in the incident that precipitated the First World War, the June 1914 murder of the Archduke Franz Ferdinand of the Austro-Hungarian Empire by a Serbian nationalist.

53. Raymond Vernon, *Sovereignty at Bay* (New York: Basic Books, 1971), 4–11.

54. For a discussion of the role multinational corporations supposedly play in promoting growth and development, see Raymond Vernon, *Storm over the Multinationals* (Cambridge, Mass.: Harvard University Press, 1977); Grant L. Reuber, *Private Foreign Investment in Development* (Oxford: Clarendon Press, 1973); Isaiah Frank, *Foreign Enterprise in Developing Countries* (Baltimore: Johns Hopkins University Press, 1980); and John M. Rothgeb, Jr., *The Myths and Realities of Foreign Investment in Poor Countries* (New York: Praeger, 1989).

55. It should be noted that the French government pressured Dresser France to participate in the pipeline deal, thereby overriding the American attempt to force Dresser to forgo cooperation.

56. Sprout and Sprout, *Toward a Politics of the Planet Earth*, 165.

57. See Dahl, "The Concept of Power," 204; Morgenthau, *Politics among Nations*, 103; and Singer, "Inter-Nation Influence," 383.

58. Singer, "Inter-Nation Influence," 383.

59. See Baldwin, "The Costs of Power," 145; David Baldwin, "Inter-Nation Influence Revisited," *Journal of Conflict Resolution* 15, no. 4 (December 1971): 476; Singer, "Inter-Nation Influence," 385; and Deutsch, *Nerves of Government*, 248.

60. See Foster Rhea Dulles, *America's Rise to World Power, 1898–1954* (New York: Harper and Row, 1963), chaps. 6–9; Lloyd C. Gardner, *Imperial America: American Foreign Policy Since 1898* (New York: Harcourt, Brace, Jovanovich, 1976), chap. 4.

61. See Cordell Hull, *The Memoirs of Cordell Hull*, vol. 1 (New York: Macmillan, 1948), chaps. 23–25; Walter LaFeber, *Inevitable Revolutions: The United States in Central America* (New York: W. W. Norton, 1984), chap. 1; Jaime Suchlicki, *Cuba: From Columbus to Castro* (Washington, D.C.: Pergamon-Brassey, 1987), chaps. 9–10.

62. Baldwin, "Inter-Nation Influence Revisited," 483.

63. Singer, "Inter-Nation Influence," 387.

64. Among many others, David Halberstam provides a stirring picture of how American decision makers miscalculated in *The Best and the Brightest* (New York: Penguin Books, 1983).

65. Knorr, *The Power of Nations*, 13.

66. Knorr, *The Power of Nations*, 9.

67. See Richard E. Neustadt, *Alliance Politics* (New York: Columbia University Press, 1970); and Anthony Eden, *Full Circle* (Boston: Houghton Mifflin, 1960), 604–26.

68. A graphic account of the Munich tragedy by a contemporary observer is provided by Winston S. Churchill in *The Gathering Storm*, chap. 17.

69. Soviet resources in this case were supplemented by a reputation for intervention, for the Soviet armed forces had interfered in both Hungary in 1956 and Czechoslovakia in 1968 when they engaged in bloody suppressions of reformist governments.

70. Churchill, *The Gathering Storm*, chap. 10 provides a good account of the British thinking regarding the imposition of sanctions.

71. See Robert Jervis, *The Logic of Images in International Relations* (Princeton: Princeton University Press, 1970).

72. The example of the Soviet confrontation with Finland also illustrates the interaction between a country's resources and its reputation. Morgenthau argues that such an interaction between resources and a country's image as perceived by other countries is a constant part of the international political game. See Morgenthau, *Politics among Nations*, 83.

73. See Robert F. Kennedy, *Thirteen Days: A Memoir of the Cuban Missile Crisis* (New York: W. W. Norton, 1971); and Graham T. Allison, *Esssence of Decision: Explaining the Cuban Missile Crisis* (Boston: Little, Brown, 1971).

74. Henry A. Kissinger, *White House Years* (Boston: Little, Brown, 1979), 227–28.

75. Churchill, *Their Finest Hour*, 256–69.

76. Jacek Kugler, "Terror without Deterrence: Reassessing the Role of Nuclear Weapons," *Journal of Conflict Resolution* 28, no. 3 (September 1984): 470–506.

77. Holsti, *International Politics*, 155.

78. See Dahl, "The Concept of Power," 204; Simon, "Notes on the Observation and Measurement of Political Power," 504; and Singer, "Inter-Nation Influence," 381.

79. John Lewis Gaddis, *The United States and the Origins of the Cold War, 1941–1947* (New York: Columbia University Press, 1972), 190–94.

80. Alexander George and Richard Smoke note that a fundamental problem for the United States in 1950 was the fact that American decision makers were not clear in their own minds just what they were and were not prepared to do with regard to Korea. This is an important reason for the lack of effective communication. See Alexander George and Richard Smoke, *Deterrence in American Foreign Policy: Theory and Practice* (New York: Columbia University Press, 1974), chap. 6.

81. See George and Smoke, *Deterrence in American Foreign Policy*, chap. 7; and John W. Spanier, *The Truman-MacArthur Controversy and the Korean War* (New York: W. W. Norton, 1965), chaps. 5–8.

82. See Lasswell and Kaplan, *Power and Society*, xvi; and Dahl, "The Concept of Power," 204.

83. See Holsti, *International Politics*, 146–48; and Singer, "Inter-Nation Influence," 380.

84. See Churchill, *The Gathering Storm*, 148–68.

85. Richard Smoke, *National Security and the Nuclear Dilemma* (New York: Random House, 1987), 175–77.

86. Trumbull Higgins, *The Perfect Failure* (New York: W. W. Norton, 1987).

87. It was understood that this American promise was coupled with a Soviet guarantee that it would not seek to place offensive missiles in Cuba.

88. Wolfers, *Discord and Collaboration*, 106.

89. David Baldwin, "Thinking about Threats," *Journal of Conflict Resolution* 15, no. 1 (1971): 77.

90. Smoke, *National Security and the Nuclear Dilemma*, chap. 9.

91. Steven Greenhouse, "Industrial Nations Agree to Push for Trade Accord," *New York Times*, June 5, 1991, C7.

92. Baldwin, "The Costs of Power," 50.

93. Knorr, *The Power of Nations*, 22.

94. Singer, "Inter-Nation Influence," 382.

95. Lasswell and Kaplan, *Power and Society*, xxi.

96. Baldwin, "Power Analysis and World Politics," 164.

97. Baldwin, "Power Analysis and World Politics," 168–69.

98. See Lasswell and Kaplan, *Power and Society*, 73; Dahl, "The Concept of Power," 203–6; Deutsch, *The Analysis of International Relations*, 28; and Baldwin, "Power Analysis and World Politics," 164.

99. Lasswell and Kaplan, *Power and Society*, 200.

100. Deutsch, *The Analysis of International Relations,* 31.

101. Deutsch, *The Analysis of International Relations,* 30.

102. See Deutsch, *The Analysis of International Relations,* 33; and Morgenthau, *Politics among Nations,* chap. 9.

103. Baldwin, "Power Analysis and World Politics," 164. Nye makes much the same point in *Bound to Lead,* 27.

104. Lasswell and Kaplan, *Power and Society,* 92–94.

105. Scholars usually discuss the existence of a threat in terms of military security affairs. Joseph Grieco has demonstrated recently that in the years since the Second World War, actors have come to perceive threats to their existence in far broader terms, and that security now encompasses economic and social matters as well. See Joseph M. Grieco, *Cooperation among Nations: Europe, America, and Non-Tariff Barriers to Trade* (Ithaca, N.Y.: Cornell University Press, 1990).

106. Holsti, *International Politics,* 151.

107. Baldwin, "Power Analysis and World Politics," 181.

3

The International System

This chapter describes the social setting in which international actors exercise power. Familiarity with this setting is important to an understanding of power in international politics and of the changes in its application in recent decades. The first part of the discussion focuses on scholars' traditional depiction of the international system. This section describes the international system from what scholars commonly refer to as the realist point of view. As will be seen, this conception usually treats the international system as anarchic and authority as decentralized, with international actors being free of any external restraints. In this kind of situation, security concerns become a fundamental motivating guide for all members of the international system. A basic function performed by all international actors is to eliminate insecurity and to seek protection from the possible threats other actors may pose. Self-interest is the driving force behind the behavior of all actors, and the resort to violence is expected and sometimes even accepted as a means for obtaining highly valued goals. Under these circumstances, morality is supposedly difficult to judge properly. Many analysts therefore regard international politics as either amoral or immoral.

This initial description of the international system will serve as a backdrop against which we may compare the current international arena. As was mentioned in Chapter 1, a number of changes over the last four decades have redefined and modified important aspects of the international system. These alterations are examined in the second section of this chapter. Among the most important are shifts in how actors define their security and envision the use of force and violence, the roles they assign to the military, and the types of conflict they engage in. Despite these changes, many things remain much as they always have been. Specifically, the essential structure of the system, the role of self-interest as a guide to an actor's behavior, the need to provide for one's own security, and problems of applying morality to international politics continue to be pertinent.

The final part of this chapter describes the emergence of parallel international universes (see Chapter 1). One of these universes consists of advanced industrialized countries that conduct one type of relations among themselves and a very different type with other members of the international system. The relationships among advanced countries are concerned primarily with nonviolently handling economic and political policy matters among equals and near equals. The interactions between advanced countries and the rest of the international arena focus on highly stratified relations that include a military component and that at times become violent. The other universe consists of a very disparate set of actors that for the most part are not nearly as wealthy as those found in the first group. These actors tend to be dominated by those in the first universe, are more prone toward both international and domestic political upheavals and violence, and do not play a large role as managers of international economic affairs. Grasping the characteristics of these parallel systems and understanding how they differ are vital aspects of determining what power is all about in contemporary international politics.

THE TRADITIONAL INTERNATIONAL SYSTEM

The international system consists of the patterns of interaction that exist among those actors that formulate and conduct a policy designed to further their foreign goals and interests. In developing policy within this system, actors respond to at least three types of factors: (1) domestically determined needs and predispositions, (2) their perceptions of the behavior displayed by other actors, and (3) their perceptions of the motivations and intentions of other actors.[1] That is, foreign policy within the international system may be viewed as a complex mix that responds to the forces that are at work within both the actor's internal and international environments. As each actor moves in response to these forces, the nature of these environments is redefined, resulting in new domestic and international situations that may elicit a counterresponse from another actor. These counterresponses redefine circumstances and create the need for further policy selections. Thus, in this ongoing set of interactions, each actor consistently reevaluates its own particular needs and monitors the behavior of other actors. It adjusts its policies in response to what is actually going on and to what it believes is going on.

As discussed briefly in Chapter 2, the members of the international system, unlike the members of the domestic political systems, are collective entities. Historically, the state has been the primary international actor, but today there are others. As a group, these actors are quite heterogeneous as to type of organization, amount of resources they control, size of their populations, level of modernization, financial capacities, and so forth. One characteristic all international actors have in common, however, is their commitment to conducting an international policy of their own and their ability to pull together what often are very substantial pools of resources to support these policies.[2] For example, many states maintain standing armed forces that include tens and even hundreds of thousands of troops and have governmental budgets of scores of billions of dollars. Some multinational corporations have total sales running to nearly $100 billion.[3] In general, the individual citizens and interest groups that operate within the domestic political sphere have neither the ability to match the resources of international actors nor the desire to conduct an international policy of their own.

The international social system is also different from domestic systems in that there is no international or world government that can operate effectively as a regulator of international political activities. As we all know, the domestic social scene is managed closely by a government that has the right to make and enforce such laws as are deemed necessary to maintain domestic order. In addition, this government usually has sufficient strength to enable it to control all the members of the political community that fall within its jurisdiction. Only in unusual instances is a government unable to control domestic political groups owing to its weakness relative to these groups. The inability of the Lebanese government to control the various religious and ethnic factions in Lebanon and of the Yugoslavian government in the early 1990s to control Slovenian and Croatian separatist efforts are two of the small handful of cases around the globe where governments cannot enforce their will when dealing with domestic challenges to their authority.

International Anarchy

The absence of a world government means that the international system is anarchic. Anarchy is defined as a situation in which there are no "formal institutions of government at the system level, and that is highly decentralized with respect to the distribution of authority and power."[4] In an anarchic arena, each actor is free to formulate its own goals and priorities and to pursue its interests as it pleases. As a result, "international politics is shaped by the anarchical context in which it takes place,"[5] for there is no international agency to coordinate the various goals that actors have and either to ensure that there are no clashes between these objectives or to act as an authoritative mediator when disputes do occur. Therefore, independence is the principle that organizes the actors in the international arena.

Restraints on International Behavior.   Restraints on an actor's behavior come from two sources. The first source is internal to the actor itself and consists of the limits that public opinion may place on policymakers, the amount of resources available for the pursuit of foreign policy, and the financial, cultural, geographical, and other characteristics of the society. For example, in the years immediately after the Vietnam War, American public opinion constrained American policymakers by its unwillingness to tolerate American interventions in Third World conflicts. As a result, the United States could not commit itself to a more active role in troubled places such as Angola, Ethiopia, and Nicaragua. In addition, the public placed restrictions on the resources it was willing to devote to the support of foreign and defense policy. Therefore, U.S. decision makers were unable to follow the courses of action they would have preferred.

The second source of restraint on an actor's behavior is external, emanating from what other actors in the international system are willing to tolerate and from what they are capable of preventing. For the most part, external restraints are loose and come into play only when an actor's behavior threatens either the independence of another actor or a right or commodity that another actor values very highly, such as its access to an important natural resource. To the extent that an actor's policy behavior threatens either the independence or vital interests of more and more members of the international system, the actor may come to be regarded as seeking hegemony, or dominance over the system. Consequently, it will meet with an ever-increasing degree of organized resistance from other actors.[6] As Hans Morgenthau notes, "since the emergence of the modern state system in the fifteenth century, no single [state] has succeeded in imposing its will for any length of time on the rest of the world."[7] Kenneth Waltz makes the same point in his observation that "in international politics, success leads to failure. The excessive accumulation of power by one state or coalition of states elicits the opposition of others."[8] Precisely this reaction greeted bids for supremacy by Napoleon in the early nineteenth century and by Germany in World Wars I and II. In each case, the reach for hegemony failed because a combination of other states resisted it strongly.

International Conflict and Security.   Many analysts point to the combination of independent policy-making and the lack of a central governmental organization as a major reason for international conflict. As Arnold Wolfers has said, "the anarchical condition inherent in any system of multiple sovereignties constitutes one of the prerequisites of international conflict."[9] Harold and Margaret Sprout agree, arguing that "the essence of statecraft . . . result[s] from efforts to defend or to promote conflicting values, goals, and objectives . . . in a milieu characterized by the absence of any overarching structure of authority."[10]

The resources that many international actors possess and the general freedom they have (within the internal and external constraints imposed on them) to use those resources in pursuit of their international objectives cast international conflict in a particularly troubling light. The absence of government means that there are few "rules" regarding what types of conflict are acceptable and what sorts of tactics are allowable. Fears regarding Iraq's potential use of chemical weapons during the Persian Gulf War in 1991 illustrate this problem well. In addition, many actors can draw on a large pool of assets and can employ them for violent purposes, if they choose to do so. As one analyst states, "any social system must contain some inevitable competition and conflict . . . in the international system they are handled in a . . . primitive fashion."[11] Thus, international conflict has the potential for far greater destruction and for much heavier loss of life than domestic disputes.

As a consequence, the international arena is often depicted as one in which war is the normal state of affairs among states. Waltz, for example, says that "in an anarchic realm, peace is fragile."[12] Morgenthau is even more explicit about this point when he claims that "all history shows that [states] active in international politics are continuously preparing for, actively involved in, or recovering from organized violence in the form of war."[13] Because of this constant violence and potential for violence, no actor is safe in the international system. At any particular time, every actor confronts an array of other actors that possess armed forces, that pursue policies that may be at cross-purposes with its own policies, and that may choose to use their military capabilities to ensure that their policies prevail over those of their competitors. Mutual antagonism therefore exists among the members of the international arena, and the end result is that "the scarcest commodity in the international system is security."[14]

Living in a world that is devoid of security, however, is unacceptable for the great majority of international actors. Hence, states act to reduce their insecurity by pursuing policies designed to provide them with a margin of safety in the event another actor seeks to compromise their best interests. One such policy is to build up a storehouse of those resources that are perceived to be most useful for guaranteeing the ability to withstand any assaults launched by another actor. The most reliable assets for ensuring safety usually are seen as those that pertain to military capabilities. A stronger military means that a state's would-be opponents may be forced to think hard before they make unacceptable moves, because the penalty for rash behavior may include harsh military punishment. Thus, the search for security invariably leads to the accumulation of ever greater levels of military resources.

John Herz has noted that such a prescription for building security contains within it an inherent problem. Specifically, when any single actor appears to become stronger as a result of the accumulation of resources, thereby supposedly ensuring its own safety, other actors may perceive this strength to be a threat to their security.[15] As Waltz observes, in the international system "the preoccupation with identifying dangers and counter-acting them become a way of life."[16] Moves by one actor to increase its security-oriented assets cannot fail to promote anxiety in others. Such anxiety may then prompt countermoves on their part, as they seek to accumulate the wherewithal to protect themselves. These countermoves lead to a renewed sense of insecurity for the state that made the initial move to increase its capabilities, with the result being further attempts to build its resources. One move thus leads to another, as the search for security merely breeds insecurity for other actors, who react by pursuing policies that undermine the original quest.

This is the "security dilemma" that Herz describes.[17] An actor can enjoy true security only if it can make all other actors accept an insecure existence. By their very nature, other actors will not accept such circumstances, and the anarchic nature of the international arena, with decentralized authority and policy-making, allows these other actors to react in such a way as to negate any one actor's true security.

Interestingly, the competition spawned as a part of the security dilemma may occur even when the actors involved are only interested in pursuing defensive measures and have no interest in or designs on the possessions of other actors. The reason is that it is nearly impossible to differentiate between defensive and offensive weapons systems and other capabilities.[18] As observed in Chapter 2, there was never any solid evidence that the Soviet Union had aggressive intentions toward Western Europe during the cold war. Thus, Soviet moves may have been largely defensive. The West was so alarmed by these moves, however, that it maintained a high level of military resources for defensive purposes, thereby disturbing the Soviet Union. Thus did two defense-minded adversaries find themselves enmeshed in security-driven competition.

Self-Interest and Self-Help.   The implications of the security dilemma extend beyond the mere buildup of armaments. In a context of strong competition and conflict, cooperating with others becomes difficult and self-interest is of paramount importance as a guide to policy-making. Cooperation is problematic due to the fear that relying on the goodwill of others and trusting them, which is the basis for any act of collaboration, may make an actor vulnerable to an act of bad faith. As Robert Jervis observes, "the fear of being exploited . . . most strongly drives the security dilemma."[19] When an actor lowers its guard, it runs risks. Caution demands that it avoid risks because of the terrible consequences that it might confront, given the strength and resources that other actors often have at their disposal.

When cooperation is difficult, actors are forced to base their policy on their own best interest. The basic motivating force for their actions must be the protection of their populations and their possessions. In fact, providing for the security of its population has long been seen as one of the most basic functions of the state. Indeed, one of the most important reasons for creating and maintaining the state was the desire to provide individuals with protection from those actors beyond the political community who might seek to do them harm. James Madison makes this very point in *The Federalist Papers* when he claims that "security against foreign danger is one of the primitive objects of civil society."[20] A more recent author agrees, commenting that

> the first duty of government is to ensure, to the extent feasible, the physical security of its citizens—a duty closely followed by the requirement that the core values, other than physical survival, of the society should be protected and, if possible, advanced.[21]

The international arena can be described as a self-help system inasmuch as international actors must take care of their own best interests and cannot look either to other actors or to an international governmental agency for aid.[22] As noted in Chapter 2, international law is based on coordinating the interests of the members of the international system rather than on subordinating those interests to the abstract principles of law. Thus, not only can actors not be forced to do what they do not wish to do, but they also cannot be obligated to do things they choose not to agree to. Even when another actor *does* agree to observe a particular set of rules, the only way to enforce compliance will be for those actors who may be affected by noncompliance to take action to compel a recalcitrant party to keep its word. This is what the term *self-help* refers to— each actor must look out for its own interests and must be prepared to use its resources to back up international agreements.

Unfortunately, too often in history the pursuit of self-interest has driven states to disregard either existing international conventions or obligations they freely accepted. German military plans on the eve of the First World War provides an example of a violation of an international convention.[23] The Germans formulated these plans on the assumption that a major war in Europe would mean that Germany would confront powerful enemies to both the east and the west. The Franco-Russian alliance appeared to assure them enemies on two fronts. The German High Command was uneasy about fighting a two-front war and believed that it would lead to disaster for Germany. The only way they believed they could avoid such a development would be to take on France and Russia one at a time, defeating one opponent first and then turning the entire weight of German capabilities against the other. This strategy was risky, however, for it required that the opponent not initially engaged be unable to wreak too much damage on Germany while German forces were dealing with the other antagonist. It also required that it must be possible to deliver a knockout blow quickly against one or the other of Germany's primary enemies.

As German military officials reviewed French and Russian capabilities, they concluded that Germany would be forced to strike at France first. They decided on France, first, because Russian transportation and communication facilities were so poor that the Russian armies would take substantially longer

Map 3. Europe in 1914

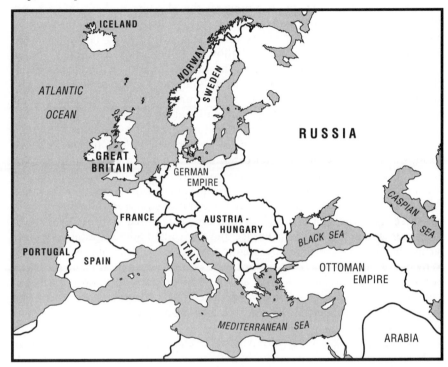

than the French to mount a threat against Germany. Second, France was compact in size, and its capital was within striking distance of the French-German frontier. Russia was a far larger country, and it might take a very long time for any military campaign to meet with success.

But in planning an attack against France, the Germans confronted difficulties pertaining to an international convention they had signed together with France and the United Kingdom in the early nineteenth century. This convention neutralized Belgium and pledged both that the signing countries would not intrude on this neutrality in any way and that they would protect Belgium in the event any other country violated Belgium's sovereignty. This convention placed Germany in an uncomfortable position, for the easiest route for quickly attacking and subduing France involved moving German forces through Belgium. The German military's proposed answer to this dilemma was to ignore the convention and to proceed with their plans to move on France via Belgium. When war broke out in August 1914, this is precisely what Germany did. Thus, when German national priorities conflicted with a long-standing international convention that Germany had agreed to, the convention was sacrificed and the German conception of self-interest took precedence.

Self-interest may also dictate that a country abrogate agreements that it has negotiated with allies or that it refuse requests made by friendly countries for assistance. During World War II, Germany abrogated a treaty of alliance.

Just before war broke out in September 1939, Germany negotiated a nonaggression pact with the Soviet Union. Known as the Molotov-Ribbentrop Pact, this alliance pledged that Germany and the Soviet Union would not engage in military action against one another. The pact also divided Poland between Germany and the Soviet Union and allowed the Soviets to control the Baltic states of Lithuania, Latvia, and Estonia. But in June 1941 the Nazis moved against the Soviet Union, launching history's largest invasion of one country by another. The Nazis did not hesitate to overturn the pact. Again, self-interest prevailed over respect for a solemn international agreement.

For an illustration of a country that turned down requests by a friendly country for assistance, we can turn to more recent events. In the spring of 1986, the Reagan administration determined that Libya was responsible for acts of terrorism against American service personnel in Europe and decided to use an air raid against Libya as a reprisal. Some of the units that President Reagan planned to use for the attack were stationed in the United Kingdom. For these units, the shortest route to their targets required that they fly through French airspace. Even though France and the United States are on very close terms, the French government refused to grant the American planes permission to fly over France. The French government's rationale was that its involvement in the attack would place French citizens and property in danger if Libyan-supported terrorists decided on revenge. The French government therefore saw its first duty as that of protecting the French people and serving the best interests of France.

In fact, when we study international events carefully, only rarely do we find that countries offer succor to those in need unless it conforms to their self-interest. At first glance, the American-led United Nations efforts in Korea and more recently in the Persian Gulf might appear to fall into the category of selfless and generous assistance provided to a country in dire straits. Further consideration of each action, however, leads to a different assessment. In the case of Korea, U.S. moves were powerfully motivated by the need to create credibility for its policy of containing communism. A failure to act in Korea would have raised questions about the United States' willingness to act anywhere.[24] And, of course, in the Persian Gulf a vital natural resource, oil, was at stake. Once more, the need to protect one's own interests was the guiding force behind the behavior.

When offering aid does not coincide with an actor's best interests, it is not extended. One such example, the French and British reaction in the mid-1930s to the Italian invasion of Ethiopia, was mentioned in Chapter 2. In that case, both France and Britain apparently perceived that they risked very little if Italy prevailed. At the same time, these countries also felt that to oppose Italy openly ran the risk of alienating a country whose help they might need in an anti-German coalition. Hence, the French and British were very hesitant to support Ethiopia, even though it was the victim of a brutal act of aggression. Chad's cry for help from the United States in the early 1980s when Chad confronted a Libyan invasion is another instance in which the lack of a stake in the victim of aggression led the would-be rescuer to demur. With Chad's shortage of key natural resources and its nonstrategic location, the United States perceived it would gain little, if anything, from extending aid.

The Effects of Miscalculation.   When discussing self-interest, we might presume that actors calculate it accurately and that they can discern the appropriate policy selections for whatever contingency they face. This is not the case, however. International actors are just as prone to miscalculate as any other human organization. The consequences of a mistake in an anarchic environment, however, are far more severe than those of an error made in the relative tranquility of the domestic arena. As Waltz observes, "in the anarchy of states, the price of inattention or miscalculation is often paid in blood."[25] Morgenthau concurs. He comments that the correct assessment of the meaning of events in the international arena is vital and that arriving at "the wrong answer has often meant deadly peril or actual destruction."[26] The penalties associated with inaccurate assessments therefore become a formidable barrier to meaningful international collaboration because, as Jervis argues, "the policies of cooperation that will bring mutual rewards if others cooperate may bring disaster if they do not."[27]

History is abundantly filled with examples of the terrible consequences of foreign policy miscalculations. The German plan to invade France via Belgium, for example, was based on the mistaken belief that the United Kingdom would accept the German move with equanimity. When the British did not, the Germans found themselves confronting an enemy they had not fully prepared for.[28] The Soviet acceptance of German assurances of peaceful intentions in the Molotov-Ribbentrop Pact was a miscalculation that cost the Soviet Union in excess of 20 million lives and untold property damage. Chamberlain was mistaken in his analysis of Hitler at Munich, and a small German neighbor, Czechoslovakia, was sacrificed. The French also made some supreme errors when drawing up their defense plans in the 1930s. First, they decided to construct a large system of fortresses, known as the Maginot Line, along the French-German border. Second, they decided to move a substantial part of their armed forces into Belgium to meet any future German attack. Third, French armored vehicles were not concentrated into armored divisions; instead they were distributed throughout the army as a whole. Finally, the Ardennes Forest was left only lightly defended, even though it was the linchpin of the French defenses.[29] As a result, the German offensive in May of 1940 caught the French woefully out of position and disorganized. The collapse of the French defense effort followed quickly, with France becoming a vassal of Germany for nearly five years.

More recently, U.S. miscalculations about the value of containing communism in Southeast Asia led to an involvement in the most unpopular war in U.S. history. Two presidential administrations were stained by the war, domestic economic and social policy was significantly altered, political campaigns were adversely affected, educational institutions were put under tremendous strain, the United States' international leadership and prestige were damaged badly, and tens of thousands of lives were lost. And all for a locale that was of very dubious value to American national security.

The Argentinian invasion of the Falkland/Malvinas Islands in 1982 provides another example of miscalculation. The Galtieri government in Argentina apparently conceived of the invasion as an opportunity to solidify the Argentine public behind the government while at the same time surprising the British and acquiring control over islands Argentina had claimed for over 150 years. The British were not expected to react. The Argentinians were wrong, however, and the end product was a sound military defeat for Argentina and the collapse of the Galtieri administration.

In surveying the effects of miscalculation, analysts traditionally single out the importance of the geographical position of the state in question.[30] As a result of geography, some states historically have been freer of the baleful consequences of miscalculation than have others. For example, in the 1930s the British were just as negligent as the French in drawing conclusions about the best defensive schemes, and the Americans were even more so. The French, however, paid the price of conquest, whereas the British and Americans did not. The difference was geographical position. Britain was protected by the English Channel and the United States by the Atlantic to the east and the Pacific to the west. France had no such protection.

Thus, the price one must pay for mistakes is not evenly distributed; some states are more heavily penalized than others. Barriers to invasion help provide security. Very small states also run risks that larger states may not. A good example is the beleaguered state of Israel. This country, which is about the size of New Jersey, illustrates how size affects a government's need to think very carefully about each move it makes. Mistakes for a tiny nation simply are not permissible in the same way that they might be for a continent-sized country, such as the United States.

Geography, Resources, and Security.   The relationship between geography and security is also seen in actors' traditional conceptions of the value of territorial possessions. The acquisition of territory is regarded as having two major benefits: (1) it puts possible enemies further from the heart of one's country, and (2) it provides greater access to the resources that an actor needs in order to compete more effectively in the anarchic international system, thereby reducing its need to depend on others for such access.[31]

The second reason has become especially important in the modern industrial era because industrialization greatly expands both the quantities and types of raw materials a country needs to keep its economy functioning optimally. Industrial and economic problems can adversely affect a country's defense posture in a world of sophisticated military weapons systems. In addition, the denial of these resources can mean great hardship for a country owing to the unemployment and the lowered standards of living that may result. In a political system marked by constant conflict, with countries maneuvering for advantage against one another, a country's opponents and would-be opponents have an incentive to use the tactic of denying it much needed resources in order to gain a political advantage. Thus, international anarchy and competition demand that countries not only seek access to important natural resources, but physically control their points of origin as well.[32]

The quest for the control of resources played key roles in starting both world wars in the twentieth century. Before the First World War, the European great powers engaged in an almost frenzied competition for empire as they sought to expand their territorial holdings to control more and more of the natural resources needed to fuel their industrial establishments.[33] Many members of the decision-making elites in each major European country believed that the failure to expand would be the equivalent of abdicating their position as a great power and would almost certainly lead to disaster in the future.[34] Thus, the Europeans seized large portions of Africa and Asia and engaged in often fierce competition when their ambitions clashed. The Fashoda crisis in the Sudan in 1898 between France and Britain and the Moroccan crises between France and Germany in 1905 and 1911 show how the pursuit of colonies and resources raised tensions to such a feverish pitch that war nearly resulted.[35]

The desire for a secure access to resources also played a large role in causing the Second World War. One important aspect of Hitler's mad vision for a New Order in Europe included German expansion to the east, so that Germany would have *lebensraum,* or living space, as well as control over greater food- and fuel-producing areas. This was a major reason for the attack on the Soviet Union in 1941.

For their part, the Japanese struck at the United States because they desperately wished to acquire the oil resources in the Dutch East Indies (now Indonesia). The need for control of these resources was created by an American oil embargo in mid-1941, which cut off the major Japanese source of this key natural resource. In moving against the Dutch East Indies, the Japanese feared that an American naval base at Subic Bay in the Philippines would pose a threat to Japanese supply routes. Thus, they needed to attack the American forces in the Far East, which meant a further need to strike at the key American Pacific base at Pearl Harbor.[36]

Concern over an unacceptable level of dependence for access to important natural resources continues to motivate foreign policy behavior in the contemporary international arena. The European natural gas pipeline controversy mentioned in Chapter 2 is one example. The Europeans decided to seek the construction of the Soviet pipeline as a means of avoiding overdependence on potentially unstable North African sources of supply. For the United States, however, the pipeline could give the Soviets an economic lever that they could use to political advantage in the future. From the U.S. point of view, the Europeans were leaping out of the proverbial frying pan of dependence on North Africa into the fire of reliance on the Soviet Union.

Natural resources also played a role in the Persian Gulf crisis and war of 1990–91. For the industrialized world the issue at stake was not only halting unwarranted aggression. Control of the oil fields of the Middle East was also perceived as riding on the outcome of events. Between them, Iraq and Kuwait account for about 20 percent of the world's proven oil reserves. If Saudi Arabia fell under Iraqi control, another 25 percent of the world's oil reserves would be in the hands of a government that many regarded as extremely unpredictable.[37] Such a circumstance was judged intolerable, especially in light of the vital role of oil in modern economies.

International Morality

As our examples demonstrate, morality is somewhat difficult to analyze in an international setting. This difficulty stems both from the anarchic nature of the system and from the makeup of the actors. Anarchy breeds a focus on self-interest and on the realization that not all actors play the game of international

Map 4. The Far East

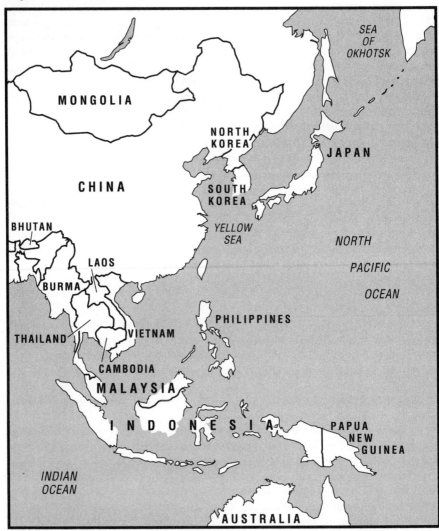

politics according to the same rules. Governments that are charged with protecting their citizens are not the equivalent of individuals, and the types of moral understandings that guide the behavior of individuals toward one another simply do not apply well to international actors. In the international arena, a government's duty to protect its population becomes its highest obligation, outweighing any requirement for correct behavior toward other actors. The diverse cultures and values that guide the varying actors throughout the world only add greater complication to an already complex matter.

Morality and Force. Morality pertains not so much to avoiding the use of force and to observing all agreements—even when they would work decisively against one's country—as it does to avoiding the sort of unnecessary bullying and resort to violence mentioned in Chapter 2 (see the discussion of the distinction between power and fate control).[38] Two examples may help illustrate these points. The first relates to the maintenance of large military establishments. The second has to do with the use of force in international politics.

In most civil societies and in almost all interactions among individuals, possessing the means to do violence is considered questionable. In addition, many people oppose expending resources on the capacity to do large-scale violence in a world where so many people lack even the basic necessities of life. Thus, scholars and humanitarians throughout the world have long argued that military expenditures are obscene and immoral. This view, however, discounts the duty of a country's government to protect its citizens from foreign dangers. It also fails to consider that a government's decision to pursue disarmament in an armed world would in itself be an act of dubious moral value. As James Madison observed two hundred years ago, "how could a readiness for war in time of peace be safely prohibited unless we could prohibit in like manner the preparations and establishments of every hostile nation?"[39] Wolfers made much the same point when he wrote that "moral advice not to submit to the necessities of survival . . . would be advice to commit suicide."[40]

Generally, force and violence are considered morally unacceptable in the domestic political arena except under the most extreme and most unusual conditions. Within the international political system, however, force plays a central role, for it enables a country to protect its interests and seek its goals. Of course, even in international politics nonviolent techniques are most often used to satisfy these two objectives. When these techniques fail, however, actors are often prepared to use force. The Japanese in the fall of 1941, for example, made lengthy efforts to obtain access to American oil through negotiations. Only when they realized that bargaining would not yield access at an acceptable cost did they turn to the use of violence.

International Change.   The Japanese example illustrates that force is an instrument of last resort. It also shows that, in the absence of any agreed-to mechanisms for obtaining and instituting change, important changes in the international environment may require a violent approach. Those who profit from the international status quo have little incentive to accept any alterations in the distribution of its benefits, and there are no legislative or judicial procedures for creating change against their will. Since any kind of meaningful peaceful change is difficult to obtain, those who feel they are wronged or harmed by the status quo may feel compelled to resort to violence.[41]

The inability to secure peaceful change through negotiations was one important motivating factor in the Argentine decision to invade the Falklands/ Malvinas. Many international terrorist groups and guerrilla organizations also use violence to dramatize their plight and to try to compel the strong to take account of their interests. The disadvantaged perceive violence in the international political arena as one of their few weapons for obtaining redress of their grievances. Without the use of force, these people would lose all hope of obtaining justice.[42]

Preemptive Violence.   In relations between individuals, while force may be acceptable in self-defense, starting fights is considered deplorable. The same is not true in the international arena where it may become necessary, and even preferable, that an actor engage in the first use of violence. Specifically, if a country in possession of evidence that an opponent was planning an assault were to await the first blow, it would be ignoring its responsibility to protect its citizens. Moreover, waiting could increase the amount of damage the opponent could inflict.

For example, in the summer of 1981, the Israeli air force launched a preemptive strike against an Iraqi nuclear research facility. At the time, there was no state of war between Israel and Iraq. Many governments from around the world condemned the Israeli act as immoral. The Israeli government, however, reasoned that if the Iraqis were to develop a nuclear capability, Israel would be a likely target. The government felt it could not ignore this supreme danger for all its citizens and so launched its attack. The morality of the Israeli act depended entirely on who was judging.

This action may have been the result of a hard-learned lesson. Eight years earlier, in October 1973, Israeli intelligence detected Egyptian and Syrian preparations for an offensive against Israel. For a number of reasons ranging from their inability to believe that these opponents would actually attack to their desire to appear as defenders instead of violators of the peace, the Israelis did not launch a preemptive attack. Thus, when the Egyptians and Syrians struck they were able to do substantial early damage to the Israeli armed forces.[43] Over a period of several days, the Israelis were able to gain mastery of the battlefield, but the early decision to stand on the defensive cost them dearly. By observing the strictures against the first use of force, they suffered more loss of life and damage to property than was necessary. Therefore, what appeared morally correct at one level was difficult to defend as morally proper at another.

In summary, conferring the ultimate authority on the state to rule the people and territory it controls means that the international system contains some very strong entities living side by side in an anarchic social setting, with few restraints on their behavior. Security is not easily obtained and peace is fragile, for competition between actors is always vigorous and mutual suspicions are inevitable. A state's military capabilities therefore play an important part in its interactions with other states, particularly when both states are strong and compete closely. Self-interest is an actor's primary guide to policymaking, its foremost obligation is to protect its citizens from physical danger, and miscalculations may carry extreme penalties. Morality is not easily assessed, friendship between countries is virtually meaningless, cooperation is at best ephemeral, and respect for international agreements is shallow. Finally, any sort of dependence on others, especially for maintaining security or for obtaining key resources, is regarded as intolerable. This then is the world we live in, at least according to the beliefs of many international theorists.

THE CONTEMPORARY INTERNATIONAL SYSTEM

The international system has undergone several fundamental changes since the Second World War. These alterations, though in many ways sweeping and even revolutionary, have not completely restructured the system, however.

This section will be devoted to considering how the world has changed. In doing this, it may be useful to reflect upon the past few pages and to see which of the characteristics just mentioned have changed and how they have been altered.

The Prominence of the State

Although the state is no longer the only actor in the international system, in many ways it remains the most formidable. As the only sovereign territorial actor, the state has the advantage of at least nominally controlling all other actors, for they all must exist in a territorial space. The state may create and enforce laws for all entities that exist within its space, making all other actors to some degree dependent on its goodwill. The state is also an important determinant of the climate of permissiveness or repressiveness, both domestically and internationally, that exists for all other actors because it is the only actor with the legitimate authority to employ force in either of these social settings.[44] For instance, nationalist groups may find either a relatively tolerant climate for their activities, as in Canada, or a much more threatening atmosphere, as in Iraq. Similarly, large corporations may be granted considerable freedom of action, as in the United States, or they may be far more closely regulated, as was the case in the former Soviet Union.

In addition, non-state actors often turn to the state for assistance when the international environment sours.[45] During the turbulent years of the 1970s, in which an unsettled international oil market buffeted the international arena, one actor after another looked to the state to prop it up and to provide it with assistance to meet its international problems. In the United States alone, the auto, steel, textile, and electronics industries, among many other international actors of American origin, turned to the state for aid. In the following decade, the international debt crisis brought one multinational bank after another to its government for help in collecting the loans it had extended to other governments around the globe. Thus, the state remains the supreme actor on the international scene.

This central role means that the anarchic characteristic of the international arena is very much present in the contemporary world. Today anarchy carries with it many of the features it had in the past: few restraints on the behavior of individual actors; mutual suspicion and competition; the need to provide for one's own security; self-interest as a guide to policy; the duty to protect one's citizens; the pain associated with miscalculation; the reluctance to depend on others; and difficulties pertaining to the judgment of what is morally proper in an international context. The many post–World War II examples presented earlier in this chapter reveal a strong continuity between the past and the present as far as international structures are concerned.

The State as Economic Manager.   Study of the current international arena indicates that some very significant changes have taken place. A good place to begin assessing these alterations is where we just began—with the state. The state remains predominant, but the nature of the state itself, including its most basic guiding reason for being, has been transformed. As noted above, in the past the state's principal international purpose was to provide security for its citizens. This purpose was almost universally seen in military terms, with the focus on foreign threats and dangers from possible attacks by the armed forces of other states. Therefore, the provision of security was best met by building a military apparatus.

Over the last several decades, much of this has been altered. Perhaps the most fundamental changes began during the years between the two world wars when for the first time in modern history the state accepted responsibility for managing the economy of its society in order to guarantee its people's social and economic welfare. One force pushing the state toward these new duties stemmed from the carnage and devastation of the First World War, which necessitated strong action geared to rebuilding the economies of the affected states. Another powerful motivation was the extreme dislocation that occurred during the Great Depression of the 1930s. As Charles Kindleberger points out in his classic study, *The World in Depression,* prior to this upheaval governments around the world had only very limited conceptions of the role the state either could or should play in regulating and managing the economy. In fact, it had a poor understanding of phenomena such as unemployment and deflation that emerged during this time.[46] The severity of the depression and the perceived threat to political stability, both domestic and international, that accompanied it compelled governments to assume an entirely new role as a provider of welfare services.

Economics and Legitimacy.   Once governments acknowledged their responsibilities in the economic area, they created a new yardstick for judging their performance. The ruled now evaluated their rulers not only according to how well they maintained order and protected them from external danger, but also according to how well they helped provide a decent minimum standard of living and promoted economic growth and greater prosperity in the future. Having embarked on the course of economic management, the state found it had to aspire to a whole new set of goals. As one analyst has observed,

> Modern governments have become increasingly sensitive to demands for a wide variety of welfare services and have taken on the responsibility for mass social and economic welfare. The improvement through state intervention of the material . . . well-being of its citizens has become one of the central functions of state activity. The satisfaction of rising claims by citizens has become a major source of the state's legitimation and of a government's continuance in office.[47]

All governments, from the most conservative to the most liberal, embraced this new role in economic activities. Fascist governments built their appeal on the idea that, based on their authority in the economic realm, they would build a new and far stronger nation that would achieve ever-greater heights of prominence in the world arena. The international communist movement claimed that centrally planned and regulated economies would outperform market economies, would be free of exploitation, and would ultimately produce a utopian cornucopia for workers all around the globe. And capitalist societies preached that Keynesian economic theory would allow governments to fine-tune economies with a minimal degree of interference, thereby assuring prosperity without infringing too much on the freedom of the marketplace. In each case, the government's new role was that of regulator and manager. It regarded such a role as an important way to buttress its authority and to undermine the credibility of the government's opponents, both domestic and international.

The Need for International Resources and Markets.   The state's greater economic role had important international implications. Now, no matter what the state's ideological predispositions might be, the rapidly increasing complexity of modern industrial societies demanded ever-greater access to foreign markets and resources in order to meet economic goals. This was as true for the capitalists who sought to relieve unemployment and increase the wealth and productivity of their societies as it was for the militarists and fascists who sought to achieve domination over so-called lesser nations and to attain their rightful place in the sun. Indeed, the Second World War determined which of the respective combatants' versions of the world economic order would be pursued over the next several decades. On the one hand, the Axis coalition favored a system predicated on dividing the world into economic spheres dominated ruthlessly by the main Axis partners. On the other hand, the Allied alliance at least formally declared its willingness to consider the more open system espoused by the United States, especially Secretary of State Cordell Hull.[48] The Allied victory did not create a solid front behind the resolve for freer trade, for there was a considerable conflict between the American views relating to the need for nondiscrimination, the British desire to preserve an imperial preference system, and the Soviet goal of communist revolution.[49] But their victory, together with the strong position enjoyed by the United States after the war, did create the opportunity for movement toward a more open system for at least some members of the international arena.

New International Structures

In the immediate aftermath of the war, the Bretton Woods system was created. This system included the International Monetary Fund, which was designed to manage currency exchange rates and to provide short-term credit to countries experiencing momentary balance-of-payments problems; the International Bank for Reconstruction and Development (or World Bank), which was supposed to extend longer term credit to states as they sought to recover from the war and to pursue economic growth and development; and, somewhat later, the General Agreement on Tariffs and Trade (GATT), which helped to enshrine the principle of nondiscrimination in international trade. Each of these institutions would play a leading role in the vast increases in economic interdependence found among many states in the decades after 1945.

These forces were not the only ones that worked to alter the international system in fundamental ways. Three other major factors complemented, reinforced, and interacted with the new goals and responsibilities of the state: namely, a basic abhorrence of war, the ability of major countries to maintain the access they needed to international markets and resources, and the deep political, military, and ideological conflict between East and West that brought on a cold war that lasted for over four decades.

The Rejection of War.   The abhorrence of war was a product of the horrors associated with the two world wars in the twentieth century. The loss of life, destruction of property, and financial expense of these wars far outstripped anything anyone had ever experienced or even imagined. Approximately ten million combatants died in the First World War and nearly fifty million in the Second World War. Such bloodletting simply could not be allowed to occur again. More importantly, the weapons that were developed in the later stages of World War II led to the horrifying realization that any such future conflagrations could even lead to the destruction of the planet. World leaders were greatly sobered by their experiences in the two wars and by the contemplation of what might happen if conflicts among the world's largest states got out of hand again.[50]

Therefore, in the years immediately after World War II, many leaders sought to develop plans that would prevent future conflicts. Chief among these plans were the United Nations and the development of structures for limiting the military, but not the economic, capacities of the former Axis states and for encouraging cooperation among the advanced industrialized countries. Nonmilitaristic democratic governments were created in Germany, Japan, and Italy, and each of these countries was included in American plans for economic recovery. The former enemies were defanged, but otherwise were allowed to participate in the newly evolving international structures. At the same time, the Europeans devised first the European Coal and Steel Community and later the European Economic Community to tie the victors to their former enemies in such a way as to prevent any repetitions of the violence that occurred in 1870, 1914, and 1939. Each of these projects involved a sort of grand experiment to determine whether the economic linkages that so many theorists from Richard Cobden in the nineteenth century to Cordell Hull in the twentieth had proposed as a solution to international conflict would indeed function effectively.[51] Thus, the horror of war led to a web of institutions, both domestic and international as well as political and economic, that were designed to create harmony between former enemies and to build formidable barriers to future outbreaks of violence by the world's largest countries.

Access to International Resources and Markets.   Reinforcing these institutional developments was the ability of the major industrialized states to gain access to what they needed internationally. Such access made it less urgent for anyone to think in terms of the New Order that Germany had envisioned for Europe or of the Co-Prosperity Sphere that Japan once had in mind for the Far East. The ability to get what one required from the international arena was largely a product of (1) the United States' willingness to enforce rules that created an open international system and (2) the increased role of large capitalist corporations in moving goods and services from producer to consumer.

Maintaining an open international economic system was a driving force behind U.S. foreign policy.[52] It rested on the American belief that an open system would ensure prosperity (especially in the United States), would guard against future conflicts, and would be the best guarantee against the spread of communism. But whatever the American motives, the end product was an international economic system in which it was "easier to obtain needed access to raw materials and markets through trade than to try to control them territorially by force."[53] At least for some countries, then, fighting for resources and markets gave way to economic exchange.

With regard to the part played by large capitalist corporations, their con-

Map 5. Europe During the Cold War

stant quest for profits and for advantages vis-à-vis their rivals led them to ever-higher levels of participation in international commerce. Such involvement has resulted in sophisticated networks of international exchange in which commodities, finished goods, services, and even capital are moved quickly from producers to consumers. Largely nonexistent before World War II, these networks have increased their capacities severalfold since the early postwar years and have reached levels of efficiency (and profitability) that were scarcely dreamed of forty years ago.[54] Again, the net result is a new set of international associations that helps redefine the relationships among states and that reinforces the search for wealth.

The Effects of the Cold War. As important as the roles of the United States and large corporations were in effecting international change, they were overshadowed by the cold war between the United States and the Soviet Union and their respective allies. The cold war followed closely upon the heels of the Second World War and spurred the creation of two groups of states that regarded one another as formidable rivals. The cold war began when the collapse of the Axis coalition in 1945 presented new and unprecedented opportunities to the victorious powers, particularly in Europe. The destruction of German strength and the exhaustion of the United Kingdom and France gave the Soviet Union a chance to exert more influence in Europe than at any time since the years immediately after the Napoleonic wars.[55] The Soviets organized firm and uncompromising control over several East European countries and sponsored active and influential Communist parties in Western Europe, with two of the strongest located in France and Italy. In addition, after the war deep difficulties arose between the Western allies and the Soviets over such issues as how Germany should be managed and governed, the creation of the United Nations organization, U.S. aid and the rebuilding of Europe, the apparent Soviet support for insurrection in Greece and Turkey, and the size of the Red Army and the ominous threat it seemed to pose for Western Europe.

In Asia, at least from the United States' point of view, the Soviets seemed no less troublesome. There were disputes over the continued Soviet occupation of Iran even after the wartime need for such control was gone, over American suspicions that the Soviets were aiding the Chinese Communists in their ultimately successful struggle against Chiang Kai-shek's Nationalist forces, over the Soviet occupation of Korea, over the presumed Soviet role in the Indochinese revolt against the French, and over Soviet demands for a hand in reorganizing Japan.

Reinforcing the United States' and Western Europe's fears were Soviet hesitations regarding the creation of an international agency to control nuclear weapons, the Soviets' ideological appeals for anticapitalist world revolution, and the formation of the Cominform, which appeared to be a successor to the Comintern, an agency that before World War II had been dedicated to the destruction of capitalist systems. From the West's perspective, Soviet leaders were absolutely determined to use the turmoil and chaos left over from the Second World War to their own advantage as they sought to begin their own drive toward world domination. World War II, it was feared, had merely created a situation in which smashing one would-be hegemon had allowed another to rise in its stead. All the dangers that had been averted by defeating the Axis alliance of right-wing totalitarian states would now reappear in equal measure as a left-wing totalitarian country began its move. Only a firm stand by the West, and more specifically by the United States, could avert the rising menace.[56]

The apparently overwhelming problems posed by the Soviet challenge convinced U.S. leaders that they had to respond. The Soviets' perceived strength and the widespread geographical area in which they could potentially take action—from Europe to the Far East and including many points in between—dictated the nature of this response. In the first place it had to be defensive; Western public opinion would not support offensive action. Moreover, any offensive action involved too great a risk of sapping Western resources while allowing action in another part of the world to go unchecked. Hence, the policy of containment was devised. This policy was designed to hold the Soviets at bay until internal change and/or decay brought their seemingly aggressive ways to an end.[57]

Another important strategy in the West's dealings with the Soviets was to bring the former primary members of the Axis coalition, Germany, Italy, and Japan, into the anti-Soviet alliance. Including these states was essential because they were strategically located. Germany, for example, is in the heart of Europe.

Control of German territory by a force hostile to the Western democracies would significantly increase their burdens of defense and would pose a grave danger. Italy is situated in a key part of the Mediterranean Sea and is well suited as a base of operations for anyone who might wish to disrupt the peace and security of the Mediterranean and of the countries that border it. Finally, Japan is located on the eastern fringes of Asia and could be used to harass those from across the Pacific that might wish to maintain close ties and commerce with Asia.

Another consideration was the status of Germany, Italy, and Japan before World War II as some of the world's leading industrial countries. Allowing these countries and their economic potential to fall into the hands of a state that might wish to subjugate the world would be supremely dangerous.[58] In addition, these three countries were judged very important to the economic recovery of Europe and Asia.[59]

A final consideration had to do with human resources. U.S. and other Western leaders saw the task of confronting the rapidly expanding communist menace as requiring a large pool of human resources. They believed that it simply would not be possible to develop the needed military forces without the assistance of the three former enemies. German cooperation was seen as particularly vital because Soviet designs were regarded as centering on Europe, and Central Europe was perceived as the focal point for any possible Soviet moves.[60]

The Emergence of the Western World

In the years immediately following World War II, the perception of a dire emergency forced Western leaders to make a Herculean effort to overcome the immediate past and to move toward ever-warmer relationships with their erstwhile enemies.

The Atlantic alliance (the North Atlantic Treaty Organization, or NATO) included full German and Italian participation by the mid-1950s, and in the Far East the Japanese were brought into the U.S.-sponsored security framework. In each arena, the United States promised to extend a nuclear guarantee to its allies while they sought first to recover from the war and later to cooperate with one another to build their own defense capacities.

These then became the twin pillars of the Western response to communism. *Militarily,* alliance networks were created and received substantial American assistance. In this way the immediate Soviet threat could be countered. *Economically,* the basic goal was a complete recovery from the ravages of war, followed by the most rapid increases possible in the economic capacities and standards of living for American allies in Europe, the Mediterranean, and the Far East. Such recovery and growth would have several possible benefits. The American allies would have increasingly greater ability to defend themselves, thereby reducing the burden on the United States. Another benefit would be a reduction in the appeal of communism, which was perceived as an ideology that seduced only the downtrodden and the poor. A third benefit complemented the U.S. policy of containment: growth and prosperity in the West would create a model that could attract those who were dominated by the Communists, providing them with a reason to rebel and to seek freedom. In addition, Western prosperity would induce the peoples of the new states that were being created as a result of the demise of imperialism to throw in their lot with the West and to reject communism.

These military and economic parts of the Western security equation complemented one another very nicely and fit hand-in-glove with the other Western measures mentioned earlier: a more open trading system and the development of economic and political structures designed to eliminate war. The network of alliances and the American nuclear umbrella provided a security shield behind which commerce could flourish with the assurance that it would not be unduly disrupted by foreign threats. A basic maxim of commerce and exchange is that it profits and grows best when it is set in a predictable, stable, and safe political and military environment.[61] The Western system provided this environment.

The American-sponsored alliance system had yet another important effect: it reined in and largely eliminated the possibility of internecine conflict between the Western coalition partners. Especially in the face of the Soviet challenge, such conflict was perceived as unacceptable. Moreover, the United States consistently used its weight to dampen all such problems among its allies. In fact, U.S. attempts in this area even went beyond intra-alliance affairs and extended to military encounters with those from outside the alliance. For example, the United States played active roles in advising the French about their efforts in Indochina and Algeria and in cautioning the Belgians about their activities in the Congo. The United States also was responsible for halting the British and French invasion of Suez in 1956. Within the American alliance system itself, the only occasion for violence between members was the Greek-Turkish conflict over Cyprus.[62]

Increased Commerce and Trade.   The need for economic growth and development and for prosperity also conformed with the desire to promote trade to build the legitimacy of the state and the welfare of its citizens and to eliminate international conflict through greater interdependence. The Bretton Woods system and the emerging European Economic Community (or Common Market), developed both to promote the growth in international commerce and to militate against future international conflicts, fit nicely with the economic needs of containment. As a result, Western nations had powerful security-oriented reasons for working together to ensure that these arrangements would function effectively. In addition, the United States and its allies had strong reasons to ensure that proper natural resources were available to them all so that their industrial plants would function effectively. Therefore, action was taken primarily by the United States to guarantee access to raw materials in such locales as Latin America, Central Africa, the Middle East, and Asia. In addition, multinational corporations were encouraged to set up shop around the globe so that they could facilitate the movement of goods, services, and capital.[63]

The cumulative effects of these forces have profoundly transformed the relationships among the members of the Western alliance system (including Japan). One major impact has to do with their involvement in international commerce. Tables 3.1 and 3.2 illustrate one of the most important of these effects by showing how much total and per capita trade have changed over the roughly seventy-five years between 1912 and 1988. These tables allow us to assess the volume of trade by each member of the Group of Seven (the United

Table 3.1. Imports for the Group of Seven, 1912–1988

	1912	1928	1938	1948	1958	1968	1978	1988
United States	12,508	19,700	6,733	24,615	37,014	78,170	231,375	319,142
	136	159	52	168	212	389	1,061	1,296
United Kingdom	28,328	25,280	14,492	27,921	28,928	44,766	99,442	131,773
	624	550	304	557	558	810	1,782	2,309
France	15,625	10,159	4,588	11,827	16,072	33,061	103,551	123,629
	395	243	109	290	360	662	1,943	2,213
Germany	20,945	16,111	7,581	4,764	21,092	47,641	152,744	173,919
	322	250	96	102	404	821	2,491	2,842
Canada	5,406	5,903	2,331	9,062	14,914	27,024	54,980	74,817
	751	573	206	702	877	1,299	2,340	2,883
Italy	5,477	5,671	2,022	5,289	9,215	24,317	71,449	96,295
	158	138	47	116	189	461	1,260	1,676
Japan	250	4,783	2,595	2,351	8,691	30,702	99,661	130,103
	5	74	36	29	95	304	867	1,061

Note: All figures are in 1980 U.S. dollars. For each country, the top figure represents total trade and is in millions. The lower figure is per capita trade.

Sources: The 1912 figures are from *The Statesman's Yearbook*. The 1928 and 1938 figures are from *The Statistical Yearbook of the League of Nations*. All other figures are from United Nations, *Statistical Yearbook*.

Table 3.2. Exports for the Group of Seven, 1912–1988

	1912	1928	1938	1948	1958	1968	1978	1988
United States	16,500	24,300	10,559	43,108	50,808	80,849	178,676	223,481
	179	197	81	294	291	402	819	907
United Kingdom	18,516	17,010	7,945	21,836	25,481	36,324	90,749	101,020
	408	370	167	437	491	657	1,626	1,770
France	13,383	9,865	3,023	6,911	14,662	30,035	96,973	116,522
	338	236	72	169	329	602	1,820	2,085
Germany	17,297	14,126	7,313	2,058	25,235	58,728	179,861	224,498
	266	219	92	44	484	1,012	2,934	3,668
Canada	3,070	6,758	3,285	10,687	14,456	29,792	58,310	78,377
	426	656	292	830	848	1,434	2,481	3,020
Italy	3,648	3,812	1,887	3,700	7,384	24,080	70,951	88,274
	105	93	43	81	152	456	1,251	1,537
Japan	89	4,280	2,613	888	8,244	30,667	123,422	183,969
	2	66	36	11	90	303	1,074	1,500

Note: All figures are in 1980 U.S. dollars. For each country, the top figure represents total trade and is in millions. The lower figure is per capita trade.

Sources: The 1912 figures are from *The Statesman's Yearbook*. The 1928 and 1938 figures are from *The Statistical Yearbook of the League of Nations*. All other figures are from United Nations, *Statistical Yearbook*.

States, United Kingdom, France, Germany, Canada, Italy, and Japan) and by the group as a whole for a representative year (1912) before World War I, before the Great Depression (1928), before the Second World War (1938), and in each decade since World War II (1948, 1958, 1968, 1978, and 1988). All seven members of this elite international club have clearly experienced continual and significant increases in their international trade since 1948. With one minor exception, no country has experienced a decline in trade since 1948.[64] This is true for both the total and per capita figures. In 1988 the Group of Seven as a whole imported at a rate that in absolute terms (adjusted for inflation) was over twelve times what it was in 1948 and exported at a rate over eleven times what it was in that year. By 1988 exports accounted for nearly 28 percent of the per capita income in Germany, 26 percent in Canada, 20 percent in the United Kingdom, and 18 percent in France. Another way of looking at the growth of trade is to compare the figures for 1988 with those for 1912, a time that historical analysts often regard as highly interdependent as far as trade is concerned.[65] In 1988 the members of the Group of Seven imported at a level that was over eleven times the 1912 level and exported nearly thirteen times what they did that year. Taken as a whole, these figures show the remarkable degree to which developments since World War II have affected the commercial relations of the world's largest countries.[66]

Conflict and Violence. The patterns and types of conflict for Western states have also changed fundamentally. Before 1945 the advanced industrial states were prone toward military encounters with one another and fought often in Europe. Since 1945, these same states have not fought one another, and there has been no fighting in the very parts of Central and Western Europe that hosted some of the bloodiest battles in history stretching all the way back to the Middle Ages. As one analyst noted, "today the European core of the international system is a vast zone of peace."[67] Insofar as these countries have fought, their attention has been directed for the most part at underdeveloped countries in Africa and Asia. Tables 3.3 and 3.4 demonstrate this change very

Table 3.3. Incidence of International War, 1945–1988, Classified According to Type of Actor and Target

Actor/Target	1945–49	1950–59	1960–69	1970–79	1980–88	Total
Developed West vs. Developed West	0	0	0	0	0	0
Developed West vs. Developing	0	2	1	1	1	5
Developing vs. Developing	1	2	6	8	3	20
Eastern Bloc vs. Eastern Bloc	0	1	0	0	0	1

Note: A war is counted more than once if it fits more than one actor/target category. Wars are counted only for the time periods in which they begin.

Source: J. David Singer, "Peace in the Global System: Displacement, Interregnum, or Transformation?" in *The Long Postwar Peace,* ed. Charles W. Kegley, Jr. (New York: HarperCollins, 1990), 60–65.

Table 3.4. Incidence of International War, 1945–1988, Classified According to Regional Location

	1945–49	1950–59	1960–69	1970–79	1980–88	Total
Western Europe	0	0	0	0	0	0
Eastern Europe	0	1	0	0	0	1
North America	0	0	0	0	0	0
Central America	0	0	1	0	0	1
South America	0	0	0	0	0	0
North Africa/ Middle East	1	1	2	1	2	7
Sub-Saharan Africa	0	0	0	2	0	2
South Asia	0	0	2	1	0	3
Southeast Asia	0	0	1	2	0	4
North Asia	0	1	0	0	1	1
Mediterranean	0	0	0	1	0	1
South Atlantic	0	0	0	0	1	1

Source: Singer, "Peace in the Global System," 60–65.

clearly: in the years since 1945 there have been no wars in which developed countries have fought one another.[68] On five occasions, however, developed countries have fought underdeveloped countries, with these conflicts centering largely on questions relating either to the collapse of imperialism or to the cold war.[69] Interestingly, developing countries, which were largely left outside of the American-designed system described earlier, have engaged in a considerable number of conflicts. They have fought twenty wars among themselves, or over three-fourths of all wars fought in the period. Moreover, the regional hot spots generally have been in the more underdeveloped areas of the globe, with seven wars occurring in the North Africa–Middle East region, four in Southeast Asia, three in South Asia, and two in sub-Saharan Africa.

The distribution of civil wars during the years since 1945 is very similar to that for international wars.[70] As Table 3.5 shows, no advanced industrialized country has experienced such a disturbance. Through 1989 all civil wars occurred within states classified as underdeveloped. Table 3.6 also reveals that, although the sub-Saharan Africa and North Africa–Middle East regions have the most conflicts, domestic problems of this sort are distributed widely among all regions of the developing world. Advanced industrialized countries have intervened in the troubles found in the developing world on eight separate occasions, most often to protect their access to vital resources by ensuring against a victory by forces sympathetic to the Soviet Union.

The overall impression gained from an examination of Tables 3.3 to 3.6 is that severe violence within and between advanced industrialized countries has receded dramatically since 1945. However, these countries are still inclined toward using violence in their relations with poorer countries and have become involved in the internal scraps found in these same countries. Thus, the advanced members of the Western alliance seem to live by a double standard: they reject violence among themselves, but at least some of them are still willing to use it in their relations with those outside their circle.

Table 3.5. Incidence of Civil Wars, 1945–1988, Classified According to Type of Country and Type of Intervention

Type of Country	Incidence of Civil Wars					
	1945–49	1950–59	1960–69	1970–79	1980–88	Total
Western Developed	0	0	0	0	0	0
Developing	8	10	14	16	12	60
Type of Intervention						
Western Developed in Developing	1	1	4	1	1	8
Developing in Developing	0	0	1	6	1	8
Eastern Bloc in Developing	0	0	0	1	0	1

Note: Civil wars are counted only for the time period in which they begin. Interventions may be counted more than once if countries from more than one category are involved.

Source: Singer, "Peace in the Global System," 66–75.

Table 3.6. Incidence of Civil Wars, 1945–1988, Classified According to Regional Location

	1945–49	1950–59	1960–69	1970–79	1980–88	Total
Western Europe	0	0	0	0	0	0
Eastern Europe	0	0	0	0	0	0
North America	0	0	0	0	0	0
Central America	1	2	2	2	1	8
South America	3	2	0	0	2	7
North Africa/ Middle East	1	2	3	4	2	12
Sub-Saharan Africa	0	0	5	3	6	14
South Asia	0	0	0	4	2	6
Southeast Asia	1	3	3	1	0	8
North Asia	1	0	1	0	0	2
East Asia	0	1	0	1	0	2
Mediterranean	1	0	0	0	0	1

Source: Singer, "Peace in the Global System," 66–75.

These facts can be juxtaposed with the greatly increased international commerce of the advanced Western allies and with the degree to which trade now contributes to individual income. On this basis, we might speculate that war and other forms of violence have been renounced in part because they threaten continued economic growth and the accumulation of wealth. As Bruce Russett and Harvey Starr put it, "high levels of wealth and equality mean that all citizens would have a great deal to lose in a war. The level of destruction from a big war among industrialized countries would be far greater than the gain realized from any victory."[71] In other words, war among at least some of the world's great states has become very unlikely because its expected utility is very low. The losses due to destruction, deaths, and interrupted commerce would be far higher than any conceivable gain.[72] The economic linkages among the members of the Western world have become so tight that warfare with one another would be the equivalent of a company killing its own best customers and destroying a substantial part of its own income. As one scholar remarks, "to attack one's best customers is to undermine the commercial faith and reciprocity in which exchange takes place."[73]

Beyond these economic interdependencies, certain political relationships have developed among these countries. During the four decades that these states have worked together as allies, their governments and peoples have become accustomed to regarding one another in friendly terms. Their cultures and political values, centering on democracy and free enterprise, have actually become somewhat homogenized. As a result, although conflicts among members of the Western world continue, violence is no longer even considered as a means for resolving differences. Public opinion simply would not tolerate a resort to arms.[74] In effect, political sentiment has powerfully reinforced economic self-interest to lower the probability of war to the vanishing point.

In areas that are less closely tied to the West, that are less familiar as political and military allies, that are far removed geographically, that adhere to different value systems, and that consequently are not as well understood, the use of violence by the West continues to receive a degree of acceptance. The poverty of the states found in these parts of the world makes them appear less able to resist the potential force of the larger and wealthier states in the West.[75] Thus, when Western states feel frustrated, annoyed, or unduly threatened by the activities of these states, they are far readier to resort to violence. In fact, "a short, small war, ending in victory at little cost in blood or treasure . . . can still produce political gains for the leaders who initiate it."[76] Although public opinion and economic bonds make it impossible to fight one's fellow members in the club of privileged countries, there are far fewer restrictions regarding violence against those outside the club, especially when they are regarded as incapable of significant resistance.

Nonviolent Coercion.   The prohibition against the use of force in the Western world extends to nonviolent coercion. Table 3.7 presents information on the use of economic sanctions between 1914 and 1990.[77] Several interesting elements emerge from this table. The first is that prior to World War II economic sanctions were seldom used as a means of coercing other states. In the twenty-five years between 1914 and 1939, which includes the World War I period, only thirteen instances of the use of economic sanctions occurred. This total is lower than for any decade since 1940.

A second point has to do with the initiators and targets of sanctions. With the exception of the 1920s, until 1949 sanctions were levied against advanced industrialized countries by other advanced industrialized countries. Since 1950, however, this particular use of economic force has become extremely infrequent. The trend is just the opposite when we consider the imposition of sanctions by developed countries against underdeveloped countries. Before 1949 sanctions were used on few occasions; since 1950 there has been a veritable explosion in their use.[78] The data for sanctions by Western states against the members of the Eastern bloc also show that the West has used economic sanctions as a part of its strategy for "fighting" the cold war.

Table 3.7. Incidence of Economic Sanctions, 1914–1990, Classified According to Type of Actor and Target

Actor/Target	1914–19	1920–29	1930–39	1940–49	1950–59	1960–69	1970–79	1980–90
Developed vs. Developed	3	0	3	5	2	0	1	1
Developed vs. Developing	0	1	2	1	4	12	28	21
Developing vs. Developed	0	0	0	0	5	0	3	0
Developing vs. Developing	0	0	0	2	1	3	3	3
West vs. East	0	0	0	7	2	2	3	4
East vs. West	0	0	0	3	2	0	0	0
East vs. East	0	0	0	1	0	3	0	1
International Organization vs. Developed	0	0	1	0	0	0	0	0
International Organization vs. Developing	0	1	2	0	0	2	0	3

Note: Sanctions are recorded only for the time period during which they were initiated. When multiple actors and targets are involved, each one is counted separately. References to East and West are made only when there is a cold war dimension to the sanction.

Source: G. C. Hufbauer, J. J. Schott, and K. A. Elliott, Economic Sanctions Reconsidered: History and Current Policy (Washington, D.C.: Institute for International Economics, 1990), 16–27.

These data further reinforce the impressions gained from examining the information regarding international and domestic violence. The patterns reveal that, although advanced Western countries engaged in close and often ferocious competition with one another prior to the end of the Second World War and the onset of the cold war, they have greatly reduced this conflict since that time. Unlike war, the initiation of economic sanctions has not halted completely, but it has slowed to a trickle. Apparently, the Western nations not only have set violence aside as a technique for resolving their disputes with one another, but they also are hesitant to employ economic force. The effects of the political, military, and economic linkages among these states seem to run quite deep, for diplomatic discourse has become the preferred tactic for resolving the problems they create for one another.[79]

At the same time, the West does not shrink from employing economic force against those countries that are not a part of their exclusive domain. Since 1950 the Western world has imposed a total of eighty economic sanctions against all targets around the world. Four (5 percent) of these have been aimed at other Western states, eleven (14 percent) have been pointed at the Communist bloc, and sixty-five (81 percent) have been directed against underdeveloped countries. Clearly, the behavior of the countries in the last two categories has displeased at least some members of the West. The "rules" regarding the employment of economic coercion permit its use in an effort to modify this behavior. Those countries that are poor and thus are unable to offer any meaningful retaliation have faced the brunt of these sanctions.

The Value of Territory.   The post–World War II era has also seen a new conception of the value of territorial possessions. As described earlier in this chapter, traditionally territory was closely associated with a state's security and with its economic prosperity. With the acquisition of land came space that could be used as a buffer to afford protection from one's enemies, people who could be pressed into the service of the state, and raw materials and productive capacities that could be used to add to the total pool of a society's resources. Therefore, territory was highly prized. Retaining or obtaining it was a reasonable foreign policy goal, and the use of force to this end was considered appropriate.[80]

Today these attitudes are no longer prominent in the West. There are several reasons why. First, the Western nations now have access to key resources and markets without actually controlling the territory in question. Wolfram Hanrieder notes that for these countries, "access rather than acquisition, presence rather than rule, penetration rather than possession have become the important issues."[81] A second reason is related to the military realities of the contemporary era. On the one hand, nuclear weapons and ballistic missile delivery systems have rendered the degree of extra safety derived from the addition of territory marginal to a country's overall security needs.[82] On the other hand, as a result of the rising tide of nationalism and the development of sophisticated guerrilla warfare and terrorist techniques for resistance, it has become increasingly troublesome to control territory taken by force, at least if it is to be used effectively.[83] Finally, much of the need to control territory to gain raw materials has been made obsolescent by the ability of advanced industrialized societies to devise substitutes for the products.[84] The substitution of nylon for rubber is a case in point. Therefore, another basic feature of the pre–Second World War international arena has been altered to such a degree as to make it qualitatively different from what previously existed.

The Western advanced industrialized states have such a special network of associations with one another and such different relationships with the rest of the world that it may be regarded as a separate international universe. These states engage in historically unprecedented levels of international commerce; they have the highest standards of living in the world; they cooperate closely with each other to guarantee their national security; they neither use violence in their relations with one another nor contemplate the use of such violence in their defense planning; they experience no domestic violence aimed at restructuring their societies; and they rarely use any other forms of coercion when interacting with each other. From a historical point of view, they have new conceptions of the purposes of foreign policy, generally eschewing territorial acquisitions and defining their national security in broad terms that include not only military but also economic, ecological, and health matters.[85] Their unusually pacific and noncoercive associations with one another, however, do not always extend to their behavior toward others. Violence, economic coercion, and interference in the domestic affairs of smaller and poorer countries all characterize these relationships at least on occasion.

The Other World

For members of the international community other than this select group of very wealthy and privileged countries, life has been, and still is, quite different. The states that compose this other international system are extremely diverse, but, as a rule, they can be said to come from two categories of countries. The first consists of the former Soviet Union and its one-time alliance partners. With the exception of Latin America, the second includes countries that before World War II were European, U.S., or Japanese colonies.

These very different countries share a common characteristic: their general exclusion from the basic economic, political, and security structures that were created to bind the advanced industrialized countries together after the Second World War. For the Communist countries, being left out of these associations occurred in part because of the fear they inspired among Western states (after all, the cold war meant that Western efforts were directed against the Soviet Union and its allies) and in part because the Soviet Union distrusted their capitalist orientations. For the underdeveloped countries, the absence of participation stemmed from their poverty, their concern with external domination, and their lack of promise as strategic assets in the cold war. Since the ideological and security reasons for not permitting a Communist role are self-evident, the discussion that follows will center on developing countries.[86]

The developing world is a very diverse collection of countries that are located primarily in Latin America, Africa, and Asia. Among these less developed members of the international community, the state regulates and manages the domestic economy in order to promote growth and development. These are much the same duties as those assumed by governments in the Western world. In many cases these responsibilities have produced a connection between the government's legitimacy and its ability to produce in the economic arena, much as has been the case in the West.[87]

International Commercial Linkages.   There is one fundamental difference between the developed and developing worlds as regards the impact of their governmental responsibilities on their views of international commerce. In the developed world, international commercial linkages have been treated as necessary and useful for promoting growth and accumulating wealth. In the developing world, the strong tendency has been (at least in the past) to see such international ties as a potential source of domination.[88]

Past developing-country views of international commercial linkages may to a great degree be attributed to the poverty found in these countries and to their prior histories of imperial subjugation. These conditions have reinforced one another, producing a suspicion of too much involvement with advanced industrialized countries, many of whom, after all, were their former imperial rulers.[89] As a result, many poorer countries have pursued policies based on deemphasizing at least some of a state's international ties, especially in the economic realm. Mexico and India are two prominent examples of countries that have selected such a course.[90] At the same time, many of these states have retained a degree of skepticism regarding the international institutions that emerged as a part of the Bretton Woods system. They perceive these institutions as instruments that the wealthier states might use to control the poor.[91] Thus, many members of the developing world have generally been reluctant to link themselves and their economies too closely to the West.

This hesitation was more than matched by the attitudes of many advanced industrialized nations. The international economic institutions and procedures established after the Second World War were largely oriented toward easing the ability of the advanced countries to conduct transactions among themselves. Exchange rate regulation, loans to cover balance-of-payments difficulties, reconstruction loans for recovering from the war, and nondiscriminatory trade all were issues of concern to the more advanced states. In the late 1940s and throughout the post–World War II period, developing countries have been far more interested in access to capital for development, the ability to tap into developed markets on favorable terms, and equitable prices for the commodities they sell internationally.[92] In addition, the decision-making and voting procedures in the International Monetary Fund and in the World Bank were heavily weighted toward wealthier states. The inclusion of developing members in these institutions appears almost an afterthought. To the extent that the leading countries in the rapidly evolving Western world conceptualized a place for developing countries, it appears that they thought of the poorer countries primarily as suppliers of raw materials, foodstuffs, and other nonfinished goods.

Therefore, most developing countries lagged far behind the Western world in the development of international commercial linkages. To reiterate, this occurred because of their poverty, which meant they had less to offer on world markets and a lower ability to consume imports; because of their concern about being dominated by others, which prompted them to close off their markets and restrict their involvement; and because of the West's unwillingness to accept them as fully equal partners and participants.

Table 3.8. Imports for Developing Regions, 1929–1988

	1929	1938	1948	1958	1968	1978	1988
Latin America	13,077	11,345	25,601	30,057	35,556	93,416	67,415
	120	87	157	153	134	272	157
North Africa	NA	2,865	6,186	7,077	6,879	33,018	20,021
	NA	50	119	107	80	317	148
Other Africa	8,208	3,333	6,186	10,172	13,688	39,176	19,385
	53	29	37	49	51	122	41
Middle East	NA	1,930	4,708	7,994	14,043	32,228	NA
	NA	79	168	195	246	432	NA
Asia	17,796	13,801	20,687	23,496	36,714	115,630	NA
	29	21	26	30	32	94	NA
Soviet Union	2,367	927	NA	12,464	22,246	63,982	74,465
	15	5	NA	60	94	245	262
Eastern Europe	6,772	4,719	NA	11,645	26,298	67,237	NA
	85	55	NA	149	309	735	NA

Note: All figures are in 1980 U.S. dollars. For each country the top figure represents total trade and is in millions. The lower figure is per capita trade.

Sources: The 1929 and 1938 figures are from The Statistical Yearbook of the League of Nations. All other figures are from United Nations, Statistical Yearbook. NA means that the relevant data were not available.

Tables 3.8 and 3.9 illustrate this lack of involvement by providing trade figures for representative regions of the developing world between 1929 and 1988.[93] Except for Asia, total trade for entire *regions* of the developing world consistently falls short of the trade for individual members of the Group of Seven. This is true both for exports ɩnd for imports. However, it should be noted that the total figures for Asia are aggregated for several countries, some of which have the largest populations in the world. When this fact is kept in mind, the total trade figures for Asia are not nearly so impressive.

The per capita trade figures show even more graphically the discrepancy between developed and developing countries. Except for the oil-rich Middle East, per capita trade figures for the developing regions are at best only about one tenth to one fifth the size of the comparable figures for the Group of Seven members. The same is true when we look at the Soviet Union and the countries of Eastern Europe.

Moreover, the developing countries in general have displayed a marginal ability to improve their positions over time. For example, Latin American per capita trade generally was stagnant or declined from 1948 to 1968. It improved dramatically between 1968 and 1978 but fell just as much over the next decade, most probably in response to the international debt crisis that occurred during those years. In fact, every developing region for which data are available experienced a decline during this decade in terms of both total and per capita trade. Another indication of their inability to improve is found in a comparison of the per capita figures for developing regions before the Great Depression with those for the Group of Seven (see Tables 3.1 and 3.2). At that time, the per capita import and export levels for Latin America were equivalent to those for

Table 3.9. Exports for Developing Regions, 1929–1988

	1929	1938	1948	1958	1968	1978	1988
Latin America	15,300	11,754	25,636	27,536	33,310	79,946	75,446
	140	90	157	140	125	233	175
North Africa	NA	2,339	4,433	4,241	9,314	26,418	16,801
	NA	41	85	64	108	254	124
Other Africa	7,164	2,690	5,979	9,054	13,901	31,790	18,892
	46	23	36	44	52	99	40
Middle East	NA	1,930	4,433	11,375	20,709	57,744	NA
	NA	79	158	277	363	774	NA
Asia	19,170	15,497	17,869	18,367	26,430	109,039	NA
	31	23	22	23	23	89	NA
Soviet Union	2,010	868	NA	12,315	25,139	66,100	76,777
	12	5	NA	59	106	253	271
Eastern Europe	6,091	5,263	NA	11,742	25,383	60,458	NA
	77	61	NA	151	299	661	NA

Note: All figures are in 1980 U.S. dollars. For each country the top figure represents total trade and is in millions. The lower figure is per capita trade.

Sources: The 1929 and 1938 figures are from *The Statistical Yearbook of the League of Nations.* All other figures are from United Nations, *Statistical Yearbook.* NA means that the relevant figures were not available.

Italy, and African countries were not far from the levels for the Japanese. Sixty years later, the Italian and Japanese figures for both imports and exports were well over ten times greater than they had been in the late 1920s. The Latin American figures, however, were only slightly higher, and the African figures had actually fallen. Given these data, it seems safe to conclude that with only a few exceptions the developing world has been left out of the international commercial boom of the past six decades.[94]

One might also recall the data for economic sanctions that were provided in Table 3.7. These figures clearly show that advanced industrialized countries consider the members of the developing world fair game for economic sanctions. Developing countries by comparison use them sparingly when interacting either with other developing countries or with developed states. In light of these data and of the trading figures, we must conclude that developing countries cannot in any way be considered a part of the new economic world that has unfolded during the post–World War II years.

Political Ties and Conflict. The political fate of these countries has in many ways been no kinder. For one thing, most of these countries were not regarded as essential strategic assets by the Western world.[95] Only selected Asian, Middle Eastern, Mediterranean, and Central American countries were in this position. The upshot was that the Western allies felt no urgent need to promote their economic development through extensive infusions of capital and preferential trade treatment. Nor did the West seek to incorporate most of these states into its alliance structures or into the institutions that proved so effective in cementing the West together.[96] For their part, many developing countries so loathed the possibility of returning to Western domination, which they feared would result from extensive participation in these Western structures, that they adopted a policy of nonalignment. This policy was designed to keep them at arm's distance from the West and to free them from the East-West conflict that fueled the cold war.[97]

Remaining at arm's length from the West, however, did not always lead to the expected end product, for their poverty and recent struggles for independence had left many of them unstable. In some cases extreme political doctrines emerged, resulting in the perceived possibility of either (1) a contagious effect, wherein trouble would spread from country to country to infect entire regions,[98] thereby depriving the rest of the world of its access to such raw materials and other goods as the region produced, or (2) a takeover by Communists who would "kowtow" to the Soviet Union, thus encouraging those who subscribed to the doctrine of world revolution. Whatever the source of the local difficulties, the temptation to intervene was great, and the outcome was a series of Western (and Eastern) interventions. The data pertaining to civil wars and interventions in Tables 3.5 and 3.6 illustrate the seriousness of this problem in the developing world. Conflicts in Vietnam, Central America, and Zaire (formerly the Congo) are but a few cases in point.

Ethnic, religious, border, and other disputes among these countries also were potent sources of international strife. Although civil and international wars were dying out in the developed world as people became too rich, secular, and tolerant to fight among themselves,[99] in the developing world the same old reasons for conflict still chugged along in deadly earnest. The figures since 1945 presented in Tables 3.3 and 3.4 show that such violence remains a deep source of concern for developing countries.

When we juxtapose the economic evidence of developing-country poverty and participation in international trade with the political documentation of the coercion used by, against, and within these states, we may conclude that they are indeed perched at a distance from the Western world. Nonetheless, not all the members of this less favored group are equally distant from the West. Some actually have extensive relations with the West and experience little or no violence. Others have renounced any Western ties and employ a great deal of violence, internally and/or externally. Singapore fits the first description, and North Korea and Iraq, among others, fall into the second group. Nonetheless, even the most Western oriented of the states in the developing world have attained virtually none of the privileges that go with full membership in the advanced industrialized club. The members of this club themselves do not recognize such states as equal participants or partners. Thus, the contention that at least two parallel international universes exist—one composed of the states in the Western world and another comprising former Communist countries and developing states—seems valid.

CHAPTER SUMMARY

The basic characteristics that set the international social system apart from other systems of human interaction have to do with the nature of the system's membership and with the absence of any governmental body that can make and enforce rules regarding the behavior of those members. The members of the international system are collective entities that have international goals and interests, that define policies, or strategies, for pursuing those interests, and that do not restrict themselves to a reliance on the good offices of others when they pursue their international interests. The strongest and the oldest of these actors is the state. Other actors include the nation, international organizations, and transnational organizations, including multinational corporations.

The human, material, and financial resources available to international actors allow them to dwarf almost all purely domestic actors, and provide them with a substantial degree of strength when interacting with one another. The fact that no governmental authority exists to regulate their behavior means that these actors exist in a state of anarchy. In turn, anarchy means that actors must seek to protect themselves and their international interests, for there is no governmental body that will do this for them, as there is domestically. The primary threats that actors face come from other actors who have goals and interests that are not in harmony with their own international designs. As a result, competition and conflict are normal in international politics, security is not inherent in the operation of the system, and self-interest must be the guiding force behind foreign policy.

When each member of the system bases its behavior on self-interest, then the trust needed for international cooperation is often hard to come by, and it becomes difficult to determine how morality applies in an international context. Thus, international politics is based on a self-help approach, and miscalculations may carry with them very devastating consequences. All international actors supposedly eye each other continuously with a high degree of suspicion and build their military capabilities as insurance against misbehavior on the part of others.

Since the Second World War, some aspects of this international picture have changed for some members of the international system. The actors most affected are the most highly industrialized and advanced members, which together make up the Western world. Certain key changes have created a new world for these states. These changes include the acceptance of a new welfare role for the state, which has had important international implications; the development of the international commercial system that was first embodied in the Bretton Woods agreements at the end of World War II; the development of a deep repugnance for and fear of war; and their alliance, led by the United States, against the Communist menace that they believed confronted them during the cold war. The convergence of these factors and their interaction with one another since 1945 have helped to mold a new international system that is qualitatively different from the one that historically existed among these states.

Members of the Western world still compete with one another and continue to engage in conflict, but they have developed a mode of interacting among themselves that is distinctly different from the one used toward nonmembers of this Western world. Several indices help illustrate these differences. For one thing, the Western world has exceptionally high levels of trade, both by historical standards and in comparison with other international actors. Second, Western states neither fight wars with one another nor arm against each other. Third, civil wars are unknown in the West. Finally, Western countries generally do not employ economic coercion in their relations among themselves. They do, however, direct violence toward those that are not in their "club," and they also intervene in the civil wars of others and direct economic sanctions toward non-Western targets.

Existing side by side with this exclusive club is another very heterogeneous international system that consists of former Communist countries and those that are less developed. These states were largely excluded from the processes that led to the creation of the Western world. The Communist states were left out because they were perceived by the West as hostile. Developing countries remained on the sidelines in part because they chose to out of fear that participation would be the equivalent of neoimperial domination and in part because they were poor and were not considered strategically important in the cold war. As a result, these countries lag far behind the West in wealth and trade; they continue to experience too much violence, both internationally and domestically; and they frequently have been the targets of the economic sanctions imposed by both the West and fellow members of this amorphous group.

Thus, considerable evidence supports the hypothesis that the world is now divided into at least two parallel international universes that, while existing together in the same international time-space, operate by very different sets of rules. In the coming chapters, the effects of these differences on the exercise of power will be considered.

Notes

1. See Oran R. Young, "Anarchy and Social Choice: Reflections on the International Polity," *World Politics* 30, no. 2 (January 1978): 243.

2. See Young, "Anarchy and Social Choice," 243; and Robert Gilpin, *War and Change in World Politics* (New York: Cambridge University Press, 1981), 87.

3. For some recent figures on the size of some of the world's largest corporations, see John M. Rothgeb, Jr., *Myths and Realities of Foreign Investment in Poor Countries: The Modern Leviathan in the Third World* (New York: Praeger, 1989), chap. 1.

4. Young, "Anarchy and Social Choice," 242.

5. Robert Jervis, "Realism, Game Theory, and Cooperation," *World Politics* 40, no. 3 (April 1988): 317.

6. Preventing domination is often characterized as a fundamental operating principle of the international system. It is regarded as an especially important part of the operation of the balance of power. See Edward Voss Gulick, *Europe's Classical Balance of Power* (Ithaca, N.Y.: Cornell University Press, 1955).

7. Hans Morgenthau, *Politics among Nations: The Struggle for Power and Peace* (New York: Alfred A. Knopf, 1948), 163.

8. Kenneth N. Waltz, "The Origins of War in Neorealist Theory," *Journal of Interdisciplinary History* 18, no. 4 (Spring 1988): 625.

9. Arnold Wolfers, *Discord and Collaboration* (Baltimore: Johns Hopkins University Press, 1962), 67.

10. Harold Sprout and Margaret Sprout, *Toward a Politics of the Planet Earth* (New York: D. Van Nostrand, 1971), 135.

11. J. David Singer, "Inter-Nation Influence: A Formal Model," in *International Politics and Foreign Policy*, ed. James N. Rosenau (New York: Free Press, 1969), 383.

12. Waltz, "The Origins of War in Neorealist Theory," 620.

13. Morgenthau, *Politics among Nations,* 40.

14. Singer, "Inter-Nation Influence," 383.

15. John H. Herz, "Idealist Internationalism and the Security Dilemma," in *The Nation-State and the Crisis of World Politics,* ed. John H. Herz (New York: David McKay, 1976), 72–73.

16. Waltz, "The Origins of War in Neorealist Theory," 619.

17. Herz coined this term to refer to the manner in which the interactions among states seeking security merely lead to greater levels of insecurity for all. See Herz, "Idealist Internationalism."

18. See Robert Jervis, "Cooperation under the Security Dilemma," *World Politics* 30, no. 2 (January 1978): 181–82, and Waltz, "The Origins of War in Neorealist Theory," 619.

19. Jervis, "Cooperation under the Security Dilemma," 172.

20. James Madison, "Federalist Number 41," in Alexander Hamilton, James Madison, and John Jay, *The Federalist Papers* (New York: New American Library, 1961), 256. John Locke also sees the provision of security from foreign danger as a primary function of government. See John Locke, *Of Civil Government, Second Treatise* (Chicago: Henry Regnery, 1955), 121–22.

21. Colin S. Gray, *The Geopolitics of the Nuclear Era: Heartland, Rimlands, and the Technological Revolution* (New York: Crane, Russak, 1977), 3. John Herz also sees the provision of physical security as a key duty of the state. See John H. Herz, "The Rise and Demise of the Territorial State," in *The Nation-State and the Crisis of World Politics,* ed. John H. Herz (New York: David McKay, 1976), 99–123.

22. Hedley Bull, *The Anarchical Society* (New York: Columbia University Press, 1977), 130.

23. One can find a useful summary of the German plans and tactics in Robert J. Art and Kenneth N. Waltz, "Technology, Strategy, and the Use of Force," in *The Use of Force: International Politics and Foreign Policy,* ed. Robert J. Art and Kenneth N. Waltz (Boston: Little, Brown, 1971), 1–25.

24. See Harry S. Truman, *Years of Trial and Hope* (Garden City, N.Y.: Doubleday, 1956), chap. 22.

25. Waltz, "The Origins of War in Neorealist Theory," 620.

26. Morgenthau, *Politics among Nations,* 65.

27. Jervis, "Cooperation under the Security Dilemma," 167.

28. See Richard Ned Lebow, *Between Peace and War: The Nature of International Crisis* (Baltimore: Johns Hopkins University Press, 1981), 130–32.

29. See Alistair Horne, *To Lose a Battle, France 1940* (New York: Penguin Books, 1979), 54–172.

30. See Jervis, "Cooperation under the Security Dilemma," 184–85.

31. See E. H. Carr, *The Twenty Years Crisis, 1919–1939* (New York: St. Martin's, 1939), 111; Jervis, "Cooperation under the Security Dilemma," 168–69; and Richard Rosecrance, *The Rise of the Trading State: Commerce and Conquest in the Modern World* (New York: Basic Books, 1986), 23–24.

32. Nazli Choucri and Robert North map this argument out in great detail. See Nazli Choucri and Robert C. North, *Nations in Conflict: National Growth and International Violence* (San Francisco: W. H. Freeman, 1975), chap. 1.

33. See Choucri and North, *Nations in Conflict,* chaps. 3–4.

34. Steven Van Evera, "Why Cooperation Failed in 1914," *World Politics* 38, no. 1 (October 1985): 85–90.

35. See William Langer, *The Diplomacy of Imperialism* (New York: Alfred A. Knopf, 1960).

36. See Peter Calvocoressi and Guy Wint, *Total War: Causes and Courses of the Second World War* (New York: Penguin Books, 1979), 686–92; and Waldo Heinrichs, *Threshold of War: Franklin D. Roosevelt and American Entry into World War II* (New York: Oxford University Press, 1988), chap. 5.

37. These figures are from the *Oil and Gas Journal Data Book* (Tulsa, Okla.: PennWell, 1990), 250.

38. See Wolfers, *Discord and Collaboration*, 51–52.

39. James Madison, "Federalist Number 41," p. 257.

40. Wolfers, *Discord and Collaboration*, 59.

41. See Gilpin, *War and Change in World Politics*, 206–9.

42. It should be noted that these comments are not meant to justify violence, but only to point out its possibly functional nature in an anarchic political system.

43. See Henry Kissinger, *Years of Upheaval* (Boston: Little, Brown, 1982), chap. 11.

44. See Wolfram F. Hanrieder, "Dissolving International Politics: Reflections on the Nation-State," *American Political Science Review* 72, no. 4 (December 1978): 1276–87.

45. See Susan Strange and Roger Tooze, "States and Markets in Depression: Managing Surplus Industrial Capacity in the 1970's," in *The International Politics of Surplus Capacity*, ed. Susan Strange and Roger Tooze (London: George Allen and Unwin, 1981), 3–24.

46. Charles P. Kindleberger, *The World in Depression, 1929–1939* (Berkeley: University of California Press, 1986). A number of other scholars also point to the Great Depression as important for inducing governments to accept new social responsibilities. For example, see Gilpin, *War and Change in World Politics*, 219; and Rosecrance, *Rise of the Trading State*, 137.

47. Hanrieder, "Dissolving International Politics," 1278.

48. Cordell Hull, *The Memoirs of Cordell Hull*, vol. 1 (New York: Macmillan, 1948), chap. 26. For a discussion of the commitments made by the leading United Nations allies to the principle of more open trade, see Richard N. Gardner, *Sterling-Dollar Diplomacy in Current Perspective* (New York: Columbia University Press, 1980), chap. 3.

49. See Gardner, *Sterling-Dollar Diplomacy*, part 2.

50. See John Mueller, *Retreat from Doomsday: The Obsolescence of Major War* (New York: Basic Books, 1989), passim.

51. Barry Buzan, "Economic Structure and International Security: The Limits of the Liberal Case," *International Organization* 38, no. 4 (Autumn 1984): 599.

52. See Robert O. Keohane, *After Hegemony: Cooperation and Discord in the World Political Economy* (Princeton: Princeton University Press, 1984). Another discussion of this point is found in Charles Lipson, *Standing Guard: Protecting Foreign Capital in the Nineteenth and Twentieth Centuries* (Berkeley: University of California Press, 1985), chap. 4.

53. Rosecrance, *Rise of the Trading State*, 159. The same basic point is made in Buzan, "Economic Structure and International Security," 603; and in Carl Kaysen, "Is War Obsolete? A Review Essay," *International Security* 14, no. 4 (Spring 1990): 57.

54. Early but still very informative discussions of the role of multinational corporations are found in Raymond Vernon, *Sovereignty at Bay* (New York: Basic Books, 1971); and in Raymond Vernon, *Storm over the Multinationals* (Cambridge, Mass.: Harvard University Press, 1977).

55. Of course, at the time of the Napoleonic wars the Soviet Union did not yet exist and the Russian Empire formed the core of what became the Union of Soviet Socialist Republics.

56. See Dean Acheson, *Present at the Creation: My Years in the State Department* (New York: W. W. Norton, 1969), chaps. 22 and 25; Winston S. Churchill, *Triumph and Tragedy*, vol. VI of *The Second World War* (New York: Houghton Mifflin, 1952), chap. 15; and Truman, *Years of Trial and Hope*, chaps. 6 and 7.

57. See John Lewis Gaddis, *Strategies of Containment* (New York: Oxford University Press, 1982), chap. 2; and Louis J. Halle, *The Cold War as History* (New York: Harper and Row, 1967), chap. 11.

58. For a discussion of how these considerations affected the U.S. foreign policy debate of the late 1940s, see Gaddis, *Strategies of Containment*, chap. 3.

59. See Halle, *The Cold War as History*, chap. 13.

60. See Halle, *The Cold War as History*, chap. 24; and James L. Richardson, *Germany and the Atlantic Alliance* (Cambridge, Mass.: Harvard University Press, 1966), chap. 1.

61. For a discussion of this point, see Buzan, "Economic Structure and International Secu-

rity," 607; Gilpin, *War and Change in World Politics*, 129; Hanrieder, "Dissolving International Politics," 1281; and Joseph S. Nye, Jr., "Soft Power," *Foreign Policy* 80 (Fall 1990): 160.

62. K. J. Holsti, "The Horsemen of the Apocalypse: At the Gate, Detoured, or Retreating?" *International Studies Quarterly* 30, no. 4 (December 1986): 369.

63. See Lipson, *Standing Guard*, chap. 4.

64. The single exception is the slight fall in per capita trade for the United States between 1948 and 1958.

65. See Gilpin, *War and Change in World Politics*, 220; and Rosecrance, *Rise of the Trading State*, 213.

66. As an aside, an examination of these figures shows how severe the Great Depression was. This may be determined by comparing the data for 1928 with that for 1938 and noting the substantial decline for all members of the Group of Seven during this time.

67. Holsti, "The Horsemen of the Apocalypse," 369. The same point is made in Buzan, "Economic Structure and International Security," 605; and in Bruce Russett and Harvey Starr, *World Politics: The Menu for Choice* (New York: W. H. Freeman, 1989), 410.

68. A war is defined as an instance of international violence in which two or more recognized states engage in armed hostilities toward one another and where there are at least one thousand battle deaths. For a discussion of wars since 1945, see J. David Singer, "Peace in the Global System: Displacement, Interregnum, or Transformation?" in *The Long Postwar Peace*, ed. Charles W. Kegley, Jr. (New York: HarperCollins, 1991), 56–84.

69. See Holsti, "The Horsemen of the Apocalypse," 369.

70. A civil war is defined as a situation in which organized armed violence occurs between a recognized government and some portion of its domestic opposition. Data relating to civil wars since 1945 may be found in Singer, "Peace in the Global System."

71. Russett and Starr, *World Politics*, 432.

72. Kaysen, "Is War Obsolete?" 49–50.

73. Rosecrance, *Rise of the Trading State*, 13.

74. See Kaysen, "Is War Obsolete?" 58; and Rosecrance, *Rise of the Trading State*, 38.

75. One should note that the appearance of an inability to resist the use of force by the advanced states in the Western world can be very deceiving. One need only reflect on the American experience in Vietnam.

76. Kaysen, "Is War Obsolete?" 59.

77. Economic sanctions are defined as a "deliberate government-inspired withdrawal, or threat of withdrawal, of customary trade or financial relations" in support of foreign policy goals. See Gary Clyde Hufbauer and Jeffrey J. Schott with Kimberly Ann Elliott, *Economic Sanctions in Support of Foreign Policy Goals* (Washington, D.C.: Institute for International Economics, 1983), 2.

78. In interpreting these figures, one should employ some caution, for the number of under-developed countries has greatly increased since 1950. This may in part account for the greater frequency of sanctions.

79. It is important to emphasize for the reader that advanced industrialized countries do still have conflicts with one another. These data do not mean that there is no conflict. The data pertain only to some of the techniques that states may use for resolving conflict on terms that they regard as favorable to themselves. In fact, Nye notes that "by the end of the decade [the 1980s] 56 percent of the American public believed that economic competitors like Japan pose a greater threat to our [American] national security than military adversaries like the Soviet Union." See Joseph S. Nye, Jr., *Bound to Lead: The Changing Nature of American Power* (New York: Basic Books, 1990), 233.

80. See Rosecrance, *Rise of the Trading State*, passim; and Keohane, *After Hegemony*, 32. For a concrete example of the value states placed on territory, Van Evera describes how territorial designs motivated the Germans on the eve of World War I. See Van Evera, "Why Cooperation Failed in 1914," 100.

81. Hanrieder, "Dissolving International Politics," 1280.

82. John Herz was among the first to recognize this new reality. See Herz, "The Rise and Demise of the Territorial State," 99–123.

83. See Rosecrance, *Rise of the Trading State,* 34; and K. J. Holsti, *International Politics: A Framework for Analysis* (Englewood Cliffs, N.J.: Prentice-Hall, 1983), 85.

84. See Buzan, "Economic Structure and International Security," 614.

85. See Nye, "Soft Power," 157; and Nye, *Bound to Lead,* 179.

86. It should be noted that early Western plans did allow for Communist participation in the postwar economic structures and aid packages. For example, Marshall Plan aid was offered to all European countries, including those in Eastern Europe and the Soviet Union. Given the rapid deterioration in East-West relations after the war, the sincerity and political practicality of these early plans and offers is debatable. See Halle, *The Cold War as History,* chaps. 13 and 14.

87. See Raymond D. Duvall and John R. Freeman, "The Techno-Bureaucratic Elite and the Entrepreneurial State in Dependent Industrialization," *American Political Science Review* 77, no. 3 (September 1983): 569–87; and K. J. Holsti, "Underdevelopment and the 'Gap' Theory of International Conflict," *American Political Science Review* 69, no. 3 (September 1975): 827–39.

88. See B. J. Cohen, *The Question of Imperialism* (New York: Basic Books, 1973), chaps. 5 and 6; and Robert L. Rothstein, *The Weak in the World of the Strong: The Developing Countries in the International System* (New York: Columbia University Press, 1977), part 2. The tendency to view international ties with suspicion has been modified somewhat in recent years as the outwardly oriented international development strategies employed by some countries, most notably Korea, Taiwan, Singapore, and Hong Kong, have led to a substantial degree of success in overcoming economic problems and promoting growth.

89. The poverty of the developing countries may be illustrated by examining the following figures for average yearly per capita income for several regions of the world. It should be noted that all figures are presented in 1980 U.S. dollars. The developing world is usually defined as including countries in Africa, Asia (excluding Japan and the Middle East), and Latin America. For the purposes of comparison, data are also provided for average income in North America (the United States and Canada) and in the European Community. As the figures show, incomes in North America and Europe are substantially higher than those found in each of the developing regions. (*Source:* United Nations, *Yearbook of National Accounts Statistics.*)

Average Yearly Per Capita Income in U.S. Dollars

	1960	1970	1980	1987
Africa	365	458	875	533
Asia	253	255	368	310
Latin America	955	1,146	2,364	1,424
North America	7,725	10,194	11,727	13,163
European Community	3,258	4,808	9,812	9,658

90. This discussion is not meant to consider the efficacy of these types of policies for securing growth and development.

91. See Cheryl Payer, *The Debt Trap* (New York: Monthly Review Press, 1974), chap. 2, for a discussion of the attitudes of many developing countries toward one of the institutions—the International Monetary Fund.

92. For discussions of the international economic goals and objectives of developing countries in the post–World War II era, see Richard N. Cooper, "A New International Economic Order for Mutual Gain," *Foreign Policy* 26 (Spring 1977): 65–139; and Ervin Laszlo, Robert Baker, Jr., Elliott Eisenberg, and Vankata Raman, *The Objectives of the New International Economic Order* (New York: Pergamon Press, 1978).

93. Some figures are missing from Tables 3.8 and 3.9 due to the difficulty experienced in

putting together data for developing countries. Pre–World War I figures of the sort found in Tables 3.1 and 3.2 for the Group of Seven were not available, nor were figures for 1928. While they are not the immediate subject of attention, data for the Soviet Union and its Eastern European satellites are also included in order to illustrate their isolation when compared with the Group of Seven.

94. This analysis seeks only to illustrate these trading trends and is not designed to explain them.

95. See Gaddis, *Strategies of Containment*, chap. 2.

96. Developing countries were included in some of the more marginal alliance structures, such as the Southeast Asia Treaty Organization (SEATO), but were not part of the primary structures that bound together the Atlantic world and Japan. Also, it is not clear that extensive efforts to draw the developing world more closely into the Western fold would have been very effective as a means for promoting development.

97. For a discussion of the nonalignment movement, see Cyril Black, Richard Falk, and Klaus Knorr, *Neutralization and World Politics* (Princeton: Princeton University Press, 1968); John W. Burton, ed., *Nonalignment* (New York: James H. Heineman, 1966); Peter Calvocoressi, *World Order and New States* (New York: Praeger, 1962); and Cecil Crabb, *The Elephants and the Grass* (New York: Praeger, 1965).

98. For a discussion of contagion effects, see Michael Mandelbaum, *The Fate of Nations: The Search for National Security in the Nineteenth and Twentieth Centuries* (New York: Cambridge University Press, 1988), 137–64.

99. One must also recall that developed countries believed that they faced a great danger from the Soviet Union and pulled together to cope with that threat. See James Lee Ray, "The Abolition of Slavery and the End of International War," *International Organization* 43, no. 3 (Summer 1989): 436.

4

Coercion and Noncoercion in Exercising Power

This chapter examines the methods that actors typically use when they attempt to exercise power in international politics. As Chapter 2 discussed, in the power relationship an actor seeks either to get a target to do what it otherwise would not do or to get the target to refrain from doing something that it wishes to do. The first scenario is a positive exercise of power in that the target responds to the actor by actively performing the actor's preferences. The second is more negative in the sense that the target forgoes or omits behavior that currently displeases the actor or that it believes would disturb the actor in the future. In either case, actor and target are in conflict with each other, for the actor wishes to modify the target's behavior in a direction that the target would prefer not to take. As a result, the actor must provide the target with an incentive for altering its behavior. This incentive may be called the actor's tool or technique for exercising power.

The techniques for wielding power traditionally have been grouped into two broad categories. The first category comprises predominantly coercive tools. Specifically, the actor attempts to force a target to adopt a particular policy by creating the expectation that the target will face dire consequences if it fails to do so. In the past, coercion was most closely associated with use of the military. In the contemporary international system, economic instruments are also used with increasing frequency (see Chapter 3). The second category of techniques may be referred to as noncoercive. In noncoercive situations an actor seeks to persuade a target to do something by reminding the target that it has an obligation to the actor.[1] As we will see, more recent discussions of power typically include a third category as well. This is the use of an exchange whereby the actor secures compliance by offering the target something in return for modifying its behavior.

This chapter focuses on these coercive, noncoercive, and bargaining devices and gives special attention to the effectiveness of each technique in the international system. The first part of the chapter presents a historical and contemporary analysis of these techniques and considers the criteria that can be employed to answer questions about the usefulness of various tools.

The second section focuses on the examination of coercion and threats as a means for getting others to do as one wishes. Communications between actor and target, the role of the actor's capability and credibility, and the effects of the target's perception of the actor are investigated to determine their impact on the efficacy of a threat. In addition, the value of threats as a way to obtain goods and services from the target and the length of the influence derived from the use of coercion are examined. The discussion in this section is designed to facilitate comparisons with the other approaches to exercising power. (For a somewhat more detailed examination of coercive tactics, the reader should consult Chapter 5.)

The exercise of power as a result of an exchange between actor and target is investigated in the third section. As will be seen, communications problems between actor and target may muddle the establishment of influence. In addition, the actor's capability and credibility are considered in the context of negotiating a bribe, and the possible effects of exchange-based influence on the actor's and the target's perceptions of one another are examined.

Finally, this chapter discusses the use of persuasion as a method of influencing others in the international system. The two types of persuasion described are propaganda and political and economic theory.

The recurrent theme of this chapter is the value of each of these techniques for exercising power in the parallel international systems described in Chapter 3.

THINKING ABOUT COERCION AND NONCOERCION

Punishment, Affection, and Bargaining

In the early sixteenth century, Niccolò Machiavelli wrote a prescription regarding the fundamental tools available to those who seek to exercise power. In this famous and extremely influential work, *The Prince*, he argued that two basic techniques may be used for this purpose: one is based on instilling fear in the target and the other on inspiring love. In considering the relative merits of each, Machiavelli said,

> From this arises the question whether it is better to be loved more than feared, or feared more than loved. The reply is that one ought to be both feared and loved, but as it is difficult for the two to go together, it is much safer to be feared than loved, if one of the two has to be wanting. For it may be said of men in general that . . . as long as you benefit them, they are entirely yours . . . [but] the friendship which is gained by purchase and not through grandeur and nobility of spirit is bought but not secured . . . for love is held by a chain of obligation which, men being selfish, is broken whenever it serves their purpose; but fear is maintained by a dread of punishment which never fails. . . . I conclude, therefore, with regard to being feared and loved, that men love at their own free will, but fear at the will of the prince, and that a wise prince must rely on what is in his power and not on what is in the power of others.[2]

Machiavelli's statements regarding fear, control, punishment, and love became extremely controversial almost from the moment that he set them to paper, in part because of the cruelty that appears to inspire them.[3] Still, the simple and almost eloquent dichotomy that he drew between fear and love, between control through punishment or control through affection, has retained its appeal to this day. At the same time, Machiavelli raised several other issues as well. First, he argues that an actor's power is greatest when it is able to use fear and love in tandem, but that punishment and affection are so different that they can rarely be employed in combination. Second, he maintains that when an actor must choose between the two techniques, the use of fear is preferable because an actor can control the fear that is created for a target but not the degree of affection that a target feels. Finally, he describes the key to fear as the actor's ability to punish the target with certainty when the target's behavior is unacceptable.

While Machiavelli expressed these thoughts well, they are not the last word on the subject. With regard to his first point, the fear and love dichotomy, we find that the thinking of scholars has evolved over time. Some contemporary analysts have adopted schemes for classifying the tools for gaining influence and strength that are similar to the fear/love dichotomy. For example, Arnold Wolfers observes that in international politics states may base their relations with one another either on amity, a feeling of friendship, or on enmity, a situation in which violence or the threat of violence guides a country's behavior.[4] An example of amity would be the United States/Canada association, whereby each country seeks to use their long-standing sense of friendship to obtain influence on important issues. An example of enmity, on the other hand, is seen in United States/Soviet relations during the cold war, when these countries treated each other as bitter rivals not worthy of trust and as controllable only through the threat of coercion.

Another variation of the fear/love dichotomy is found in the work of Karl Deutsch and Harold Lasswell and Abraham Kaplan, who speak of the dual nature of politics and power. They note that compliance with authority may be based on the perceived legitimacy of those who issue orders or on their ability to coerce.[5] That is, (1) power may rest on the consent of the target who believes that it must obey the actor out of a sense of obligation and the conviction that the decisions are best for the political system as a whole, or (2) power may be a product of force. The problem in an anarchic political system is that the feeling of community spirit needed for a sense of legitimacy to develop is rare. This means that all too often power may be derived from the second source: some type of force. There are, however, some contemporary examples of legitimacy guiding behavior. In the Western world both the North Atlantic Treaty Organization (NATO) and the European Community (EC) have gained the loyalty of their members, who believe they have a duty to honor the rules of these bodies. For instance, NATO has commanded remarkable adherence to its rule that member countries not withdraw their contingents from the unified command structure without authorization from the NATO commander. The EC countries routinely pay into the EC treasury and observe the Common Agriculture Policy (CAP), even though the benefits from each are thought to be distributed in a lopsided fashion. In each case, legitimacy would appear to be at work.

The friendship and obligation as opposed to the fear and force dichotomy deals with only two of the tools that may be used to wield power. The friendship/obligation dichotomy conceptualizes power and influence as something that is either given by or forced on a target. Many scholars argue, however, that power may be acquired through an exchange relationship. As an example, we might consider the 1947 treaty by which the United States acquired the use of the Subic Bay naval base in the Philippines in exchange for yearly rental payments to the Philippine government. The United States' goal was to obtain the rights to a base from the Philippines. These rights were gained neither through the use of force nor through the Philippine government's feelings of friendship or obligation to the United States. Instead, a transfer of assets was one important reason for the Philippine government to agree to comply with American requests.

Hans Morgenthau speaks of this kind of trade-off when he indicates that an actor's economic wealth gives it the means to exert influence over others.[6] J. David Singer and David Baldwin share much the same idea when they describe an actor's promises of rewards to a target in exchange for compliance with a demand as a potent source of power.[7] Bruce Russett and Harvey Starr put it somewhat differently. They maintain that bargaining, which is based implicitly on an attempt to come to terms regarding an exchange of goods and services, is often a useful means for getting one's way when dealing with another member of the international system.[8] Joseph Nye uses the familiar colloquial expression of the carrot and stick to make much the same point.[9] K. J. Holsti also includes offers and grants of rewards as important features in any arsenal of tools for exercising power.[10] C. W. Maynes, however, probably provides the catchiest and most honestly blunt categorization scheme when he says that power and influence may be acquired through the use of logic, bribes, and threats. He defines bribes as transfers of resources designed to entice a target to follow the course of action that the actor prefers.[11]

Thus, a trichotomy may be used to group the devices that actors employ when exercising power. That is, techniques may be classified according to whether they are based on (1) political and psychological resources that are designed to convince a target to act in a particular way, (2) economic or other resources that may be used to buy off a target in order to obtain the preferred behavior, or (3) intimidation and/or violence (which usually means the military but may be based on another resource) to force a target to do something. In essence, such a scheme divides the tools for exercising power according to what an actor does to the target in an effort to obtain compliance, focusing on whether the actor aims at the target's mind, its pocketbook, or its security. The mind may be influenced by convincing elite decision makers and/or public opinion that the actor's goals are legitimate and that it is in the target's best interests to comply with the actor's wishes. Such efforts may include using propaganda, which is intended to sway public opinion, or diplomacy, and/or political and economic theory, which may affect the perceptions of policymakers. Focus on the target's pocketbook entails efforts to create a trade-off between target and actor, where the target receives a tangible (e.g., money) or an intangible (e.g., protection) resource in exchange for an alteration in behavior to conform to the actor's desires. It may consist of offering or granting rewards, ranging from foreign aid to arms transfers to military protection from a rival. Finally, actions that are oriented toward security are those in which the actor concentrates on the target's ability to maintain its preferred way of life and its autonomy and standing within the international arena. Attempts to acquire influence through compulsion may include warnings about the use of coercion, both military and nonmilitary, or may involve the actual use of force.

Considering Relative Efficacy

Each of the tools for affecting the behavior of others—logic, bribes, and threats (to use Maynes's attention-getting terminology)—is often used best when reinforced by one or more of the other tools. In other words, the attempt to influence the actions of others is most likely to yield the desired results through the combination of two or more instruments.[12] Robert Keohane notes that this is especially true when strategies based either on the use of punishment and threats or on promises of rewards are used. He argues that the two are most effective when used together.[13] In other words, a menacing action yields the best results when it is combined with the prospect of some gain for the target if it complies with the actor's demands.

An example of combining threats with inducements can be found in the 1962 Cuban missile crisis. During this incident the United States publicly insisted that the Soviet Union remove its missiles from Cuba immediately and threatened that if the Soviets did not do so the United States would use its armed forces to accomplish the task by force. This was a direct challenge to the Soviet Union and to its policy of placing missiles in Cuba. Few countries accept such threats with equanimity, especially when they are superpowers.[14] Thus, the Soviets could have been expected to refuse to yield. The U.S. ultimatum, however, was accompanied by secret proposals that sought to provide the Soviets with an inducement to remove their missiles. These inducements came in two forms: the United States promised that it would not sponsor future attempts to overthrow Fidel Castro's Communist regime in Cuba, and would shortly withdraw American missiles stationed in Turkey. As a result, Soviet leaders were not just confronted by threatening American behavior, but also found that they were offered a way out of their dilemma. Neither the threat of U.S. military action alone nor the promises offered, in themselves, would likely have been sufficient to secure the desired change in Soviet behavior.[15] In this case, the carrot and the stick reinforced one another.

Political and economic tools may also obtain a greater effect if used together than if either is used separately. For instance, U.S. diplomatic influence in the Middle East, most notably with Israel and Egypt, has been strongly bolstered by the very large levels of economic and military aid that the United States grants to these countries.[16] In the absence of this aid, both Israel and Egypt would undoubtedly feel freer to disregard American initiatives that they considered imperfect. Indeed, without the prospect of U.S. assistance the treaty of peace signed by these two countries in 1978 would never have become a reality.[17]

Another example of the interaction between diplomatic argument, or logic, and economic incentives, or bribes, is provided by the U.S./Philippines agreements permitting an American naval base at Subic Bay. The treaty granting the United States the rights to a base was negotiated in 1947. At that time, the cold war between the United States and the Soviet Union was beginning and the Soviet threat seemed real and immediate. The U.S. offer of payment for base privileges was magnified by diplomatic reminders regarding the potential menace posed by the Soviet Union. In such a situation, an American presence gave the Philippine government significant protection from any designs that the

Communists might have had on the Philippines. Political persuasion worked hand in hand with the economic advantages that would be derived from the deal, and an agreement was reached. Forty-five years later, in 1992, the end of the cold war has robbed the earlier diplomatic arguments of much of their punch. As a result, even though the economic incentives for maintaining the American base remain, the agreement has come under attack within the Philippine government. For the Filipinos, keeping the base simply has begun to look too much like an overreliance on American tutelage, no matter how great the economic gains.[18]

With regard to questions relating to the relative efficacy of individual techniques, Machiavelli asserted that forceful and coercive techniques should be preferred to those based on persuasion because their effectiveness can be controlled by the actor seeking to gain influence. In effect, this argument is based on the premise that a tool is superior if its use and its impact on others can be controlled. One can supposedly control the degree to which punishment is administered to a target, but cannot regulate either affection or the acceptance of a bribe. Therefore, punishment is the preferred tool for exercising power.

Many international political theorists agree with this approach. They point out that, because of the anarchic nature of the international system and the severe penalties associated with committing errors in foreign policy–making, coercion and/or the threat of force is the preferred basis for conducting foreign relations. After all, countries presumably are able to determine their own levels of safety (within the limits imposed by resource availability) when they adopt policies that give prominence to the use of force and acts of violence against those who would do them harm. Preparing for the worst enables a country to avoid the unnecessary risks associated with relying on the persuasion of logic or on another's willingness to deliver as promised when bribed. As Wolfers states, "there is no substitute for coercion—even less for the threat of coercion."[19] Robert Art and Kenneth Waltz concur, maintaining that

> the web of social and political life is spun out of inclinations and incentives, deterrent threats and punishments. Eliminate the latter two, and the ordering of [international] society will depend entirely upon the former—an anarchic ideal that is unworkable this side of the Garden of Eden.[20]

Such arguments are, of course, impressive, particularly when we accept both the traditional conception of the international system (see Chapter 3) and the basic premise that accompanies these assertions, as noted above. Both elements, however, are debatable. As noted elsewhere in this book, traditional notions about the international arena are at least partially flawed, especially when applied to the Western world. The fundamental premise that underlies statements regarding the benefits of relying on force are also problematic. The difficulties arise not so much because seeking to be safe is an unreasonable standard as because additional criteria should be applied when judging the value of influence techniques.

International political theorists who have analyzed the efficacy of threats have provided one set of such additional criteria. According to these theorists, at least four elements affect the degree to which the threat of coercion is successful: (1) the communications between actor and target; (2) the actor's capabilities, or resources, relative to those of the target; (3) the actor's credibility, or its willingness to do what it says it intends to do; and (4) the target's willingness to comply with the actor's demands or to suffer the consequences (if any) of refusing to do so.[21] These factors are closely related to weight, domain, range, and scope, which were described in Chapter 2 as useful for assessing the limits of an actor's strength. To refresh the reader's memory, weight is defined as the probability that a target will behave as the actor desires; domain refers to the number and types of targets the actor dominates; range is the kind of rewards and punishments an actor has at its disposal; and scope is the kind of target behavior the actor controls.

Several factors were depicted in Chapter 2 as useful for examining weight, domain, range, and scope. These relate to the definition and consistency of the actor's goals, the target's perception of the actor, the quality of the communications between actor and target, the actor's ability to locate the target and the aid the target receives from other actors, and the actor's resources. Clearly, there is a close match between these elements and the four mentioned above. The communications that occur between actor and target and the resources available to the actor are found on both lists. As I will discuss below, the actor's ability to locate the target is an essential component of the actor's capability; the target's perception of the actor is related strongly to the willingness of the target to go along with the actor's wishes; and the definition and consistency of the actor's goals are important to the communications process and to determining the actor's credibility.

Thus, at least four other factors must be included along with the considerations pertaining to safety and security that often guide the traditional analysis of the techniques for exercising power. These are (1) communications between actor and target, (2) the actor's and the target's capabilities, (3) the actor's credibility, and (4) the target's willingness to comply with the actor's requests. When taken together, these elements help determine both the duration of any control that an actor obtains over a target and the risks an actor incurs when seeking control. These factors also affect the target's desire and ability to resist the actor's demands.

LOOKING AT THREATS

Let us begin our assessment of relative efficacy by examining the technique that is often regarded as most appropriate in international relations—threats. As mentioned earlier, threats involve statements or actions by an actor that are designed to compel a target to do something by indicating the consequences of failure to comply. The actor threatens to impose a punishment or deprivation that will undermine the target's ability to pursue its preferred domestic pattern of social organization and/or its autonomous existence as an international actor.[22] Threats are usually made when an actor (1) expects that the target may not be prepared to acquiesce and (2) thinks threats will work and will cost less than the gains that will be reaped.[23]

Baldwin notes, however, that such rational calculations are not always at the root of a threat and that threat-making has a powerful emotional component. Emotion becomes a factor when the frustrations of stymied leaders combine with their notions of glory, honor, and prestige. As a result, foreign policy—makers are pushed toward menacing behavior even when calm and careful thinking might suggest they would not benefit from such acts.[24] For example, the Japanese decided to risk war with the United States in the fall of 1941 when they found that they could not negotiate an end to the United States' trade restrictions against Japan. Apparently, the Japanese leaders were aware of the United States' potential material superiority, but despite the very bad odds, they decided on war rather than accept what they perceived as continuing American interference.[25] In this case, emotion overcame the assessment by some Japanese leaders of the risks associated with war against the United States, and they resorted to coercive behavior knowing that they courted disaster.

Communicating Threats

One may begin the consideration of the effectiveness of threats by looking at communications. The actor needs to inform the target of what it wants and what it plans to do if the target does not comply and, alternatively, if the target does comply.[26] To communicate this information effectively, the actor must have well-organized goals and a clear understanding of how it plans to pursue these goals. Such information conveys to the target the actor's preferences regarding acceptable and unacceptable behavior and the potential cost to the target of compliance or noncompliance.[27] Targets are more likely to give in if they think they are confronted with a marginal change in their own behavior, and if they perceive that the actor will be generous if they comply but very cantankerous and perhaps even violent if they do not.[28]

A good example of these principles is the Munich conference in the fall of 1938 between Adolf Hitler, Neville Chamberlain, and Edouard Daladier. As described in a previous chapter, Hitler demanded that the French and British agree that Germany be granted the Sudetenland, which was part of Czechoslovakia. If the French and British did not agree, Hitler threatened to plunge Europe into an all-out war. If the French and British did agree, Hitler promised to sign treaties guaranteeing the peace in Europe into the distant future. Thus, Daladier and Chamberlain were confronted with what they considered a relatively marginal demand, affecting only Czechoslovakia and apparently having little to do with the French and British positions in Europe or in the world. At the same time, they were informed that the consequences of refusing to agree would be extremely high but that there would be substantial benefits if they went along. When all of these considerations were weighed, the scales tipped toward accepting Hitler's demands and offers. The threat was successful.

An example of a failed threat is found in the German demands on Belgium in August 1914. The Germans insisted that they be allowed to occupy Belgium and use it as an invasion route against France. They threatened that noncompliance would mean violence. For the Belgians, these German requests meant that they would at least temporarily lose their independence. Moreover, they envisioned being caught up in a war whether or not they agreed to the German demands. Thus, major changes were expected and a high cost would be paid for either compliance or noncompliance. Therefore, the Belgians refused to accede to the German terms.[29]

More recently, U.S. interactions with Iraq regarding its threats against Kuwait in the summer of 1990 also illustrate a failed communication. On the one hand, the U.S. government did not believe the Iraqi warning to Kuwait that an invasion would occur unless Kuwait fully supported Iraq's demands that international oil prices be forced sharply upward. For their part, the Iraqis had a hard time understanding the degree of U.S. concern for Kuwait's safety and independence. The message that U.S. ambassador April Glaspie was instructed to convey to the Iraqi government was vague and appeared to suggest that good relations between the United States and Iraq would take precedence over any Iraqi behavior toward Kuwait.[30] To the Americans, the threat of an Iraqi invasion seemed little more than a rhetorical flourish designed to induce Kuwait to take Iraqi demands more seriously. To the Iraqis, the American message seems to have left the impression that American actions toward Iraq would change only marginally if Iraq decided to invade Kuwait. The American message was so imprecise that it utterly failed to convey a meaningful signal to Iraq.

This example also reveals some of the problems associated with communications between advanced Western states and poorer developing countries. The U.S. government apparently found it inconceivable that any nation would launch a war simply to overcome the obstacles to negotiating economic agreements. After all, within the Western context, economic and diplomatic resources are used to resolve economic disagreements; military resources rarely play any role. The possibility that cultural and other differences between the West and this particular member of the developing world might mean that Iraqi behavior would follow a very different pattern never seems to have occurred to the U.S. decision makers. As this example illustrates, the values and motivations that guide foreign policy in one international context appear, at least on occasion, to be quite different from those that guide behavior in another. This makes it hard to understand the meaning of the signals that are sent.

Threats and Capabilities

The second characteristic of a threat is associated with the relative capabilities of actor and target. Capability refers to an actor's possession of a sufficient range of resources that enables it to do whatever it says it is going to do in the event of noncompliance. In general, this means being able to hurt the target and to raise the costs of noncompliance.[31] Threats that are not backed up by the actor's ability to carry them out are hollow. Similarly, when targets can counter the capabilities that an actor plans to use to carry out a threat, the threat loses much of its meaning.[32]

The Cuban missile crisis constitutes an instance in which the actor making the demand, the United States, clearly had the capacity to do what it said it would do and the opponent, the Soviet Union, had little, if any, ability to counter that capacity. The threat was that the United States would forcibly remove the missiles if the Soviets did not do so promptly. Given the size of the

American military, the proximity of Cuba to the United States, and the great distance between Cuba and the USSR, this threat was backed up by an impressive American capability that the Soviets could not counter. During the Munich crisis of 1938, on the other hand, the British lacked the capability to counter possible German offensive moves in a meaningful way. Therefore, they did not have the forces in hand to get Hitler's attention. The Gulf War of 1991 presents another situation. Although the American-led coalition had the capability to do as it threatened, the Iraqi government apparently believed that it possessed the military muscle needed to neutralize any moves by the coalition. Thus, Iraq largely ignored the American threats made in the fall of 1990 and the winter of 1991.

Of course, even when an actor possesses the capacity to inflict pain on a target for not doing as it is told, success is not guaranteed, for the actor must be able to locate the target. As mentioned earlier, one of the most fundamental problems in dealing with many of the non-state actors in the contemporary international arena is their ability to avoid detection by those with whom they are in conflict. Terrorist and guerrilla organizations are especially adept at posing this difficulty. Under such circumstances, the actor's ability to damage a target and inflict considerable pain on it may be almost meaningless. The end result is that actors sometimes turn to an alternate target that they associate with the actual source of their problems and use their capabilities to retaliate against those that can be located.[33] For example, the United States attacked Libya in the spring of 1986 in response to terrorist incidents against American citizens in Europe. The United States had what it regarded as sufficient evidence of Libyan complicity, and since the terrorists were not at hand, it attacked a target that could be found.

Threats and Credibility

To be effective, an actor's capability must be coupled with credibility—the ability to convince the target that it has the willpower to do what it has threatened to do. The possession of a tremendous capability has almost no significance vis-à-vis making threats if the target simply does not believe that the actor intends to use those resources.[34] After all, the United States could use its nuclear arsenal to obliterate any society on earth. But this capability did it no appreciable good during the Vietnam War, the Iranian hostage crisis, or the events leading up to the Gulf War of 1991. In each case, the targets simply did not believe that the United States would use its nuclear forces because they felt that the U.S. government and the people it ruled had no stomach for such action. Therefore, in each case the United States' adversaries felt free to ignore the vast destructive potential of the American nuclear war chest and pursued their plans as if it did not exist.

Establishing credibility thus becomes one of the most important aspects of the threat-making formula. At least two factors stand out as keys to doing so: (1) a comparison between the actor's and the target's capabilities; and (2) the actor's past and present behavior.

Relative Capabilities.   Threats become less believable when it is apparent that the target has the capacity to inflict substantial damage on the actor in retaliation for attempts to carry out threats. To the extent that the target's ability to respond is assured, and that response would be particularly painful, the actor would be running very severe risks if it carried out its threat. Thus, the threat loses a lot of its credibility. Few people are prepared to believe that an actor will carry out a threat of punishment if it will result in extreme discomfort and damage for that actor.[35]

For example, during the cold war the U.S. policy was to defend Europe against possible Communist aggression by threatening to launch a massive nuclear strike against the Soviet Union in the event of a Soviet attack on Western Europe.[36] This policy was formulated in the 1950s when the United States enjoyed a decisive nuclear superiority over the Soviet Union. Thus, at its inception, the policy had some credibility, for the United States could inflict considerable damage on the Soviets without finding itself on the receiving end of a comparable Soviet effort. By the mid-1960s, however, these American advantages had deteriorated as the Soviet Union engaged in a crash program designed to catch up with the United States. Once the Soviets possessed the capacity to strike back at the United States in the event of a nuclear engagement, questions naturally arose regarding the credibility of American policy. In effect, the Soviets' increased capability in comparison with that of the United States meant that carrying out the American policy might be the equivalent of committing national suicide. Since few political leaders have any interest in inflicting such horrors on their own societies, the policy of massive retaliation for protecting Europe became very questionable. As the balance between Soviet and U.S. forces shifted, and as it became ever more certain that the Soviets could indeed strike back in a horrible way, the credibility of the American threat was lost. In such a situation, the security of the actor becomes intertwined with that of the target, and the two become security interdependent. It becomes impossible for one to seek to coerce the other without bringing substantial damage down on itself.[37]

Interdependence in the economic realm has created a similar effect among members of the Western world. These countries have reached a point in their relations with one another that they rely on each other as customers, suppliers, and investors. As a result, threats by one member of this exclusive group of countries to take extreme action leading to substantial damage for other members of this group have lost their credibility. Efforts by any one of these actors to severely hurt other Western countries would simply boomerang and the actor's own society would be harmed. The economic interdependence found among these countries means that almost all of them have the capability to hurt one another. At the same time, many of these countries have military establishments that could wreak a good bit of destruction on fellow Western countries. These very capabilities to harm one another in an unacceptable way undermine the credibility of threats to do so. As was true in the case of the security interdependence between the superpowers, a high degree of capability to do mutual harm has reduced the credibility of any dire threats that one actor in the Western world may direct toward another. Interestingly, the lower degree of interdependence between the West and the rest of the world helps threats between these two groups of countries remain credible.

Past and Present Behavior.   Some analysts note that an actor's past and present behavior are important indicators of a threat's credibility.[38] Such behavior may be important in at least two ways. First, an actor may build credibility if it has actually carried out similar threats in the past. A problem for the United States in the above example regarding the protection of Western Europe was that its threat was so extreme that it never had been implemented in any form, at least not with nuclear weapons. Of course, an actor could at least partially reinforce its credibility if it had established a reputation for tough responses in the past. Creating policy credibility was one reason why the United States responded as it did to the Communist invasion of South Korea in 1950 and during the Cuban missile crisis in 1962.

Past behavior may also help build credibility through brinksmanship— excessive risk taking. An actor who exhibits either an unbalanced or an overly committed reaction to a particular policy outcome might succeed in convincing an opponent that he or she was more committed to that policy than to anything else, including survival. As an alternative, one might at least signal that one may tend to get out of control, and therefore would be unable to rein oneself in at critical moments. A metaphor often used to illustrate brinksmanship has to do with a game of chicken (where two automobiles race toward each other, the purpose being to see who panics first and swerves). One player might purposely disable the steering mechanism in his or her car. Doing so signals the player's commitment, creates instant credibility for the threat to crash if necessary, and presumably leads to victory.

In the international arena, the same type of effect may be achieved by adopting a position from which it is hard to retreat. An example is found during a 1955 crisis between the United States and the People's Republic of China over the islands of Quemoy and Matsu (which are located just off the Chinese coast opposite Taiwan). In order to create credibility for the U.S. policy of protecting these small and not very important islands, members of the Eisenhower administration provided background briefings to the press in which they said that an American nuclear response to Chinese behavior was being contemplated and might be imminent unless the Chinese backed down.[39] Such reports backed the United States into a policy corner and left it with few options, short of being severely embarrassed, if the Chinese did not alter their behavior. To further heighten the pressure, President Eisenhower confirmed the reports shortly after they were published.[40] Rather than take chances and find out if American leaders were bluffing, the Chinese backed down. This is what brinksmanship is all about.[41]

The Target's Will

The final component that determines the degree to which a threat is successful is the target's willingness to suffer rather than change its behavior to conform to the actor's expectations. No matter how dire and credible a threat may be and no matter how well it may be communicated, in the end its success rests on the target's decision to comply or not to comply with the demands made. The decision to comply in turn is a product of whether the target is prepared to suffer the consequences of refusing to go along with the actor. As one analyst notes, "frightening others . . . can be effective only if the pain anticipated or suffered is greater than the opponent is willing to tolerate."[42] One must also consider the degree to which leaders who succumb meekly to an external threat may lose their own credibility with their followers.

In other words, when all is said and done, the target's will becomes the key to the success of any threat. Highly committed or determined targets can force an actor to expend a larger volume of resources in the pursuit of its goal. One of the most difficult tasks that any actor can set for itself is to attempt to compel a recalcitrant opponent to behave in a particular way. Ultimately, the actor must ask itself if the goal is worth the cost.

This was precisely the problem that the United States faced in Vietnam, where the insurgents in the south and their allies in the north were prepared to accept substantial punishment rather than abandon their goal of destroying the U.S.-backed regime in Saigon. In fact, the level of violence that the Americans inflicted in their attempt to compel increased so enormously that it eventually unnerved not the recipients but the deliverers. American public opinion, many members of Congress, and even some participants in both the Johnson and Nixon administrations came to be shocked by the degree of force delivered in Southeast Asia. They began to question whether anything was worth the creation of so much misery. In the end, American behavior became the issue, and whatever Vietnamese transgressions had inspired it were almost entirely forgotten or dismissed as irrelevant. The United States was forced to withdraw its demands and to wind down its participation in the war. Its Vietnamese opponents prevailed because their refusal to back down led to what was eventually perceived both at home and abroad as a U.S. overreaction.

Attempts to use economic coercion may also fail when a target refuses to go along with the demands being made. The United Nations sanctions applied against Iraq before, during, and after the Gulf War in 1991 are a case in point. These sanctions were applied to virtually all goods entering and leaving Iraq, and they were vigorously enforced by an impressive international coalition. From all reports, the United Nations efforts greatly disrupted the Iraqi economy and caused severe problems. Yet the Iraqi government never gave in to the United Nations demands regarding Kuwait. Later, it stalled and attempted to evade United Nations requirements pertaining to the inspection of its weapons capabilities. As in the case of Vietnam, pain was no assurance of success.

The Target's Perception of the Actor. The use of threats and coercion has a fundamental effect on the target's perception of the actor who makes the threat. Since a threat contains the expectation of punishment and pain, the target's normal reaction is to feel fear and/or anxiety. The greater the promised punishment, the more that fear is felt. Because of the fear and anxiety associated with threat making, the target often tends to conclude that the actor's goal is not solely to modify the target's behavior. Rather, the target comes to believe that a sadistic element is involved as well. Under these circumstances, resentment and resistance are likely to guide the target's response, for "influence attempts based solely on negative sanctions provide [the target] with no incentive to comply with [the actor's] demands if [the target] can find a way to avoid detection."[43]

As a result of the target's hostility, the actor's efforts to affect the target's actions may merely cause the target to modify the form of its unacceptable behavior. As Deutsch puts it, those who urge the use of threats as a policy instrument "first propose that we should frustrate our opponents by frightening them very badly and that we should then rely on their cool-headed rationality" to guide them in the proper direction.[44] Such a happy outcome rarely occurs, for the target is far more likely to switch from one form of unacceptable conduct to another form of equally undesirable behavior.[45]

Stephen Van Evera provides an excellent description of just such a situation in pre–World War I Europe.[46] At the turn of the century, Germany had become the strongest industrialized country in Europe. German prestige within the European state system did not match its strength, however. Consequently, the German government decided on a policy of intimidation, wherein a large German navy would be built to serve as an implied threat to any country that might choose to ignore German might. This policy was particularly designed with the British in mind, for the British were regarded as especially unwilling to accept the Germans' desired changes in the European hierarchy.

This policy backfired when the British exchanged one form of unwanted behavior for another. Alarmed by the German naval buildup, the British began to construct a new fleet and initiated discussions with the French that led to an implicit military agreement. The German bluster was designed to force the British to stop ignoring German importance and to recognize Germany's position. Instead, it drove the British to move from the unacceptable conduct of ignoring German status to the undesired behavior of fleet construction and a closer alliance with the French.

A more recent example may be found in the economic realm. In the late 1970s U.S. automobile makers, alarmed by the rapid growth in competition from small, fuel-efficient cars imported from Japan, put strong pressure on Congress and on first the Carter and later the Reagan administrations to restrict Japan's ability to export cars to the United States. The U.S. government obliged, and spurred on by the hint of severe congressional action if no agreement was reached, the Japanese were ultimately forced to accept "voluntary" quotas regarding the number of cars they could ship to the U.S. market each year. In the face of these restrictions, the Japanese adopted a two-pronged strategy. They exported more "upscale" cars instead of the smaller and cheaper cars they had previously sent to the United States, and moved some production facilities to the United States, thereby evading import restrictions altogether. In this case, one form of unacceptable behavior (the sale of too many small cars) was followed after a veiled threat (possible import restrictions) by another type of unwanted conduct (larger and more expensive cars were sent, and production was set up in the United States). American automobile makers found that mobilizing the U.S. government to make an implied threat on their behalf only meant that their opponent invaded new and more profitable parts of the market.

This example also illustrates two other points. One has to do with the ability of the United States and Japan to understand and appreciate the subtle communications they sent to one another. As noted earlier, actors frequently misinterpret the meaning of the signals they send back and forth, especially when the messages must overcome formidable cultural barriers. Such was the case when the United States attempted to warn Iraq about Kuwait in 1990. These problems are muted considerably when the signaling is between countries that have a similar understanding of the international system and that share many of the same international goals.

The second point involves the nature of both the threats and the responses made between fellow members of the Western system. When imports from Japan were perceived as harming American manufacturers, the American threat was that Congress might act unless Japan compromised by voluntarily restricting its exports. It was merely suggested that action could be taken, and there never was a demand that Japan stop selling cars altogether. The incomes of too many Americans relied on the sale and maintenance of Japanese cars for this type of threat to be made. Once again, economic interdependence considerably muffled the nature of the confrontation.

Let us compare this U.S.-Japanese interaction with that between two developing countries, Iraq and Kuwait. The issue precipitating the Iraqi invasion of Kuwait was in large measure economic. Kuwait had given Iraq significant amounts of foreign aid during the Iran–Iraq war in the 1980s. With the end of that war, the aid slowed, leaving Iraq short of the money it needed to rebuild from the war. In addition, oil prices in 1990 were soft. Iraq wanted higher prices and saw Kuwait as a stumbling block to a price rise. Thus, Iraq threatened Kuwait with invasion if it did not resume aid and take action to force up oil prices. When confronted with economic trouble, the Iraqis took a far more severe course of action than the United States did with regard to Japan. In part, this happened because the interdependence between Iraq and Kuwait was very shallow. Few Iraqi domestic interests depended on the existence of normal commercial relations between the two countries. At the same time, the nearly five-decades-old tradition of cooperation found in the Western world did not exist to tone down the confrontation.

The Costs of Using Threats. When coercion is the basis for the actor's influence on the target, the target will only begrudgingly cooperate with the actor and will seek to free itself of the domination imposed by the actor whenever it feels able to do so. As Richard Rosecrance notes, when the exercise of power is based on repression, the actor faces the "problem of popular laxity, indifference, and lack of support."[47] Morgenthau makes the same point when he says that "no dominion can last that is founded upon nothing but military force."[48] Robert Gilpin agrees, arguing that, although the ability to use coercion may seem to represent the actor's substantial strength, simply using force to obtain influence means that one is "able to enlist and secure the loyalty of only a small fraction of [the target's] inhabitants. This lack of identification . . . [is] a source of serious weakness [and] accounts for the ultimate fragility of empires in the face of internal revolts and external pressures."[49] And, of course, as targets become ever more reluctant to do an actor's bidding, the cost of control can begin to skyrocket as the actor has to expend greater amounts of resources to achieve the desired effects.

An Eastern European Example. The rise and fall of the Soviet empire in Eastern Europe illustrates the problems inherent in relying on coercion, threats, repression, and other strong-arm tactics for controlling targets.[50] The Soviet domination of Eastern Europe began in the closing months of the Second

World War as the Red Army chased the German Wehrmacht first out of the Soviet Union and then out of the countries that it occupied to the west of the Soviet Union. The liberation of Eastern European countries from Nazi rule, however, resulted not in the restoration of the prewar governments but in the imposition of regimes that in some cases were handpicked by the Soviet Union. They were subservient to Soviet wishes and based their authority on the support they derived from a substantial Soviet presence and from a large amount of Soviet aid. In Poland, the regime that came to power consisted of Communists who for the most part were imported from the Soviet Union for the task of governing a country deemed vital to Soviet territorial security. Communist regimes were also imposed in Bulgaria and Romania and came to power with Soviet sponsorship after popularly elected governments were subverted in Hungary in 1947 and in Czechoslovakia in 1948. The lineup of Soviet clients was completed when a Communist East German government was set up in the wake of the Berlin Blockade of 1948–49.

In sponsoring the creation of these governments, the Soviets displayed little concern for popular sentiment in the countries involved. Where elections were allowed, either they were rigged, as in Poland, Romania, and Bulgaria, or they were eventually overturned by a Communist coup d'état, as in Hungary and Czechoslovakia. In each case, the end product was a totalitarian state. The Soviets made it plain that they expected the regimes they supported to adhere closely to Soviet demands. Accordingly, they assisted in the development of secret police organizations to ensure against organized opposition and rebellion from the local population. In addition, units of the Red Army were stationed in each of the satellite countries to assist in keeping order and to guard against deviations from Soviet interests. The availability of information was closely controlled, propaganda praising the local Communist rulers and their Soviet masters was widely disseminated, and each country's society and economy were set up along lines that conformed to patterns established by the Soviet Union.

Within their Eastern European empire, the Soviets monitored the foreign policy initiatives of the satellite states and limited their contacts with non-Communist countries.[51] Popular disturbances aiming at the introduction of more representative governments were labeled capitalist subversion and were handled in a severe way. Three of the more notable instances involving the suppression of disruptions occurred in 1956 in Hungary, in 1968 in Czechoslovakia, and in the early 1980s in Poland. On the first two occasions, Soviet troops were sent to quell insurrections that were about to undermine and topple the Soviet-backed governments. On the third, menacing hints of potential Soviet action were used to induce the Polish government to crack down on the Solidarity trade union movement. In each case, the Soviets claimed that they were merely lending such "fraternal socialist assistance" as had been requested by the local governments. This euphemism was designed to hide the exceedingly brutal and harsh nature of Soviet actions. In fact, after the 1968 invasion of Czechoslovakia, the Soviet government attempted to clothe its interventions, both present and future, with respectability by announcing the Brezhnev Doctrine. This doctrine asserted the right of Communist countries to aid one another with force, if necessary, to prevent backsliding toward capitalism.

Thus, over a period of thirty-five years beginning in the late 1940s, the Soviet Union established an iron-fisted grip on the countries along its western borders. The Soviets' rule had little appeal to those who were governed, and the result was sullen, and in some cases outwardly hostile, populations and allies whose dependability was at best questionable. The governments that ruled on behalf of the Soviet Union were not accepted as legitimate by the local populations, and they required extensive Soviet aid and assistance to keep themselves afloat. The Soviet empire was therefore a continual source of concern for its masters and served as a constant drain on Soviet resources.

During the years when the Soviet economy experienced reasonable growth, the strain of sustaining the empire was tolerable. In the mid-1970s, however, the dismal performance of the Soviets' own economy began to have a telling effect on their ability to preserve their hold on Eastern Europe. By the late 1980s, the Soviets were faced with hard choices, for they could no longer hold Europe, compete with the United States as a superpower, and at the same time provide the goods and services demanded by an increasingly restive domestic audience. Despite the distaste of many in the Soviet hierarchy for doing so, it became necessary to repudiate the Brezhnev Doctrine and to cut back on aid given to the European satellites.[52]

The winding down of Soviet aid and the now uncertain support of the Red Army left the satellite governments in the lurch. Having never been able to establish themselves as the legitimate rulers of their societies, they now found themselves face to face with disaffected populations. Solidarity reemerged as a political force in Poland. In rapid succession, the Communist parties in Hungary, Czechoslovakia, and East Germany reorganized, and elections were scheduled. In Romania, the Ceausescu regime, refusing to accede to the winds of change, was deposed and its leaders were executed. By the end of the revolutionary year of 1989, the political complexion of Eastern Europe had been significantly altered with the sudden end to four decades of Soviet-dominated Communist rule in the satellite countries. Once the threat of intervention was gone, Soviet influence was instantly repudiated. Soviet power, having been based on fear and intimidation, left Eastern Europeans with bitter feelings toward both their former overlords and their puppet governments.

This example also illustrates that the type of goal an actor pursues strongly conditions the tactics it feels are required for the proper exercise of power. After the Second World War, the Soviet Union's paramount objective was to safeguard its national security; the need to promote the spread of international communism, though important, was secondary to this desire. In 1945, the Soviets felt that, with the possible exception of Czechoslovakia, the USSR was confronted with unfriendly and potentially troublesome neighbors. After all, the Germans had invaded and nearly destroyed the Soviet Union, the Poles had traditionally demonstrated animosity toward the Soviets, and the Romanians, Hungarians, and Bulgarians had been German allies. Therefore, the Soviets had ample reason to adopt a forceful approach rather than simply trust these countries to spawn governments that would respect Soviet security needs and would be amenable to Soviet concerns.

The same could be said for the Soviet desire to propagate communism. Only in Czechoslovakia and to some extent in Hungary did the local Communist party enjoy any significant degree of popular support. The other countries exhibited a substantial amount of conservative and anti-Communist sentiment. Spreading the communist faith again necessitated some amount of coercion.

The Soviets' use of coercion to get their way may have borne fruit in the long term if they had not also based their influence almost entirely on intimidation, repression, and fear. As noted earlier, over time it is important that an actor build some sort of acceptance for its domination of a target. In the case of the Soviets, they might have allowed their Eastern European satellites increasingly greater autonomy and freedom of action and might have gradually withdrawn the Red Army from these countries. Hence, instead of crushing the Hungarians in 1956 and the Czechoslovakians in 1968, the Soviets might have accepted their attempts to introduce greater variety into the Communist bloc. During World War II and for a considerable time thereafter, communism was a very attractive ideology and had considerable appeal around the world, Eastern Europe included.[53] This mood might have been built upon. But then, as Louis Halle reminds us, "Hamlet need not have suffered the fate that befell him—but only if he had not been Hamlet."[54] By its nature, the Stalinist system could not tolerate a looser sort of leadership and domination. Fear was in many ways its lifeblood, in both domestic and foreign policy. The result was a form of influence that appeared virtually complete but was paper thin, with the repressed just biding their time until their opportunity to rid themselves of their oppressors came. Targets placed in such a circumstance almost invariably have this reaction.[55]

Summary of Threats

Coercion and threats as tools for exercising power may be summarized by a brief consideration of their relationship to weight, domain, range, and scope. In the case of all four factors, the simple use of force is a relatively poor technique for accomplishing one's purposes. Weight, or the probability that a target will do as the actor wishes, is significantly altered only to the degree that the target complies with the actor's demands. And this is in many ways a product of the actor's ability to communicate its message in such a way that the target's way of life is not apparently menaced. But threats quite naturally tend to instill anxiety in a target, which often translates into fear and an unwillingness to comply, or else into modification of behavior in a direction that presents new problems for the actor. The examples given earlier regarding German and British actions before World War I and Japanese and American conduct vis-à-vis imported automobiles illustrate this principle. At best, coercion produces only a sullen performance of the tasks demanded, as in the case of Eastern Europe under Soviet domination.

The actor's domain, or the set of targets that it controls, is also limited by the use of tactics built on intimidation. Again, the reason has to do with the way targets tend to react. Few enjoy being frightened and dominated. Hence, the domain of an actor who employs such a technique is likely to extend only as far as its physical reach allows. Beyond that, few will be inspired to follow.

This observation has important implications for range, the resources at the actor's disposal. When influence is based on the ability to produce fear, then the actor's resource base becomes important because it is the defining element of the actor's reach. As discussed earlier in this chapter, an actor's capabilities relative to those of the target are an essential component of the successful threat.

Finally, scope—the type of behavior the actor controls—is also affected by the target's reaction to the actor's behavior and by the actor's resources. To the degree that the actor's conduct is considered unacceptable, the target will keep its cooperation to a minimum, and the actor will be forced to expend larger amounts of resources to obtain the desired effect. The Eastern European example is a case in point.

Many of the more lasting examples of influence through the use of this tactic come only when it is employed in conjunction with bribes or when an effort is made to use political or psychological resources to convince the target that it will benefit from going along. The first of these two techniques is examined in the next section.

THE VALUE OF BRIBES

Inducing a target to perform a desired act by offering a reward may be referred to as a bribe. It is based on a trade in which an actor transfers a resource to a target in exchange for a modification in the target's behavior. For some, the use of bribes is an indicator of moral turpitude, a display of the actor's weakness, and constitutes evidence of the lack of willpower in the face of adversity.[56]

For instance, in the early years of the American republic, pirates operating off the Barbary Coast of modern-day Libya requested that the Jefferson administration make a payment in exchange for a guarantee of safe passage for U.S. merchant ships. American opinion was outraged by the demand, regarding it as depraved, and backed a policy built on the use of force as a means of handling the problem. Similar dismay was expressed during President Reagan's second term in office when the American public learned that the president was involved in the payment of what amounted to a bribe to Iran in exchange for the release of American hostages who were held by a pro-Iranian terrorist group in Lebanon. Many saw the U.S. government's behavior as a case of cowardly appeasement.

Despite the emotions it evokes, such bribery has a long tradition: bribes "have long been important as a means by which some states get other states to do things they would not otherwise do."[57] Since ancient times, international actors have used royal weddings, preferential trade agreements, and similar inducements to cement good relations with one another and to influence each other's conduct. Indeed, the Barbary pirates example is a case in point. Whereas the Americans were upset by the pirates' insistence on a payment, the French quietly agreed to compensate the pirates if they kept their hands off French vessels. Thus, what constituted offensive behavior for one country was seen by another as a convenient way of avoiding the expense and pain of warfare.

Bribes are typically used in international politics when the actor's goal requires cooperation from the target and the actor perceives that the target also has goals that require the actor's cooperation. Under such circumstances, the two may work out a mutually beneficial exchange. Of course, such negotiations occur only when both actor and target see a basis for an exchange and when, as the American examples here show, both feel that an exchange is an acceptable way to resolve their individual policy needs.

Communicating a Bribe

Negotiating a successful bribe involves many of the same characteristics associated with a successful threat: careful communication between actor and target, considerations relating to the actor's capabilities and its credibility, and the target's degree of receptiveness to the actor's proposals. The communications process must at a minimum include a statement of the behavior the actor seeks and of the offer it is making in order to obtain that behavior. In effect, when making a bribe, the actor tries to create a linkage between its behavior and that of the target, "making [its] own behavior on a given issue contingent on [the target's] actions toward other issues."[58] For example, in the 1947 negotiations between the United States and the Philippines regarding the lease of Subic Bay and Clark Air Force Base, a clear agreement was made for the United States to pay the Philippines a given sum in exchange for the use of the bases. Each side understood its obligations, and each knew what to expect of the other. The communications process therefore functioned effectively.

This technique, though apparently straightforward, may result in considerable confusion if actor and target are not explicit with one another as to the nature of the exchange. Vague transactions occur in part because "gifts [are] a way of establishing superiority, and not rarely, the recipient feels degraded."[59] This is especially true when the target is a sovereign state. Such feelings can be avoided by obfuscating the kind of service the actor expects of the target. In the process, however, just how much influence the actor is supposed to receive becomes unclear, and future recriminations may be the result.

One example of such confusion occurred in 1987 when the U.S. government offered to have its navy escort Kuwaiti petroleum tankers in the Persian Gulf in order to protect them from the Iranian armed forces during the Iran–Iraq war. The offer clearly was motivated by the U.S. government's desire to obtain influence with the Kuwaitis and to block the Soviet Union from doing the same. This proposal was in line with a general American policy of seeking influence with Arab governments, particularly those that controlled large petroleum deposits, by transferring weapons to them. One of the primary recipients of this policy was Saudi Arabia, which received sixty F-15 fighter aircraft in the late 1970s and five AWAC (Airborne Warning and Control System) planes in the early 1980s.[60]

The United States carefully attempted to avoid offending those who benefited from American actions by not making any explicit linkages between American offers and expected Arab behavior. Still, the Americans believed that the arms transfers and the protection of Kuwaiti tankers gave them a measure of influence with the governments involved. Therefore, the United States was both surprised and dismayed when an American naval ship, the U.S.S. *Stark,* was attacked by an Iraqi plane while protecting Kuwaiti vessels in the Persian Gulf and neither the Kuwaitis nor the Saudis proved of any help. After the attack, it was learned that a Saudi AWAC had spotted the Iraqi jet on its way toward the *Stark* but had made no effort to inform either the *Stark* or other nearby U.S. units. In addition, the Kuwaiti government displayed little concern for the stricken American ship, insisting that it could not seek refuge in a Kuwaiti port.

For many Americans, the Saudi and Kuwaiti behavior represented a clear case of ingratitude and a violation of the implicit agreement that accompanied the arms transfers and the offer to protect the petroleum tankers. The problem, however, lies not in a lack of Arab graciousness but in the clouded communications that accompanied the American deeds. As mentioned, the kind of behavior expected in return for the American actions was not explicitly defined in order that the exchanges would not come to be seen as crass. But many American analysts thought they would be able to count on Arab assistance, especially if the United States was providing assistance to an Arab country.

The Arabs had quite a different point of view. They saw the American escorting of Arab tankers as payment for something the Arab country in question had already done, or else for something it wished to do but refrained from doing to please the United States. In other words, the Americans had already received their payoff and had no right to expect more. The Saudis had already expressed a willingness to invest heavily in U.S. government bonds, to pump oil at a rate that exceeded Saudi needs, to acquiesce in American Middle East peace initiatives, and to buy American defense products instead of weapons made by another country, such as the United Kingdom or France.[61] For the Kuwaitis, the exchange involved their willingness to forgo an appeal to the Soviet Union for naval assistance, a degree of cooperation with American peace plans, and an agreement to pump oil. In addition, the United States was seen as being forced to protect Kuwaiti ships by its need to keep oil flowing to international markets. Thus, the American escorting of tankers was regarded as making a virtue out of necessity.[62] When we consider these Arab views, the problem of communications stands out more clearly.

A failure of communications in the area of bribery may either sour relations between actor and target by violating the sensitivities of one or the other, or it may lead the actor to believe that it has bought more influence than it has in fact secured. When communications are effective, however, bribes help to create a greater degree of mutual interests between actor and target than previously existed because it sets up a situation in which both may hope to benefit. Nonetheless, the exchange in itself is merely instrumental. That is, it is designed to help the actor accomplish its goal, and it does not guarantee that a deeper friendship between actor and target will ensue. Indeed, assuming that some type of affection and close relationship will result from the exchange is precisely the sort of mistake that helped lead to the confusion that enveloped the *Stark* incident.

Capability, Credibility, and Bribes

Just as was true with threats, an actor's capabilities and its credibility play a role in the bribery process. Two keys to a good bribe are the target's belief that the actor can deliver as promised and the target's perception that the actor can be relied on to do so. If the actor does not have a sufficient resource base, the target is not likely to regard any offers as reasonable. At the same time, if the actor has a reputation for reneging on its promises, then the target will have little incentive to take the actor's offers seriously.

Two examples of proposals that have capability and credibility problems come to mind: the American program of assistance for Europe after World War II, better known as the Marshall Plan, and President Lyndon Johnson's proposal to the North Vietnamese for a massive American-financed development of Southeast Asia. In both instances, it was not at all clear that the money existed to make the program a reality, which meant that capability was questionable, and American behavior in other areas made the sincerity of the United States debatable, thereby affecting American credibility.

The Marshall Plan was designed to foster the recovery of Europe from World War II, the most devastating war in history. The destruction of this war was so intense that even after two years of peace the situation in Europe had not improved and actually seemed to be going downhill rapidly. With the economic conditions in Europe going from bad to worse, communism gained great appeal. To many analysts, communism appeared to be on the verge of subverting all hopes of restoring the democratic institutions in Western Europe, much as it was already doing in Eastern Europe.

These circumstances led the Truman administration to propose on June 5, 1947, an American-financed program to assist in the recovery of Europe, both East and West, and including the Soviet Union. The Communist countries of Europe were included in the program so that the program could not be labeled as anti-Russian or as biased in some other way. In addition, it was perceived as a last-ditch means of inducing the Soviets to follow a more cooperative course in reorganizing Europe. Thus, the primary goal of the Marshall Plan was to aid in reconstructing Europe, but one additional goal was to induce the Soviets to alter their behavior.[63]

The American capability to finance the program came into doubt because of the potential involvement of the Soviet Union. Anti-Communist sentiment was on the rise in the United States, and Congress, on whom the funding of the Marshall Plan depended, reflected this mood. At the same time, the plan's credibility also came into question because of the announcement in March 1947 of the Truman Doctrine. This proposal offered assistance to Greece and Turkey in their struggles against Communist subversion and held out the prospect of similar assistance to any other European countries that confronted the same problem. Beyond this, the very day that the Marshall Plan was announced, President Truman was featured in newspapers throughout the United States as denouncing Communist efforts to undermine the democratically elected Hungarian government.[64]

These characteristics of the American offer tended to destroy any value it might have had in producing a shift in Soviet behavior, for the Soviets believed first that the plan had little substance behind it and second that the American decision to include the Soviet Union was insincere. Of course, even if the plan had not contained these flaws, the Soviets would probably still have rebuffed it because their plans and goals in Eastern Europe were predicated on the need for near total control.

The second example is President Johnson's offer to use American economic and financial muscle to promote the rapid development of Southeast Asia, especially Vietnam.[65] This proposal was made in a speech delivered at Johns Hopkins University on April 7, 1965, and was part of a U.S. effort to prop up the American-backed South Vietnamese government. In the spring of 1965 U.S. foreign policy decision makers were convinced that Hanoi was sponsoring internal subversion in South Vietnam, and the Americans wished to protect the Saigon government from what they perceived as North Vietnamese acts of aggression. American policymakers firmly believed that only an American effort could protect South Vietnam and that a commitment of U.S. forces would be necessary. Fearing that such a move would have unpleasant political repercussions, both at home and abroad, U.S. leaders attempted to secure a policy change from Hanoi. This attempt was in the form of an offer to aid in developing Vietnam "on a scale to dwarf even our own [the United States'] TVA [Tennessee Valley Authority]" by asking "Congress to join in a billion dollar American investment."[66]

From Hanoi's point of view, this apparently bold and generous initiative lacked both capability and credibility. Capability was a problem because financing would be available only if Congress agreed to provide it. Just eight months earlier, however, both the House of Representatives and the Senate had overwhelmingly passed the Gulf of Tonkin Resolution, which authorized the president to act to prevent further aggression in Southeast Asia and was clearly aimed at North Vietnam.[67] Given this prior action, the possibility of money being made available for a billion-dollar grant for Southeast Asia most probably seemed remote to Hanoi. The United States' credibility was rendered debatable by the rapid buildup of American military and advisory forces that was under way, by a bombing campaign then in progress against North Vietnam, and by the massive amounts of American money for military assistance being provided to the Saigon regime. Such militarily oriented moves made it appear that the Johns Hopkins speech was little more than a fig leaf designed to cover actual American intentions, which were to fight instead of giving aid.[68]

The Target's Receptivity to a Bribe

These two examples also show how the target's receptivity is involved. In order for a payoff to succeed, the actor must have not only capability and credibility, but a receptive audience as well. In the case of the Marshall Plan, the Soviet Union would probably not have traded a revision of its behavior for any amount of Western monetary assistance. The Soviets simply were too convinced that they needed to control Eastern Europe in order to guarantee their security. As far as the North Vietnamese were concerned, they had an overriding commitment both to the unification of the country under the rule of the Hanoi government and to the need to purge Vietnam of colonial and neocolonial influences. Thus, in neither case was the target particularly interested in the trade-off that the American proposal implied.

For the most part, a target has such an interest only when actor and target share some common value. The value may be ephemeral, as was the case during the Cuban missile crisis, when both the United States and the Soviet Union wished to avoid nuclear war, or it may be more permanent, as was true of the Western European and American interest in the recovery of Europe in the late 1940s. As these examples portray, these mutual interests can exist either between bitter rivals or between staunch friends and allies. The important consideration pertaining to a successful exchange is that a shared value must exist.[69] It was, after all, their desire to avoid war that led the Soviets to agree to withdraw their missiles when the United States gave them private assurances that it would leave Cuba alone and would pull its own missiles out of Turkey. If the Soviets had not shared the American desire to avoid war, then the American offer, whether made privately or publicly, would have fallen on deaf ears.

When bribes are viewed in this light, one of their most prominent problems becomes relatively clear. The very nature of the anarchic international system, with its tendency toward distrust and suspicion, and the tremendous diversity in the actors found within the world arena, with their varying goals, cultures, and value structures, both work to mute the climate in which bribes are most likely to be successful. In general, international theorists often note that bribery is preferable to threats as a means of gaining influence because both actor and target may be expected to gain from the bribe. Therefore, they may come away from the exchange with a better impression of one another and may feel better disposed to cooperate with each other in the future.[70] When this is the outcome, the fear, anxiety, resentment, and resistance associated with threats are less likely to cloud the relationship between actor and target. And on many occasions this is the result. For example, after the peaceful resolution of the Cuban missile crisis, the superpowers began inching toward better relations with one another. The Limited Nuclear Test Ban agreement, the establishment of better communications for crisis management (the "hot line"), and the Strategic Arms Limitation Talks all followed this crisis as the superpowers learned that they should and could bargain with each other.[71]

Problems arise, however, when actor and target regard each other as insincere. In an anarchic world where actors constantly maneuver for advantage, the perception of insincerity by either actor or target may merely increase their mutual suspicion. The Soviet reaction to the Marshall Plan and the North Vietnamese rejection of President Johnson's offer both produced such a development. In the case of the Marshall Plan, the Soviets apparently believed that the American proposal was designed to pull Eastern Europe away from Soviet influence and to force the Soviets to allow Americans to have a chance to inspect the Soviet economy, and thereby to uncover Soviet weaknesses. To the Americans, the Soviet rejection of the Marshall Plan and their obstructionism as regarded Eastern European participation served as confirmation of Soviet hostility and the Soviet desire to rope off and exploit Eastern Europe. Thus, far from improving Soviet-American relations, the Marshall Plan helped fuel the downward spiral.

The same was true of Johnson's offer. To the American president, the proposal represented an extremely generous attempt to help an impoverished nation even in the face of its unprovoked and unacceptable aggression. To the North Vietnamese, the offer was nothing less than an attempt to continue Western colonialism and to build international support for the policy of force that the United States obviously preferred. Hence, the Vietnamese rejection enraged some members of the Johnson administration and confirmed their belief that the only way to deal with the Vietnamese was through overwhelming force. Once again, when an actor and a target are entirely at cross-purposes, bribes do not smooth relations but become the excuse for more bitterness.

In the presence of a commitment to a set of common values, it is possible for an exchange to lead to greater stability and to a relatively long-lasting degree of influence—provided, of course, that both actor and target keep their end of the bargain. The forty-four years during which the United States had generally nonacrimonious access to the Subic Bay naval base and to Clark Air Force Base in the Philippines is a case in point. During that period, the United States traded rental payments and military protection to the Philippines for use of the bases. A large number of jobs for local workers was also generated. This example also shows, however, that when the basis for exchange ends, then so, too, might the relationship. As noted earlier in this chapter, after the Soviet threat disappeared, the Philippine government began to reevaluate the lease arrangements for the bases. One implicit part of the trade-off had been protection of the Philippines from Communist aggression. With the termination of the cold war and the improbability of a Communist attack, this part of the original deal no longer applies. Thus, the basis for the exchange had been altered, and as a result the agreement had become questionable.

An analogous set of conditions is found in U.S. policy toward Western Europe and Japan in the first two and a half decades after the Second World War. During these years, the United States was profoundly interested in the recovery of these countries from the effects of the war and in their development as dependable allies in the cold war against communism. Hence, the United States extended economic and military assistance in order to create a strong network of partners to aid in the protection of the Free World. In effect, an implicit exchange was set up in which the United States provided assistance to its fellow democracies in order that they might get their internal "houses" in order and become close associates in the campaign to contain communism. By the mid- to late 1960s and the early 1970s, most members of the Western world were fully recovered from the war. In fact, many had become strong enough economically that they were able to compete effectively with the United States. At this juncture, a new set of relationships was needed to reflect the alterations that had occurred. It was in this context that American analysts began to call in the early 1970s for a toning down of U.S. commitments to Europe and Japan and for a reappraisal of the existing trading and investment arrangements. Basically, American "payments" had acquired the sort of allies they were designed to buy, and now it was no longer necessary to continue making the "payments."

Thus, exchange relationships tend to mellow either because the target feels it no longer is receiving appropriate compensation (as in the case of the U.S. military bases in the Philippines), or because the actor believes it is not getting adequate value for its payments (as in the U.S. reevaluation of its economic and military relations with the other members of the Western world). Whatever the reason, the relationship either is terminated or must undergo substantial alterations. Bribes last only as long as both actor and target continue to make the appropriate payment.

Summary of Bribes

Bribes are a reasonably effective way for an actor to increase the weight of its influence when actor and target have a common interest in making an exchange, when suspicion does not cloud their perceptions of one another, and when the two can reach an agreement regarding the terms of the transaction. The greatest problem the actor is likely to confront in trying to get a target to act as desired has to do with imprecise communications, as the Kuwaiti and the Saudi Arabian examples showed. The same basic observations apply as far as scope is concerned, for the types of target behavior controlled by the actor are also strongly affected by careful communications and the circumstances surrounding negotiations.

The domain that the actor controls when using bribes is in part affected by some of the same factors, especially the existence of mutually held values and the absence of animosity. The range and sum total of the resources available to the actor also have an important role, for they help to determine how many targets the actor can hope to influence. A larger resource base and a greater scope of resources are the key both to influencing a wider group of targets and to controlling more types of behavior by those targets.

In summary, a bargain involving an exchange between an actor and a target is a useful means of exercising power in international relations when the two share a basic set of reference points, or values. Under these circumstances, the actor can obtain influence without encountering the degree of resistance that usually occurs when it uses more coercive tactics. In addition, the actor often comes closer to modifying the target's behavior in the desired direction, as opposed to merely obtaining a change in the type of undesirable conduct that the target displays, as may happen through force. Moreover, the use of bribes generally does not harm the relations between actor and target and may promote greater understanding between the two.

Bribes are not without shortcomings, however. First, when poor communications exist, the actor's understanding of the situation may not coincide with that of the target, and recriminations may result. Second, actors may make apparently generous offers of assistance to targets for which they harbor animosity as a means of legitimizing a more violent approach for seeking a change in behavior. At the same time, bribes that are proposed when mutual suspicion distorts the perceptions of actor and target can merely serve to heighten the trouble rather than to cool it. Finally, even when successful, bribes last only a limited period of time because conditions shift, and eventually one or both of the parties to the agreement will feel that it is no longer receiving sufficient payment for its efforts.

THE ART OF PERSUASION

Persuading a target to perform tasks that are in accordance with the actor's preferences is a third method for exercising power in international politics. Using this technique requires the actor to convince the target that it is in the target's best interests to do what the actor wishes. Over time, two approaches to persuasion have stood out as the most effective: the use of propaganda and the employment of political and economic theory. For each, the communications between actor and target, the actor's capability and its credibility, and the target's perception of the actor's motives determine the effectiveness of the technique.

Propaganda

Lasswell and Kaplan state that "propaganda consists of political symbols manipulated for the control of public opinion."[72] In essence, propaganda revolves around the distorted or incomplete presentation of information and ideas to a group of subjects in an attempt to alter their beliefs about political reality. By definition, propaganda is aimed at a mass audience, with the central purpose being to affect the thinking of as many people as possible. Manipulating information in this way can be an overwhelmingly effective means of securing a desired pattern of behavior because the target will act out of a sense of conviction instead of being motivated by either fear or the desire for a payoff. In fact, Morgenthau describes states that use propaganda properly as especially strong because of their ability to "exert strict control and guiding influence over the thoughts and actions of their citizens and foreign sympathizers."[73] According to this line of thought, regulating a target's perceptions and beliefs leads to the actor's almost complete ability to get whatever it desires.

Propaganda has played an increasingly important role in the contemporary international system because public opinion and mass audiences play a greater part in the modern political process.[74] Before the nineteenth century, when the public had a relatively small role in the public policy decision-making process, propaganda was almost unknown. With the public's greater participation, propanganda-like appeals aimed at a mass audience began to have more political relevance. Among the first messages built around the use of propaganda were those that appealed to the audience's sense of nationalism and its lack of ease at being controlled by nonnationals. Local culture was glorified, and all things foreign were depicted as the source of trouble and even of degradation.

In addition to mass participation, freedom of information within a society facilitates the use of propaganda by allowing an actor the opportunity to get its message across to its target. A carefully controlled flow of information and a regulated press and mass media present propagandists with severe problems, for they block their access to their audiences and place obstacles in the path of their ability to convince.

Communicating a message to a mass audience is often very difficult, for as Holsti notes, most people are too apathetic to pay attention to political messages.[75] Moreover, the uneducated and politically most unsophisticated members of society, who compose the group that is least likely to listen to political arguments, are usually the most susceptible to propaganda. The only exception occurs when people confront a crisis, such as severe economic dislocation and imminent foreign danger. Propaganda is most effective when the actor is able to seize the target's attention and to convey its messge in a simple manner that the audience can understand.[76] In the current international setting, terrorism, hostage taking, political assassinations, public demonstrations, riots, and strikes have been used as attention-getting devices, thus linking persuasion to violence in some cases.

Breaking the target's apathy also requires that the actor be credible, which means that the target must believe that the actor's claims conform to reality as the target understands it. Finally, the actor must seem to be motivated by a political program or set of principles that the audience can understand and relate to, and it must conduct itself in such a way that the target believes that the actor wishes no more than justice for itself and for those it represents. Actors that are able to do this can go a long way toward calming the audience's fear that the actor wishes to subjugate others for the mere pleasure of it.

In its crudest manifestation, propaganda is akin to a form of coercion directed at the target's mind. In this case, the actor fundamentally attempts to appeal to the audience's basest emotions in an effort to persuade the target to support the policy the actor prefers. The National Socialist, or Nazi, program in Germany in the interwar years serves as an excellent example. The Nazi plan of action took advantage of the national disillusionment that followed defeat in the First World War and combined it with concern for the economic woes that befell Germany first during the hyperinflation of the early 1920s and later as a result of the skyrocketing unemployment brought on by the Great Depression of the 1930s. As the bewildered and embittered common people in Germany sought an explanation for their troubles, they found a political party with a message that claimed to explain all: the German Jewish population and communism—both domestic and international—were to blame for Germany's woes. The solution the Nazis offered included rebuilding German military strength, settling scores with foreign foes, and purging Germany of its impurities. The Nazis deliberately used this disgusting message of hatred to take advantage of the audience's vulnerabilities, and exploited these troubles to secure support for the policies they desired. Outright lies and misleading information were provided to an insecure audience to obtain its support. Those who might object were silenced by the stampede of acceptance by those around them. In effect, a mob psychology was created and employed to suit the actor's purposes.

Propaganda may also be used to convince the citizens of another country that their government has embarked on a wrongheaded policy. Such activities are designed to bring pressure to bear on the government to change its actions.[77] By denying the government its base of public support, the actor hopes to compel a government to change its policy. History presents numerous examples of this tactic. For instance, both Germany and the United Kingdom attempted to influence American public opinion during both the First and Second World Wars, the German effort being less effective than the British. More recently, the Vietnamese directed propaganda at American public opinion during the Vietnam War with a reasonable degree of efficacy. In the early 1980s, the Soviets sought to use propaganda to affect Western public opinion during the debate regarding Euro-missiles, only to find that it did not produce the intended result.

The use of propaganda has varying degrees of effectiveness because its success is related to whether it conforms to facts as the audience perceives them.[78] As Lasswell and Kaplan have observed,

> propaganda in accord with predispositions strengthens them; propaganda counter to predispositions weakens them only if supported by factors other than propaganda . . . [for] propaganda cannot operate to alter the power structure except in directions to which the participants in the power process are already predisposed.[79]

In effect, this difficulty centers on problems associated with the actor's credibility and sincerity. When an actor's arguments stray too far from the target's conception of reality, then the target will question both the actor's credibility and its sincerity.

The illustrations presented earlier support these contentions, for in each example of failure the actor's claims flew in the face of reality as understood by the target, whereas in each case of success the actor's assertions reinforced reality as the target perceived it. In the two world wars, Germany maintained to the rest of the world that it was a victim of the plots and machinations of the other European great powers and that Germany wished only for peace. These messages failed because the facts belied their claims. The world had ample access to accounts of German cruelty during the invasion of Belgium in World War I and during action in Poland, in Scandinavia, in the Low Countries, and in France in World War II.

The Soviet use of propaganda during the Euro-missile debate also ultimately failed because the message seemed to be at odds with reality. In this case, the Soviet Union attempted to manipulate public opinion to oppose the United States' installation of Pershing II and cruise missiles in Western Europe. The American missiles were designed to counter the Soviets' prior basing of missiles in the western part of the Soviet Union and in Eastern Europe. The Soviet weapons were capable of striking at virtually any part of Europe. Of special concern was the SS-20, a mobile Soviet missile that was highly accurate and that could arrive on target with tremendous speed. The Soviet decision to place these missiles at these sites caused grave concern among Western European governments and led them to consider the counterdeployment of the American missiles, which could target the Soviet Union. The Soviet leaders tried to block the Western missiles by using propaganda portraying the governments in Western Europe and in the United States as aggressive and not worried about keeping the peace.

These Soviet ploys failed for two basic reasons: (1) the Soviet missiles preceded the American missiles; and (2) the Western proposal to negotiate the elimination of all Euro-missiles, both Soviet and American, was refused by the Soviets for a long period of time. In light of these circumstances, the Soviet arguments fell on fallow ground.[80]

Thus, in both examples of failed propaganda the most fundamental difficulty centered on the target's perception of the actor's credibility and sincerity. The instances in which propaganda was reasonably successful bear this out. During both the First and the Second World Wars, the British cleverly wove examples of German brutality in Europe and toward neutral shipping on the high seas into their appeals for aid from neutral countries. The British presented themselves as the bulwark of civilization against such behavior. Conveniently omitted was any information relating to Britain's own questionable behavior, such as boarding and seizing neutral vessels. Prior public awareness of German actions and the extremely repugnant nature of the Germans' actions reinforced the British message and gave it credibility. At the same time, the revulsion toward Germany created a need for a figure who would protect the audience the British wished to influence. This need also made many receptive to the British and helped convince them of British sincerity.

In the case of Vietnam, the message was aimed at the American public and depicted Vietnam as a poor, small, nonaggressive, and underdeveloped Asian country that was being subjected to merciless attacks from the greatest power on earth—the United States. The world press reinforced this presentation through its daily coverage of the war in Vietnam and its detailed reports on the extent of the U.S. military efforts against the Hanoi regime. This helped give the Vietnamese message credibility. The absence of a sound and widely accepted logic for American military involvement in Southeast Asia, problems relating to the stature and viability of the U.S.-backed government in Saigon, and the lack of any convincing reason to believe that events in Vietnam would have any appreciable effect on U.S. security all worked to bring American actions into question. By implication, many saw Hanoi's behavior as that much more reasonable. Hence, some Americans were receptive to the Vietnamese message because it seemed both credible and sincere.[81]

One of the most fundamental problems associated with the use of propaganda is that, by distorting ideas in order to gain influence, the actor limits its ability to maintain influence. As time passes, the target generally gains access to an ever-greater volume of information, even when information is tightly controlled. As more information becomes available, the target invariably will begin to see discrepancies between the message of the propaganda and the impressions it is gaining from other sources. As a result of these discrepancies, the target usually questions the propaganda and often rejects it. As an example, we might consider the general disillusionment with communism in Eastern Europe and even in the Soviet Union, where access to information from the outside world made many realize that Communist propaganda about the horrors of capitalism was farfetched.

Another limitation to propaganda is associated with the type of audience that is most easily swayed by such appeals. As noted earlier, the disadvantaged and uneducated are most easily influenced. Such individuals usually are least inclined toward political participation and tend to be apathetic. Thus, even if initially propaganda leads them to participate, over time they tend to become bored and to lapse into apathy. Hence, this audience is an unreliable base on which to build political support.

Political and Economic Theory

Unlike propaganda, which is aimed at a mass audience and often borders on psychological force,[82] political and economic theory as a method for convincing others usually is aimed at the target's elite decision makers and is far more subtle. This technique is built on the actor's attempt to establish a degree of group consciousness, or mutual identification, in which the target comes to see itself as sharing values and interests with the actor.[83] When an actor is successful in this attempt, the target begins to believe that the actor's goals are mutual goals. It confers a degree of legitimacy on the goals and perhaps even on the means that the actor wishes to use to pursue these goals. In such a situation, the actor's influence is magnified considerably because the target becomes a willing and even an enthusiastic aid in helping the actor to attain its objectives.[84] As Russett and Starr put it, "persuasion can occur when one appeals to the values that others hold dear. By demonstrating that one also holds these values, an appeal based on neither promise nor threat can still result in others doing what one wishes."[85]

Communicating Theory.   As noted earlier, the actor's ability to communicate effectively, its capability and credibility, and the target's willingness to accept the actor's message are key determinants of the actor's success in promoting a doctrine. Communicating theoretical conceptions of what are supposedly widely applicable political and economic value systems is far different from transmitting threats, bribes, and propaganda. In the cases of threats, bribes, and propaganda, the message is fairly narrow, and usually the behavior that the actor wants from the target is relatively specific. In the case of communicating theory, the message is often broader and far more complex, and the desired behavior may be much more vague.

For example, in the mid-1940s the United States took the lead in promoting the adoption of an international economic system that was organized around the principles of free trade. In its simplest terms, free trade involves a situation in which countries agree not to construct political barriers, such as tariffs or quotas, which will obstruct the movement of goods and services between countries. Many argue that the absence of such obstacles has both economic and political benefits. Economically, removing barriers is treated as ensuring larger markets, more efficient production, higher employment, better-made products, and lower inflation. Politically, dropping restraints is regarded as tying countries and corporations more closely together, thereby reducing the probability of violent international conflict. Simply put, it would be unprofitable to fight since they would be destroying their own customers and suppliers.

Transmitting such a theoretically complex set of ideas to others is not easy. For one thing, free trade theory is based on assumptions that pertain to the target's awareness of the operation of a market economy. In cultural environments that place little emphasis on such organizational principles, the free trade message is not easily understood. In addition, free trade assumes that countries are prepared to live in and can comprehend an international economic arena that is based primarily on competitive principles and in which trade is not used for political purposes. The communication of the free trade message also requires an understandable blueprint for putting into practice the procedures needed to monitor and administer such a system. Moreover, the behavior expected from the target is vague, for differing countries might devise many apparently acceptable and yet incompatible ways to meet their obligations under free trade arrangements. As an example, let us consider the debate regarding trade imbalances during the Bretton Woods negotiations in 1944. One proposal called for placing the onus for eliminating imbalances on the buyer, requiring that it reduce imports and increase exports. Another focused on the seller, obligating it to slow its exports and increase its imports. Both proposals would help solve imbalances, but they were incompatible.[86]

This is just a sample of the problems associated with the communications process. Thus, although great influence may be derived from convincing others to accept one's system of beliefs, the obstacles relating to the communications process are daunting.

Theory and Capability.   Within the context of molding beliefs, an actor's capability refers to whether adhering to the system of values that the actor espouses will lead to the expected payoffs. Gilpin argues that one of the most important ingredients in the process that leads others to regard an actor's value preferences as legitimate is the degree to which they benefit from it.[87] Deutsch concurs in this judgment, noting that no matter how compelling the arguments, they will carry scant weight with other international actors unless those actors are convinced they will reap substantial gains from adopting them.[88] Logic can go only so far in persuading others. At some point the target must believe that it is getting something in return. Otherwise, the target will have little incentive to follow, and the anarchic nature of the international arena, with its lack of governmental machinery needed to enforce rules that others do not choose to obey, will allow the target to defect and to refuse to go where the actor wishes to lead. Moreover, in an anarchic environment, suspicions about an actor's motives often are overcome only if the targets see benefits for themselves.

Capability is therefore a second formidable requirement that must be met if an actor is to exercise power by way of persuasion based on shaping another's system of preferences. Great difficulties are associated with capability, as became clear to the United States after the Second World War when it sought to convince other members of the international system to accept new commercial arrangements based on freer trade. At that time, the United States was far and away the strongest country on earth, both economically and militarily. Its casualties during the war were lighter than those of any other major country, and its industrial capacity emerged virtually undamaged. Not only had the United States supplied the American war effort in Europe and in the Pacific, but it had also contributed significantly to the war efforts of four other major countries: the United Kingdom, the Soviet Union, France, and China. At this time, the American economy was so strong that it accounted for approximately one half of all international trade (see Tables 3.1 and 3.2 in Chapter 3).

Thus, if any country ever had the ability to guarantee that the acceptance of its preferred system of values would lead to gains for others, the United States was that country in the years just after World War II. And to a large extent, the United States was able to deliver, at least as far as some countries were concerned. Marshall Plan aid to Western Europe, the establishment of the Atlantic alliance under the aegis of NATO (the North Atlantic Treaty Organization), and U.S. efforts to maintain open international markets all contributed to this end. The Marshall Plan helped the Europeans rebuild and once again become productive international actors, the Atlantic alliance provided a military screen behind which commerce might flourish in security, and an open international marketplace meant that goods could be bought and sold with an ease that facilitated prosperity.

Hence, through its immense strength at this time, the United States could put into practice its theoretical notions with a reasonable prospect of success. Not many countries ever enjoy the degree and margin of superiority that the United States had during those years. Few, therefore, are ever in the position to provide what the United States could provide.

Even at the peak of its strength, however, American capabilities had their limits, and these limits affected the acceptance of its international commercial agenda. We may illustrate this point by comparing the reactions of the Western and developing worlds to the system of freer trade. Whereas free trade theory purports to be universalist in its effects (see Chapter 3), the benefits from the operation of the new international economic arrangements were not evenly distributed. An examination of both trade and average income figures (see Chapter 3, Tables 3.1, 3.2, 3.8, and 3.9 and note 89) shows that the advanced industrialized nations have benefited far more than have the developing countries. For the West, international trade, both imports and exports, has increased continually and dramatically since the Bretton Woods system was inaugurated. Indeed, for these countries trade has come to represent a significant and growing source for augmenting the incomes of average citizens, which also have grown rapidly.

In the developing world, the situation has been very different. These countries were not included in the Marshall Plan and the Atlantic alliance. Their volume of trade has increased far more slowly and has even declined substantially in recent years. Average individual income has followed a similar course, having increased slowly and fallen off over the last decade. In addition, both the trade and income levels of these countries are only a fraction of the comparable levels of the West, and the gap between these groups of countries has not closed much over the last forty years.

Not surprisingly, then, the two groups have reacted very differently to the free trade doctrine pushed by the United States. The advanced nations have grumbled about the technical features associated with implementing the theory, and most of them have on several occasions felt compelled to break with orthodoxy in order to protect one or another domestic interest that has been harmed by more open trade. In general, however, the West has displayed a broad degree of satisfaction with, and acceptance of, the system as it has evolved since World War II. In contrast, developing countries have been much less interested in the doctrine and in the system created to put the theory into practice. They do not see that either the theory or the system contributes to their economic well-being. As a result, developing countries have challenged the theory, and many have rejected not only free trade, but also the capitalist system of free enterprise that they believe goes hand in hand with it. Those that have benefited from the application of the theory tend to accept it, whereas those that have not benefited tend to reject it.

Debates revolving around capability and the distribution of advantages not only center on the differences between groups of countries, but also vary across time.[89] For instance, political and economic theorists in the United Kingdom took the lead in creating free trade theory. Adam Smith, David Ricardo, and Jeremy Bentham all contributed to the early development of some of the principles that serve as the supporting foundations for this body of ideas. During the latter part of the nineteenth century, when the United Kingdom enjoyed substantial economic dominance over its would-be international competitors (and therefore would derive the greatest advantages from the application of the theory), its government tended to promote free trade as the only natural means of organizing international commerce. At the same point in time, the United States, which was more economically backward and would not benefit much from a more open international trading system, opposed free trade vehemently.

Approximately a half-century later, the situation changed completely. By the mid-1940s the government of the United States, which had become the world's dominant economic actor, was a strong proponent of free trade. For their part, the British were now far more hesitant to accept the doctrine that they had in large part developed, because with their weakened economic position after two world wars they could no longer obtain the same benefits that had accrued to them five decades earlier. The British felt that a system based on the acceptance of preferential trade with the members and former members of their empire made far greater sense. They now perceived free trade as an impractical body of theory that was not workable when applied to the hard realities of international politics. Once again, the actor's view of theory depends on whether it believes the theory will enhance its position.

Theory and Credibility.   The credibility of the actor's theoretical propositions constitutes another element that affects their value as a means for swaying others. In order for an actor to have credibility, it must appear to be committed to its own principles, applying them domestically where appropriate and taking actions internationally that appear designed to facilitate the proper functioning of the ideas that it favors. In the context of the free trade example mentioned here, the fact that its domestic economic system is based on the free enterprise principles that are at the heart of free trade was an asset that built credibility for the United States. The Marshall Plan, the Atlantic alliance, and U.S. moves to maintain an open international commercial system also contributed to American credibility. The same was true of the strong American leadership role in the negotiations leading to the creation of the International Monetary Fund (IMF), the World Bank, and later the General Agreement on Tariffs and Trade (GATT). In each case, the United States placed either its prestige or its considerable resources behind its theoretical preferences. In that way, the United States conveyed a sense to others that it was highly committed to their implementation.

Interestingly, each of these credibility-building moves had far greater impact on the Western world than they did on developing countries. The reason is simply that these American policies pertained largely to developed countries. The Marshall Plan and the Atlantic alliance in particular were aimed at demonstrating that the United States was committed to a select group of international actors. The negotiations leading to the IMF, to the World Bank, and eventually to GATT could not help but deliver the same message: once again Western countries were treated as full partners, and many developing countries either were left on the sidelines or were consulted only sporadically. The issues that the developing countries found most pressing, such as economic development and commodity agreements, were omitted from the discussions.[90] Thus, from the non-Westerner's point of view, the new system based on the concept of freer trade not only had capability problems, but also suffered from a credibility gap.

Capability and credibility problems also plagued the recent Uruguay Round of GATT negotiations regarding international trade. Among others, two issues played an important role in these negotiations. For the West, and for the United States in particular, the protection of intellectual property rights and a greater degree of freedom of trade in services, such as banking and insurance, were key parts of the bargaining process. The basic argument was that international commerce increasingly involves services and ideas and that these had to be respected and protected under the GATT code. Otherwise, international trade would eventually be stunted and prosperity all over the world would be undermined, which would have deleterious effects for all countries and all international corporations.

Among developing countries, a very pressing issue related to trade in agricultural goods. The United States had a strong interest in this issue as well. Here, the argument was that production and trade subsidies by advanced industrialized countries in general, and by the European Community in particular, were drying up markets for the food produced in the less developed parts of the world and in the United States, thereby denying income to these countries. In addition, subsidies drove the prices of agricultural goods upward. As a consequence, consumers both in the advanced countries and in other parts of the world were forced to pay billions of dollars more to purchase their goods than they would pay without the subsidies.

Thus, the United States argued that economic theory dictated that all members of the international system would benefit if intellectual property rights and trade in services were respected and if agricultural subsidies were terminated. The major problem in negotiating this outcome had to do with the capabilities of key actors, which ultimately affected the credibility of any concessions they offered. As far as the West was concerned, domestic groups tied to agriculture exerted tremendous pressures that limited their ability to reduce subsidies, especially in the European Community. At the same time, it was expected that the governments in many developing countries would be unable to control local businesses that profited from disregarding intellectual property rights. Hence, negotiators from all sides doubted that their partners could deliver on any promises that they made simply because they apparently lacked the domestic capacity to do so. At the same time, no international actor was capable of offering sufficient inducements to entice others to try to overcome these domestic problems.

The absence of this capability, together with the strong domestic pressures against concessions, hurt the credibility of all negotiators. Many of them suspected that false promises might be made simply in an effort to induce others to make concessions. Apparently, many negotiators thought that any concessions they made on one issue would be pocketed by others, who would then refuse to offer reasonable counterproposals of their own. The upshot was a collapse in negotiations. While theory pointed toward the need for a deal, capability and credibility problems blocked it.

The Target's Receptiveness to Theory. The fourth factor affecting an actor's ability to use theory to exercise power is the target's receptivity, or its willingness to accept the logic of the actor's arguments. A vital part of such a strategy is based on convincing the target that the actor's theoretical and value preferences are legitimate and therefore should be used as a guide for the target's behavior. The ability to convince the target is closely tied to whether the actor's preferences appear relevant to the target's concerns and to be a useful means of addressing the target's problems. As has already been noted, many perceived the new international commercial system created after the Second World War as having fundamental problems in this regard. Thus, they resisted the new arrangements and sought to overturn or to bypass them.[91]

In general, theoretical preferences are most likely to achieve widespread acceptance when they are based on precepts that allow other international actors to make their own choices and to set their own policy courses. Two examples come to mind. The first is President Woodrow Wilson's promotion of national self-determination at the end of the First World War. Simply put, national self-determination proposed that all peoples who constituted a nation should have the right to form a state and to become a recognized member of the international system.[92] This message had an appeal that went to the heart of the international troubles confronting many people all around the world. Fascination with it transcended culture, region, level of development and wealth, size of the society in question, and ideology. People everywhere either yearned for self-rule or could understand the desire others might have for such rights.[93] And almost everyone expected that the application of self-determination would lead to a better way of life for those who achieved self-rule. Thus, the United States gained considerable prestige and potential influence when President Wilson proclaimed his support for the doctrine.

The second example is found in the American/British announcement in late 1941 of the Atlantic Charter. This document outlined the principles that would be followed in the effort against the Axis coalition in World War II.[94] Specifically, the United States and the United Kingdom pledged that as victors they would seek no territorial aggrandizement, that territorial changes after the war would occur only with the consent of the people concerned, that all peoples would have the right to select their own form of government, that trade should be freer in order to benefit all peoples, that freedom of the seas would be respected, that arms limitations should be pursued, and that all peoples should be secure and free of social and economic deprivation. Once again, these statements contain ideas that have nearly universal applicability. Few would object to the rejection by the strong of any desire to dominate, or to pledges that the rights and freedoms of the weak must be respected and protected.

In both examples, the universality of the doctrine and the targets' willingness to accede to it were closely related to the degree to which the targets of the pronouncements perceived that their freedom of action would not be encumbered, and would in fact be enhanced if the principles went into effect. In the case of the Atlantic Charter, later American and British actions demonstrated their capability and credibility, at least as regarded the application of their principles to Western Europe. As the war ended, the peoples of this region were indeed offered the opportunity to select their own governments. They were allowed to play a role in the creation of a new international economic framework based on free trade and designed to ensure prosperity. In addition, they were treated as partners in an alliance system to guarantee their security. These actions greatly augmented British and especially American prestige. In addition, the announcement of the Truman Doctrine in March 1947 reinforced the United States' credibility, as far as the principles of the Atlantic Charter were concerned, by pledging that the United States was prepared "to support free peoples who are resisting attempted subjugation by armed minorities or by outside pressures."[95] Moreover, the United States also assured the world that it would use its vast military might properly. President Truman announced that "the possession in our hands of this new power of destruction [atomic weapons] we regard as a sacred trust. Because of our love of peace, the thoughtful people of the world know that trust will not be violated."[96]

Taken in combination, these and other events (such as the Marshall Plan and NATO) brought the United States a historically unprecedented degree of leadership and allowed it to rally Western states to its goal of opposing the spread of communism. Public opinion polls in Europe confirmed the special regard of Europeans for the United States. In France in 1945, 47 percent of those polled said they favored American influence in Europe, while only 23 percent favored Soviet influence. In the United Kingdom in 1947, 63 percent of all respondents said they trusted the United States government, 45 percent said they trusted their own government, 4 percent trusted their neighbor across the Channel, France, and none trusted the Soviet Union.[97]

Clearly, when the ideals expressed in the Atlantic Charter and in later American pronouncements were combined with the United States' commitment and ability to put at least some of these concepts into practice, the effect on American stature and strength was incalculable. As a result, the United States was catapulted into a position as the preeminent leader of the Western world. This role rested not so much on the United States' tremendous economic and military muscle as on its theoretical preferences and the values it represented.

Because so many parts of the world, especially Europe, North America, and Japan, share these values, the United States continues playing its part as a leader even after nearly five decades have passed. In addition, many of the international institutions that the United States took the lead in establishing in the wake of World War II remain vital to the operation of the international arena. Indeed, a comparison of the fate of the Warsaw Treaty Organization alliance in Eastern Europe, which was set up by the Soviet Union and rested on coercion, with that of NATO, which was created under American sponsorship, is instructive. Whereas NATO may actually be on the verge of expanding its horizons toward a greater global role, the Warsaw Treaty Organization has been disbanded. In fact, many former members of the Warsaw Treaty Organization in Eastern Europe have applied for NATO membership. Clearly, the nation that represents values held dear by others and that is able to deliver at least some of the benefits supposedly associated with these values may gain a considerable degree of lasting influence.

Theory and Context.   The strength derived from the effective presentation of theory and values is severely limited by context, as shown by a consideration of weight, domain, range, and scope. As described earlier, a theory- and value-oriented approach may affect a relatively wide scope of behavior by a target. Specifically, those who are attracted by the system of principles and preferences that an actor stands for may be inclined to follow the actor's lead in many areas. U.S. leadership in the Western world since World War II illustrates this thesis. Although the actor may not have its way in all matters, its influence under such conditions may extend to many issues and the target may take the actor's desires into account when reaching decisions in a variety of areas. Hence, the scope of the actor's strength may be considerable.

The weight and domain of the strength, however, are a different matter. They may be more limited and may be greatly affected by the range of resources available to the actor. The examples in this chapter relating to the developing countries' reaction to the Bretton Woods system and the worldwide reaction to the Uruguay Round of GATT negotiations show that the weight and domain of the influence gained by an actor may be narrow. The problems that affect both the degree to which an actor can affect the probability of a given outcome and the set of targets that the actor controls include communications, cultural variations among targets, and the actor's capability and credibility. As has already been discussed, the communication of theoretical concepts and value systems is very complex. Differing domestic patterns of social organization, value systems, and traditions create formidable barriers to the employment of persuasion as a means of exercising power. The high degree of homogeneity (by international standards) found in the Western world facilitates the use of persuasion within this group of countries. Even in that context, however, some problems remain, as the differences between the United States and the European Community during the Uruguay Round show. When more heterogeneity is encountered, as is common in the non-Western world, and when we compare Western and developing countries, then the problems relating to communications become so enlarged that persuasion through the use of theory is a daunting proposition.

At the same time, the vast benefits expected from the application of almost any theory are usually far beyond the capabilities of any actor and serve as another formidable limitation. Only rarely does an actor achieve the resource dominance enjoyed by the United States in the years immediately after World War II. As a result of these resource deficiencies and communications problems, the domain of the actor's influence will likely be circumscribed. Only a limited number of targets will both understand the actor's message and benefit sufficiently from it that they will be inclined to follow the actor's lead. These factors also affect the weight of the actor's influence. Once again, understanding the actor's message and the target's expectation of gain are important to a target's decision to change its behavior to conform to the actor's preferences.

Hence, under the proper conditions it is possible to derive considerable strength from persuasion based on the communication of economic and political theory. Nonetheless, the effective employment of such a technique is limited and can be used only with certain types of targets under certain types of circumstances. Moreover, this approach is useful only when a limited set of goals are pursued. Few would feel comfortable with the attempt to employ this technique when dealing with an implacable foe or when confronted with imminent invasion.

CHAPTER SUMMARY

This chapter has investigated some of the techniques that actors use to exercise power in international politics. An actor might use three basic methods to influence the behavior of others: coercion, bribery, and propaganda or political and economic theory. The use of these approaches is affected by such factors as the communications process between actor and target, the resources available to actor and target, the target's perceptions of the actor's intentions, and the target's willingness to conform to the actor's preferences.

With regard to coercion, in order to function well the communications process must transmit a clear idea to the target of what the actor wants, and what the actor proposes to do if the target fails to comply or does comply. Using these criteria, we find that threats appear to be most effective when they require only a marginal change in the target's behavior and when the consequences of failing to make the change seem enormous. Threats seem more likely to fail when they demand that the target make major changes or when the target believes that the actor is not prepared to respond vigorously to the target's failure to comply.

When looking at exchange as the basis for exercising power, the communications process becomes more difficult. An important reason why is that the exchange must avoid hurting the recipient's pride. Therefore, the nature of the trade-off between actor and target is often deliberately vague. This tendency to obfuscate may result in misunderstandings between actor and target as to the degree of influence that the actor is supposed to have over the target. The result may be a situation in which the target fails to deliver what the actor believes it has a right to expect. When the actor and the target have very different social cultures and traditions, these communications problems appear to be exacerbated.

The communications associated with the attempt to persuade a target to conform to an actor's preferences are even more complex than those associated with making bribes. When propaganda is the chosen instrument of persuasion, the primary difficulties relate to the type of audience that is most easily swayed and to the need to ensure that the message does not differ too greatly from the reality that the target perceives. When an actor wishes to employ political and economic theory, the communications process is even more intimidating: the message must explain the principles underlying the theory and how they may be applied properly to the international arena. In each case, cultural and other social differences between actor and target magnify the barriers associated with the communications process to the point where an actor may find it virtually impossible to use persuasion-based techniques effectively.

The actor's resources are the key to its ability to deliver on the threats and promises made and on the visions conveyed. In the context of coercion, the actor's capabilities usually refer to its capacity to locate the target and to inflict pain on it. When the actor is unable to do either, then its threats are hollow. With bribes, the actor's resource base is important to making the payoff that the actor promises. Again, the inability to do this makes the offer of a bribe meaningless. Resources also play a role in the attempt to persuade, especially when an actor seeks to use theory to build legitimacy for its preferences. Here, targets are likely to accept the actor's views only if they have reason to believe they will benefit from such acceptance. Producing those benefits can be a prodigious task that very few actors ever have the capability of doing.

The actor's capabilities, particularly in relation to those of the target, and its past and present behavior are keys to the actor's credibility. Credibility is the degree to which the actor can convince others that it will do as it says. With threats, credibility is enhanced when the actor is able to do as it wishes without fearing retaliation from the target and when the actor is known to have engaged in similar acts of coercion in the past. The same is true with bribes, for an actor's promises are more easily believed when the actor has previously made the same type of payoffs. The credibility of an actor's offers is also affected by concurrent behavior. That is, if an actor is preparing for coercion while at the same time offering an exchange, the target may regard the bribe as merely a means of justifying the ultimate use of force. Persuasion follows an analogous path—the actor's credibility rests in large measure on its willingness to introduce programs and to help create international institutions designed to guarantee the provision of the benefits that supposedly accompany the application of the actor's ideals.

Finally, the target's willingness to comply with the actor's wishes is closely related to the degree to which the target believes that such compliance will negatively affect its well-being and its freedom of action in the international arena. In general, it is difficult to avoid creating the impression that adverse effects will occur when one makes threats. As a result, the actor often succeeds only in modifying the form of the target's unacceptable behavior when it makes threats. The greatest problems associated with bribes center on the target's fear that the bribe may make it a junior partner in its relations with the actor. When persuasion is the centerpiece of the actor's influence attempts, the most important effect on the target's view of the actor's argument has to do with (1) whether the target believes that the principles advocated are relevant to the target's problems and (2) whether the target suspects that the principles are designed to convince the target simply to make sacrifices that will benefit only the actor.

The value of each of the three techniques examined in this chapter is closely related to the type of goal the actor is pursuing, the type of target it wishes to influence, and the international circumstances under which the attempt to exercise power occurs. Coercion appears best suited to those situations in which a high level of prior animosity exists between actor and target, there is a perception that the target threatens the actor's existence, and actor and target hold few values in common. Bribes are successful only when animosity has fallen off considerably, actor and target do not regard each other as threats, and actor and target have some common foundation of shared values that may be used as a basis for negotiating a deal. Persuasion based on the communication of theoretical principles and ideals demands that any animosity and sense of threat between actor and target be virtually eliminated (at least as far as violence is concerned). It also demands that a common understanding exists as regards the type of international society each prefers.

In conclusion, all the techniques investigated in this chapter have played an important part in recent international politics, and there is every reason to believe that they will continue to do so. If the world continues to evolve along the lines described in Chapter 3, we can expect that bribes and persuasion will play increasingly greater roles in the Western world and that only subtle nonviolent threats will be found in the relations among these countries. In the developing world, however, the full panoply of threats and coercive devices that historically have plagued the interactions among international actors most likely will continue to be used in the attempt to exercise power. Influence based on the use of persuasion will play only a marginal role in the relations both among these actors and between these actors and the members of the Western world.

Notes

1. Some authors use the techniques employed as the basis for distinguishing between power and influence, with coercive tools being the key to the exercise of power and the noncoercive being regarded as leading to influence. As was noted in Chapter 2, this distinction is not made in this book, because power is defined according to whether a target's behavior is modified, and is not determined by the sorts of tools used. See Harold Sprout and Margaret Sprout, *Toward a Politics of the Planet Earth* (New York: D. Van Nostrand, 1971), 168; and Arnold Wolfers, *Discord and Collaboration* (Baltimore: Johns Hopkins University Press, 1962), 103.

2. Niccolò Machiavelli, *The Prince and the Discourses* (New York: Modern Library, 1950), 61–63.

3. The impression of cruelty is reinforced when Machiavelli instructs rulers that "when the prince is with his army . . . then it is extremely necessary that he should not mind being thought cruel." Yet, in a neighboring passage, Machiavelli reminds rulers to avoid being unnecessarily brutal by stating that "a prince should make himself feared in such a way that if he does not gain love, he at any rate avoids hatred." See Machiavelli, *The Prince and the Discourses,* 61–62.

4. Wolfers, *Discord and Collaboration,* 53.

5. See Karl Deutsch, *The Analysis of International Relations* (Englewood Cliffs, N.J.: Prentice-Hall, 1978), 21; and Harold D. Lasswell and Abraham Kaplan, *Power and Society* (New Haven, Conn.: Yale University Press, 1950), 99.

6. Hans J. Morgenthau, *Politics among Nations: The Struggle for Power and Peace* (New York: Alfred A. Knopf, 1973), 59–61.

7. See J. David Singer, "Inter-Nation Influence: A Formal Model," *American Political Science Review* 57, no. 2 (June 1963): 420–30; and David A. Baldwin, "Inter-Nation Influence Revisited," *Journal of Conflict Resolution* 15, no. 4 (December 1971): 471–86.

8. Bruce Russett and Harvey Starr, *World Politics: The Menu for Choice* (New York: W. H. Freeman, 1989), 131.

9. Joseph S. Nye, Jr., *Bound to Lead: The Changing Nature of American Power* (New York: Basic Books, 1990), 31.

10. K. J. Holsti, *International Politics: A Framework for Analysis* (Englewood Cliffs, N.J.: Prentice-Hall, 1983), 155–56.

11. C. W. Maynes, "Logic, Bribes, and Threats," *Foreign Policy* 60 (Fall 1985): 111–29.

12. Klaus Knorr, *The Power of Nations: The Political Economy of International Relations* (New York: Basic Books, 1975), 20.

13. Robert O. Keohane, *After Hegemony: Cooperation and Discord in the World Political Economy* (Princeton: Princeton University Press, 1984), 53. Other scholars also make this point. For example, see Robert Axelrod, "The Emergence of Cooperation among Egoists," *American Political Science Review* 75, no. 2 (June 1981): 306–318; Richard Ned Lebow, *Between Peace and War: The Nature of International Crisis* (Baltimore: Johns Hopkins University Press, 1981); and

Glenn H. Snyder and Paul Diesing, *Conflict among Nations: Bargaining, Decision Making, and System Structure in International Crises* (Princeton: Princeton University Press, 1977).

14. See Knorr, *The Power of Nations*, 10; and David Baldwin, "The Power of Positive Sanctions," *World Politics* 24, no. 1 (October 1971): 35.

15. See Graham Allison, *Essence of Decision: Explaining the Cuban Missile Crisis* (Boston: Little, Brown, 1971); and Robert F. Kennedy, *Thirteen Days: A Memoir of the Cuban Missile Crisis* (New York: W. W. Norton, 1971).

16. Maynes, "Logic, Bribes, and Threats," 121.

17. See Jimmy Carter, *Keeping Faith: Memoirs of a President* (New York: Bantam Books, 1982), 269–429.

18. See "Philippine Senate Moving to Bar Lease for U.S. Base at Subic Bay," *New York Times*, September 12, 1991, A7; and "Aquino Revokes Eviction of U.S.," *New York Times*, September 18, 1991, A6.

19. Wolfers, *Discord and Collaboration*, 107.

20. Robert J. Art and Kenneth N. Waltz, "Technology, Strategy, and the Use of Force," in *The Use of Force: International Politics and Foreign Policy*, eds. Robert J. Art and Kenneth N. Waltz (Boston: Little, Brown, 1971), 4.

21. For descriptions of these factors, see Robert Jervis, *Perception and Misperception in International Politics* (Princeton: Princeton University Press, 1976), chap. 3; Lebow, *Between Peace and War*, 82–97; Thomas C. Schelling, *Arms and Influence* (New Haven, Conn.: Yale University Press, 1966), chap. 2; and Frank C. Zagare, *The Dynamics of Deterrence* (Chicago: University of Chicago Press, 1987), 79–81.

22. David Baldwin describes the nature of threats in some detail in "Thinking about Threats," 71–78.

23. See Knorr, *The Power of Nations*, 12; and David A. Baldwin, "The Costs of Power," *Journal of Conflict Resolution* 15, no. 2 (1971): 148.

24. David A. Baldwin, "The Power of Positive Sanctions," *World Politics* 24, no. 1 (October 1971): 34.

25. See Waldo Heinrichs, *Threshold of War: Franklin D. Roosevelt and American Entry into World War II* (New York: Oxford University Press, 1988), chap. 7; and Peter Calvocoressi and Guy Wint, *Total War: Causes and Courses of the Second World War* (New York: Penguin Books, 1979), 686–91.

26. Baldwin, "Thinking about Threats," 75.

27. Knorr, *The Power of Nations*, 10.

28. See Knorr, *The Power of Nations*, 10; and Baldwin, "Thinking about Threats," 74–75.

29. See Barbara Tuchman, *The Guns of August* (New York: Macmillan, 1962), 75–90.

30. Descriptions of the talks between American ambassador April Glaspie and the Iraqi government may be found in Elaine Sciolino, "Deskbound in U.S., the Envoy to Iraq is Called Scapegoat for a Failed Policy," *New York Times*, September 12, 1990, A19; Elaine Sciolino and Michael R. Gordon, "U.S. Gave Iraq Little Reason Not to Mount Kuwait Assault," *New York Times*, September 23, 1990, A1; and "Excerpts from Iraqi Document on Meeting with U.S. Envoy," *New York Times*, September 23, 1990, A19.

31. See Zagare, *The Dynamics of Deterrence*, 34; and Baldwin, "Inter-Nation Influence Revisited," 476.

32. Russett and Starr, *World Politics*, 129.

33. Robert Axelrod and Robert O. Keohane, "Achieving Cooperation under Anarchy: Strategies and Institutions," *World Politics* 38, no. 1 (October 1985): 235.

34. See Knorr, *The Power of Nations*, 18; and Wolfers, *Discord and Collaboration*, 113.

35. For a complete discussion of the theory surrounding retaliation and threat making, see Thomas C. Schelling, *The Strategy of Conflict* (New York: Oxford University Press, 1960); and Karl Deutsch, *The Nerves of Government* (New York: Free Press, 1966), 67–68.

36. Much of the following is based on Henry A. Kissinger, *Nuclear Weapons and Foreign*

Policy (New York: W. W. Norton, 1969); John Lewis Gaddis, *Strategies of Containment: A Critical Appraisal of Postwar American National Security Policy* (New York: Oxford University Press, 1982), chaps. 5–6; and Richard Smoke, *National Security and the Nuclear Dilemma* (New York: Random House, 1987), chaps. 5–6.

37. For discussions of security interdependence, see Baldwin, "Power Analysis and World Politics," 179–80; Richard Rosecrance, *The Rise of the Trading State: Commerce and Conquest in the Modern World* (New York: Basic Books, 1986), xi; and Russett and Starr, *World Politics,* 490.

38. The following discussion draws on Schelling, *The Strategy of Conflict;* Deutsch, *Nerves of Government,* 67–68; and David A. Baldwin, *Economic Statecraft* (Princeton: Princeton University Press, 1985), 107–12.

39. For examples of articles based on these briefings, see *New York Times,* March 9, 1955, 1; and *New York Times,* March 26, 1955, 1.

40. See Dwight D. Eisenhower, *Mandate for Change* (Garden City, N.Y.: Doubleday, 1963), 477.

41. It should be noted that brinksmanship may have very serious and untoward side effects, for the exceedingly strident nature of the behavior needed to force one's opponent to back down may greatly frighten public opinion both in one's own country and in allied countries. In the case of the offshore islands crisis, many Americans were shaken by the Eisenhower administration's apparent willingness to resort to nuclear war over Quemoy and Matsu. The governments of the United Kingdom, Canada, Japan, France, India, and the Philippines also were deeply concerned and protested to Washington. See O. Edmund Clubb, "Formosa and the Offshore Islands in American Policy, 1950–1955," *Political Science Quarterly* 74, no. 4 (December 1959): 527.

42. Wolfers, *Discord and Collaboration,* 110.

43. David A. Baldwin, "The Power of Positive Sanctions," *World Politics* 24, no. 1 (October 1971): 35. The typical reaction that one may expect a target to have when threatened is also discussed in Baldwin, "Thinking about Threats," 71–78; and Deutsch, *Nerves of Government,* 70.

44. Deutsch, *Nerves of Government,* 70.

45. Singer, "Inter-Nation Influence," 389.

46. Stephen Van Evera, "Why Cooperation Failed in 1914," *World Politics* 38, no. 1 (October 1985): 87–88.

47. Rosecrance, *Rise of the Trading State,* 162.

48. Morgenthau, *Politics among Nations,* 64.

49. Robert Gilpin, *War and Change in World Politics* (Cambridge: Cambridge University Press, 1981), 117.

50. The following discussion draws on several sources: Stephen E. Ambrose, *Rise to Globalism: American Foreign Policy since 1938* (New York: Penguin Books, 1988); A. W. DePorte, *Europe between the Super-Powers: The Enduring Balance* (New Haven, Conn.: Yale University Press, 1979); John Lewis Gaddis, *The United States and the Origins of the Cold War, 1941–1947* (New York: Columbia University Press, 1972); Louis J. Halle, *The Cold War as History* (New York: Harper and Row, 1967); Walter LaFeber, *America, Russia, and the Cold War, 1945–1984* (New York: Alfred A. Knopf, 1985); Vojtech Mastny, *Russia's Road to the Cold War: Diplomacy, Warfare, and the Politics of Communism, 1941–1945* (New York: Columbia University Press, 1979); and Adam B. Ulam, *The Rivals: America and Russia since World War II* (New York: Penguin Books, 1978).

51. See John M. Rothgeb, Jr., "Loose vs. Tight: The Effect of Bloc Structure upon Foreign Interactions," *Journal of Politics* 43, no. 2 (May 1981): 494–511.

52. A factor that most likely facilitated these cuts was a reevaluation of the potential threat from the West. While this threat may have seemed imminent when control over Eastern Europe was established in the 1940s, it probably was perceived as vastly diminished by the 1980s. As a result, there was far less need for a cushion of subservient countries that might serve as a barrier to the West.

53. Nye, *Bound to Lead,* 71.

54. Halle, *The Cold War as History,* 76.

55. The Soviet Union's use of repression did allow it to buy over forty years of security on its own terms. In the context of the anarchic international arena, this is not an accomplishment to be dismissed lightly. At the same time, one must also note that when Soviet influence did begin to falter, the fact that it was based so completely on repression meant that its collapse was nearly complete, both abroad and, more interestingly, at home.

56. Baldwin, "The Power of Positive Sanctions," 34.

57. David Baldwin, "Power Analysis and World Politics: New Trends vs. Old Tendencies," *World Politics* 31, no. 2 (January 1979): 183. The same point is also made in Knorr, *The Power of Nations,* 7; and Baldwin, *Economic Statecraft,* 43.

58. Axelrod and Keohane, "Achieving Cooperation under Anarchy," 239.

59. Knorr, *The Power of Nations,* 7.

60. For discussions of these weapons transfers, see Andrew J. Pierre, *The Global Politics of Arms Sales* (Princeton: Princeton University Press, 1982), 181–88; and John Spanier and Eric M. Uslaner, *American Foreign Policy Making and the Democratic Dilemmas* (Pacific Grove, Calif.: Brooks/Cole, 1989), 244–48.

61. See Pierre, *The Global Politics of Arms Sales,* 181–88.

62. Robert Jervis notes the potential for bribes to be viewed by the target as merely providing a service to the target that the actor would be compelled to provide even if the target did not compensate the actor. See Robert Jervis, "From Balance to Concert: A Study of International Security Cooperation," *World Politics* 38, no. 1 (October 1985): 77.

63. See Halle, *The Cold War as History,* chaps. 13 and 14.

64. Halle, *The Cold War as History,* 128.

65. The text of President Johnson's speech can be found in Marvin E. Gettleman, ed., *Vietnam: History, Documents, and Opinions on a Major World Crisis* (New York: Fawcett, 1965), 323–30. An abbreviated version is in William Appleman Williams, Thomas McCormick, Lloyd Gardner, and Walter LaFeber, eds., *America in Vietnam: A Documentary History* (New York: W. W. Norton, 1989), 242–44.

66. Quoted in Gettleman, *Vietnam,* 328.

67. The text of this resolution may be found in Williams et al., *America in Vietnam,* 236–37.

68. In thinking about the North Vietnamese response to Johnson's proposal, one should consider, first, the North Vietnamese goals, which were to unify the country under the Hanoi government's rule and to eliminate undue foreign influence, and, second, the role of the insurgents in South Vietnam, who were in many ways the key to the problem that the United States faced in 1965, and who were not the target of Johnson's offer. Thus, Johnson's speech was directed in part at the wrong target and at the same time was not relevant to the purposes of the audience that the speech was aimed at. For an excellent discussion of American military planning for Vietnam, see Andrew F. Krepinevich, Jr., *The Army and Vietnam* (Baltimore: Johns Hopkins University Press, 1986). Many sources describe the planning that led to the American escalation of its efforts in Vietnam. One concise treatment is found in Larry Berman, *Planning a Tragedy: The Americanization of the War in Vietnam* (New York: W. W. Norton, 1982).

69. Interestingly, shared values are also a key to meaningful threats. For example, the American threat in Vietnam to bomb the North Vietnamese industrial infrastructure was not as potent as many Americans believed because of the agrarian nature of Vietnamese society at that time. The Vietnamese simply did not place the same emphasis on preserving industry as did the far more industrialized United States.

70. For authors who regard bribes as producing these sorts of beneficial effects, see Baldwin, "The Costs of Power," 150; Baldwin, "The Power of Positive Sanctions," 33; E. H. Carr, *The Twenty Years Crisis, 1919–1939* (New York: St. Martin's Press, 1939), 131; and Knorr, *The Power of Nations,* 8.

71. At the time of the Cuban missile crisis and for years thereafter, it was widely believed that the resolution of the crisis had little to do with a bargaining process between the superpowers,

and that it was for the most part a situation in which the United States used its military superiority to force the Soviet Union to back down. More recent analysis suggests, however, that an exchange between the superpowers in which the United States promised to remove its missiles from Turkey and to let Castro be in return for the pullout of the Soviet missiles did indeed play a key role in settling the crisis peacefully. See Raymond L. Garthoff, *Reflections on the Cuban Missile Crisis* (Washington, D.C.: The Brookings Institution, 1989).

72. Lasswell and Kaplan, *Power and Society,* 111.

73. Morgenthau, *Politics among Nations,* 63. Russett and Starr also note the possible strength of the dominance that may result from the careful management of information. See Russett and Starr, *World Politics,* 134.

74. See Carr, *The Twenty Years Crisis,* 132–33; and Holsti, *International Politics,* 193.

75. Holsti, *International Politics,* 196–97.

76. Lasswell and Kaplan, *Power and Society,* 111.

77. Harold Sprout and Margaret Sprout describe this use of propaganda in *Toward a Politics of the Planet Earth,* 142.

78. Carr, *The Twenty Years Crisis,* 144.

79. Lasswell and Kaplan, *Power and Society,* 113–14.

80. This does not mean that there was no reaction whatever to the Soviet propaganda, for there was quite a political stir in Europe. This died down over time, however, as the Western offers to negotiate came to be seen as sincere and the Soviet refusals became ever more difficult to explain.

81. It is not clear how many of the American people actually were swayed by North Vietnam. Most of those who opposed the war were very likely unaffected by Hanoi's propaganda, or at best only found that the Vietnamese message simply reinforced beliefs they already held.

82. K. J. Holsti notes that in some cases propaganda has become very sophisticated and now uses modern advertising techniques and professional consultants to package the message in a manner that will enhance its appeal to its audience. See Holsti, *International Politics,* 193.

83. The ability to establish a feeling of group identification is described by many as an important way to gain influence over others. See Lasswell and Kaplan, *Power and Society,* 45–46; and Deutsch, *Nerves of Government,* 121–23.

84. Nye, "Soft Power," 167.

85. Russett and Starr, *World Politics,* 130.

86. During the negotiations, the first of these proposals was advanced by the United States and the second was favored by the United Kingdom. See Richard N. Gardner, *Sterling-Dollar Diplomacy in Current Perspective: The Origins and the Prospects of Our International Economic Order* (New York: Columbia University Press, 1980), 88–95.

87. See Gilpin, *War and Change in World Politics,* 34.

88. Deutsch, *The Analysis of International Relations,* 49.

89. See Carr, *The Twenty Years Crisis,* 80–82.

90. For a description of the negotiations leading to the creation of the Bretton Woods system, see Gardner, *Sterling-Dollar Diplomacy,* passim. The lack of a complete discussion of the issues that were of greatest concern to developing countries is discussed in Joan Edelman Spero, *The Politics of International Economic Relations* (New York: St. Martin's, 1981), 78.

91. For an examination of these points, see the discussion in Chapter 3 of developing country protectionism and of the new international economic order.

92. For a more complete discussion of national self-determination and President Wilson's role in promoting it, see Alfred Cobban, *The Nation State and National Self-Determination* (New York: Thomas Y. Crowell, 1969), passim.

93. Of course, national self-determination was not universally accepted for some countries held empires that would be threatened by the application of the principle. In addition, many political and economic theorists wondered about the problems that would arise when attempting to apply the doctrine to reality—problems such as determining where international borders should

be, deciding on the validity of rival claims to the same piece of territory, and knowing whether a particular new country would be economically and politically viable.

94. For a discussion of the Atlantic Charter, see Robert F. Ferrell, *American Diplomacy: The Twentieth Century* (New York: W. W. Norton, 1988), 195–96; and Robert D. Schulzinger, *American Diplomacy in the Twentieth Century* (New York: Oxford University Press, 1990), 177–78.

95. Quoted in Harry S. Truman, *Years of Trial and Hope,* vol. 2 of *Memoirs by Harry S. Truman* (Garden City, N.Y.: Doubleday, 1956), 106.

96. Quoted in Geir Lundestad, "Empire by Invitation? The United States and Western Europe, 1945–1952," *Journal of Peace Research* 23, no. 3 (September 1986): 265.

97. These figures are presented in Lundestad, "Empire by Invitation?" 272–73.

5

Another Look at Coercion

This chapter provides a somewhat closer examination of the approach to power that is most often associated with international politics—coercion. Chapter 3 noted that force plays a major role in international politics because the international social setting is essentially anarchic. Because of the absence of an international government and the immense resources available to many international actors, actors must diligently protect themselves from the harm others might do to them. At the same time, when an actor's international goals are at odds with the objectives of other actors, it must have the means to pursue those goals in the face of opposition. At the most basic level, protecting oneself and one's interests and pursuing objectives even when others resist require the capacity to coerce. Of course, as discussed in Chapter 4, the use of threats and force is no guarantee of success, and it usually encounters resistance from the target. Still, in an anarchic world, many actors continue to advocate the use of force when persuasion and exchanges fail.

This chapter examines two very broad categories of coercion: use of the military and use of economic resources. In the discussion of the military, three basic tactics are considered: defense, deterrence, and compellence.[1] Defense and deterrence constitute what we have described in Chapter 4 as a negative exercise of power because both seek to prevent an opponent from doing something that the actor would find undesirable. Compellence, on the other hand, involves a more positive use of strength, for it is designed to force an opponent to carry out the actor's wishes and to help the actor attain its goals. A fundamental difference between these negative and positive tactics is whether the actor is specific about what it wants to prevent or about what it wants to produce. In the case of defense and deterrence, actors are more precise about what they do not want, whereas with compellence, they are more specific about what they do want. This distinction, though seemingly minor, sheds a great deal of light on how an actor behaves and on the actor's probability of success.

With regard to the second category, economic-based force, in general, economic resources have in the past been viewed as ineffective for coercive purposes. Indeed, with the exception of economic sanctions, the employment of economic resources is usually not conceptualized as involving the use of force.[2] Nonetheless, economic resources are often used much like military resources, playing a defensive, deterrent, or compellent role in an actor's arsenal of weapons for coercing others. Each of these approaches to economic coercion is examined, with special attention to determining the conditions under which they might be expected to achieve the greatest probability of success.

This chapter is organized into five parts. The first is devoted to defining compellence, deterrence, and defense. In the second, the criteria developed in Chapter 4 are used to compare these tactics when they are used in a military setting. The third looks at the problems associated with the use of the military in contemporary international politics. The fourth briefly considers how the use of economic resources as a means for coercion has evolved over time. Finally, the efficacy of economic resources for defense, deterrence, and compellence is examined.

DEFINING COMPELLENCE, DETERRENCE, AND DEFENSE

Through compellence, an actor wishes to attain a goal and regards a particular target as important to enabling it to achieve it. Therefore, it seeks to force the target to contribute in such a way as to facilitate the actor's ability to accomplish its purpose.[3] This effort usually involves requiring the target to provide the actor with some tangible or intangible resource. As Glenn Snyder puts it, compellence is "used in an aggressive way; it is designed to persuade the opponent to give up some value."[4] Thomas Schelling concurs, noting that compellence is "intended to make an adversary *do* something (or cease doing something)."[5] By way of example, the Iraqi invasion of Kuwait in August 1990 was a clear case of an attempt to compel. The Iraqis wanted Kuwait to assist in forcing oil prices up. When Kuwait appeared to hesitate, Iraq tried to use force to obtain the outcome it desired.

Defense and deterrence, on the other hand, center on avoiding undesirable outcomes, but they do so in very different ways. With deterrence, the focus is on stopping an opponent from ever engaging in the unwanted behavior. The means used is to convince the opponent that acting in an unacceptable manner will lead to costs disproportionate to the gains expected. As Alexander George and Richard Smoke define it, "deterrence is simply the persuasion of one's opponent that the costs and/or risks of a given course of action he might take outweigh its benefits."[6] The action one wishes to prevent may take any form, but theorists usually see it as being of a military nature. Indeed, Snyder says that "deterrence means discouraging the enemy from taking military action by posing for him a prospect of cost and risk outweighing his prospective gain."[7]

Compellence versus Deterrence

At first glance, compellence and deterrence may seem quite similar. Both involve altering the behavior of a target by using, or threatening to use, force.[8] One important key to distinguishing between the two is found in the sequencing of the actor's and target's behavior. As Schelling argues, "the distinction is in the timing, in who has to make the first move, in whose initiative is put to the test."[9] When an actor seeks to compel, then it usually must take the initiative because it desires a change in a pattern of behavior that the target has already established. When an actor wishes to deter, then the first move is left to the opponent because the actor is largely willing to accept the target's current pattern of behavior and only wants to prevent an unacceptable change in that behavior.

Thus, the Iraqi invasion of Kuwait in 1990 constituted compellence because Iraq was taking action in the attempt to change Kuwaiti behavior. In the circumstances that confronted Iraq, deterrence was inappropriate since it was *current* Kuwaiti policy regarding the production and pricing of oil that Iraq judged to be unacceptable. Hence, Iraq felt the need to initiate action in order to secure its desired outcome—a change in Kuwaiti production and pricing behavior. By contrast, the Carter Doctrine, in which the United States announced that it would react militarily to any Soviet move to seize control of the oil fields surrounding the Persian Gulf, was deterrence because it was aimed at a potential future course of action, and not at current Soviet behavior.

Whatever type of behavior is involved, the basic idea behind deterrence is prevention.[10] That is, the actor believes that a certain type of behavior by the target would be so repugnant that it commits itself to ensuring that the undesired behavior never occurs. This may be done in one of two ways. In the first method—deterrence by denial—the actor makes it clear to the opponent that it will be unable to attain its goals. In the second—deterrence by punishment—the actor indicates that it will punish the opponent severely if the opponent engages in unacceptable behavior.[11] Robert Art and Kenneth Waltz describe the two approaches as follows:

> One way to counter an intended offensive is to build fortifications and to muster forces that look forbiddingly strong. The other way to inhibit a country's intended aggressive moves is to scare that country out of making them by threatening to visit unacceptable punishment upon it.[12]

In either case, a rational opponent will presumably forgo the proscribed behavior because of the overwhelming costs associated with going ahead.[13] With denial, the actor convinces the opponent to hold off by demonstrating that any attempts to proceed would be futile and would reap few, if any, benefits. With punishment, prevention occurs because the target fears the damage that the actor threatens to heap on it if it goes ahead.

An example of denial is the commitment of American troops to South Korea for the last four decades, which was designed to convince North Korea that any assault would fail abysmally. Punishment may be illustrated with the American nuclear posture that was designed to forestall a Soviet attack on American territory by threatening an all-out American nuclear response. In Korea, an assault is prevented because the North Koreans know that it would not succeed and that it therefore would be pointless. In the case of American territory, prevention occurred not because the Soviets could never accomplish their purpose, but because they were frightened by what the United States would do to the Soviet Union if they went ahead with an attack.[14]

Defense versus Deterrence

When an actor engages in defense, it adopts an entirely different course. With deterrence the emphasis is on prevention; with defense it is on damage limitation. As Snyder defines it, defense means reducing our own prospective costs and risks . . . defense reduces the enemy's capability to damage or deprive us; the defense value of military forces is their effect in mitigating the adverse consequences for us of possible enemy moves.[15]

Basically, an actor's defense posture revolves around what it does to protect itself and to limit the harm that it would experience once an opponent began to exhibit threatening and unacceptable behavior. In effect, defense is how an actor meets someone's attempt to engage in compellence when deterrence fails. As mentioned earlier, compellence is an attempt to force someone to give up something he or she values. Deterrence is designed to convince someone not even to try to engage in compellence owing to the adverse consequences that such an effort would create. Defense is action taken to protect oneself when an opponent ignores or fails to understand one's deterrent efforts and initiates the act of compellence anyway. Under such circumstances, defense usually centers on the ability to defeat the opponent in a test of strength.[16] In the traditional international system composed of sovereign territorial actors, "the essence of defense [has been] keeping the other side out of your territory."[17]

Interestingly, both defense and deterrence try to avoid being compelled, but they do not necessarily complement one another. In fact, the very instruments that may best serve a deterrent purpose may prove to be of little value for defense. As an example, let us consider the American commitment to NATO and to the defense of Western Europe during the cold war. From the American point of view, Western Europe was of vital importance. Not only was it a home to many fellow democracies, but it was also an economic powerhouse with vast military potential. The health of the American economy was heavily dependent on access to European markets and on the ability to purchase European goods. Geopolitically, Europe is on the opposite side of the North Atlantic where it could serve as a base for disrupting American shipping, and it sits astride American access to the Mediterranean. The loss of Western Europe to Soviet aggression would have been a severe, and perhaps fatal, blow to the United States. Thus, the U.S. government committed itself to protecting Western Europe from the earliest days of the cold war.

In implementing its decision to safeguard Europe, the United States was forced to concentrate on a deterrent strategy because of the expense associated with defense. In the European context, deterrence could be achieved with nuclear weapons, whereas defense required a substantial deployment of much more costly conventional forces. Using nuclear weapons meant that the United States could threaten the Soviet Union with both denial and punishment tactics. Deterrence by punishment could be achieved by stating that any Soviet moves against Western Europe would be met by an immediate massive strike by the United States against the Soviet homeland. Such a strike might not stop the Red Army, but it would wreak incalculable damage on the Soviet Union. This cost would surely be far higher than any benefit that the Soviets could possibly gain from obtaining Western Europe. Deterrence by denial focused on the possible NATO use of tactical nuclear weapons, devices designed for use against an opponent's conventional forces. In Europe, then, they would be used to destroy Red Army formations as they moved to seize Western Europe. Their use would invariably lead to the virtual annihilation of the Red Army, thereby making it impossible for the Soviets to attain their goals. Therefore, as far as deterrence was concerned, the Western strategy seemed complete.[18]

From the point of view of defense, however, these tactics could prove disastrous. Recall that defense is oriented toward self-protection and damage limitation. Both the punishment and the denial tactics associated with deterrence created serious problems in this area. Punishing the Soviet Union with a massive nuclear strike would lead to vast amounts of nuclear radiation that could be swept to the west by the wind, thereby contaminating and badly hurting the very areas the United States wished to protect. The Chernobyl nuclear accident in the Soviet Union in April 1986 served as one shocking indicator of just how potent this danger can be. The use of tactical nuclear weapons posed an even more serious problem, for, by their very nature, such weapons are directed at enemy formations that are on the attack. Hence, they are employed in the very midst of the territory one wishes to defend. We can only imagine how devastating this would be.

As this example shows, defense and deterrence do not necessarily go hand in hand. In Europe, the tactics that were best suited to the one would have been wholly inappropriate for the other. Being able to frighten an opponent into not doing something clearly is not the same as being able to protect oneself in an appropriate manner if that opponent is able to overcome its fear.

An actor will also seek to deter another even when it has no capacity for defense. Indeed, when the actor's ability to defend its interests is questionable, deterrence becomes the only recourse. Two examples come to mind. The first occurred in the spring and summer of 1939 when the United Kingdom and France felt it was vital that they assist Poland in the face of a dire threat from Germany. They had almost no ability to defend Poland, however. Moving their military forces to Polish territory would entail immense difficulties, and generally, they lacked proper military preparations. Both of Poland's would-be saviors therefore perceived that their positions were distinctly inferior to Germany's. As a result, British and French actions necessarily had to center on deterrence of German action.[19] They did so through a guarantee that in the event of German aggression they would aid Poland by declaring war on Germany. Apparently, British and French leaders expected that this guarantee would give the Germans pause. After all, it would raise the specter for Germany of the excessively costly and savage fighting that dominated the action between Germany, Britain, and France in World War I. The universal horror that the British and French believed governed everyone's memories of the First World War would certainly prevent the Germans from taking action against Poland.

In the end, the British and French effort to deter the Germans failed, and the Nazi attack on Poland was launched on September 1, 1939. Once the war was under way, the hollowness of the Western pledge was revealed, for the British and French were unable to do anything to come to Poland's rescue. In effect, the British and French promise was little more than an attempt to induce such fear in the minds of German decision makers that they would incapacitate themselves psychologically. Had this happened, the absence of a British and French ability to defend Poland would not have mattered because the Germans would have been frozen, unable to engage in the unacceptable assault. When deterrence failed, however, and the matter of defense became supremely important, the Western powers' nakedness was revealed.

The second example is found in the Carter Doctrine, which was announced in the wake of the Soviet invasion of Afghanistan in 1979. The invasion produced considerable alarm throughout the Western world about possible Soviet intentions in the Middle East. In response to the invasion, the United States cautioned the Soviet Union to steer clear of any efforts to acquire control over the vital Persian Gulf region. It issued this warning despite the fact that it had only a very limited ability to defend the area if the Soviets decided to ignore the American wishes. Hindering the American ability to create a reasonable defense were the restricted air- and sea-lift capacities for delivering the needed troops and equipment to the area, the lack of military units that had been designated and trained for such a mission, and the need for military bases and support facilities in the area. Without these capabilities, sending American forces into the Gulf would have been suicidal.

Still, the Persian Gulf was judged to be so extremely important to American interests in particular, and to Western needs in general, that President Carter felt it essential that the United States do all it could to forestall unacceptable Soviet behavior. Hence, the Americans issued a warning that the United States would go ahead with something it clearly would have severe difficulty doing successfully. As it turned out, American capabilities were never put to the test, because the Soviets did not seek to defy the American warning.

A comparison of these examples reveals one of the basic problems associated with evaluating deterrence. On the face of it, these cases might show that in 1939 deterrence failed in Europe and that forty years later it worked in the Persian Gulf. Such a conclusion, however, would be presumptuous at best and could, in fact, be entirely inaccurate, because "claims for the success of deterrence must rest on assertions about why something did not happen."[20] It was noted earlier that deterrence is aimed at encouraging a target to maintain, rather than change, its current pattern of behavior. When a target acquiesces, we can never be sure why. In arguing that deterrence has succeeded, we are assuming that the target of the deterrence effort intended to take the forbidden course of action and that it decided not to when confronted with the actor's warnings.[21] If this is the case, then deterrence did succeed. But it is also possible that the target never wished to do what it was ordered not to do. If this is so, then the deterrent effort was irrelevant to the target's behavior.

We know that deterrence failed in 1939 because the British and French *did* try to stop Germany, and the Germans invaded anyway. We are left uncertain about 1979 because, although the United States did issue a warning, the Soviets did *not* do anything. And perhaps they never planned to. Perhaps they did but were loath to face a direct confrontation with the military of the other superpower. They may have feared that, while they might win in the Gulf, events elsewhere in the world might spin out of control with disastrous consequences for Soviet society. In order to evaluate the success of deterrence, we must know precisely what the Soviet intentions were.

Hence, an important part of appraising deterrence revolves around uncertainties regarding the target's intentions. Interestingly, corresponding but not identical problems affect the assessment of both compellence and defense. These are examined shortly.

COMPARING DETERRENCE, DEFENSE, AND COMPELLENCE

At this point, it may be illuminating to consider how the communications between actor and target, the relative capabilities of actor and target, the actor's credibility, and the target's willingness to go along with the actor's demands impact on the use of deterrence, defense, and compellence.

Communications

Beginning with the communications process, we might recall from Chapter 4 that effective communications consist of a process wherein the actor informs the target of what it wants, and what it plans to do if the target does not comply and, alternatively, if it does comply. As noted at that time, the most effective communications process involves a situation in which an actor states clearly what it wishes the target to do, is explicit about the penalties it will apply for noncompliance, and is definite about how it will react if the target does go along. Wider ranges of acceptable behavior and narrower bands of unacceptable behavior and larger differences between the adverse consequences to the target, depending on whether the target complies, were posited as important determinants of the target's reaction to the communications process.

These earlier comments were designed to apply to a situation in which an actor sought to induce a target to adhere to its verbal demands. The question of subsequent tactics was set aside at that time. When we consider the general military approach that the actor may need to take in order to enforce its demands, the communications formula changes and depends on the type of tactic considered.

Deterrence is the tactic that comes closest to a classic threat in which the actor seeks to obtain compliance on the basis of its verbal (and sometimes nonverbal) signals and has no desire to be forced into doing what it says it will do in the event of noncompliance. Since through deterrence the actor wants to avoid an unacceptable change in the target's current pattern of behavior, it becomes essential that the actor communicate clearly to the target both that it would find a change unacceptable and how it would respond to such a change. The actor's failure to do this would be self-defeating, for it would leave the target in the dark and therefore might give the target the impression that the actor was unconcerned.[22] Under such circumstances, the target might out of ignorance make a move that the actor would find very distasteful, which, of course, would be a problem. Indeed, without the prior communication of the actor's preferences, we might say that deterrence was never even applied.

Two examples illustrate this problem very well. The first pertains to the Korean War and the second to the Gulf War of 1990–91. Many critics of U.S. foreign policy have argued that in the months before the Korean War, the U.S. government was negligent in its communications about its intentions with regard to South Korea. During this period, the United States failed to state explicitly that it valued South Korea and was prepared to react forcefully to any effort to seize that country. Moreover, U.S. policymakers actually indicated publicly on more than one occasion that they had little interest in Korea. The best known of these public statements was made in January 1950, when Secretary of State Dean Acheson defined American interests in the Far East in such a way as to appear to exclude any possible future American action to protect South Korea.[23] In the Persian Gulf, as was stated in Chapter 4, the United States never indicated adequately to Iraq that it valued an independent Kuwait and that it would frown on any Iraqi moves to undermine Kuwaiti sovereignty. In fact, American messages apparently sent the opposite signals.[24] In both cases, the actor's prior communication to the target was an essential component in the deterrence process, and the American failures meant that there would be a breakdown.

With compellence and defense, the communications process is often different. While deterrence consists of making a threat that one neither expects nor wishes to carry out, both compellence and defense potentially involve situations in which the actor may believe that action will be necessary. With compellence, action would be required if the target ignored initial demands. With defense, action geared toward self-protection is virtually automatic if the opponent makes an unacceptable move. This expectation of the need for action changes the communications process. In fact, an actor may actually prefer clouded communications under two conditions: (1) if it feels that verbal warnings will not work, and (2) if it believes that secrecy or the ability to make a first move in any confrontation will produce an advantage. That is, clear and careful communications are most likely when the actor neither wishes to carry out its threats nor believes that the target would be able to mount an effective counter if the actor felt it had to act. Secrecy and a lack of communications tend to occur when the actor believes it will need to act and when it perceives that the target could counter its moves effectively.[25] Indeed, when the latter conditions apply, the actor has a reason not only to keep its planning secret, but also to pretend that it has no genuine claims against the target. Stephen Van Evera explains this situation when he notes that

> if the state that strikes first stands to gain an important military advantage, all states have an incentive to conceal their grievances against one another, because complaints could provoke a preemptive strike by alerting the other side that the conflict is serious.[26]

Thus, when all actors believe that they need to get in the first blow (or act of compellence) in the event of conflict, then they may downplay the extent of their complaints, much as the Germans did in the months before the outbreak of the First World War, as the Japanese did before they struck at Pearl Harbor, and as the Israelis did before they unleashed their ferocious assault on the Egyptians in the Six Day War of June 1967. This is true not only for compellence, but for defensive efforts as well. An actor has a powerful reason to mute communications when it believes that its preparations will work only if the target is unaware of them. An excellent example is found in the Israeli defenses against the Syrians along the Golan Heights in the October War of 1973. In that conflict, Israel's devastating flanking moves against Syrian armored thrusts could be a successful

Map 6. Israel and Its Neighbors

defense only if the Syrians were unprepared.[27] And a lack of Syrian preparations could be achieved only if Israel surrounded its plans with secrecy. Publicizing one's defense preparations makes most sense when an actor wishes to communicate its ability to prevent the target from attaining its goals, thereby achieving a degree of deterrence by denial. When the actor is not interested in deterrence by denial, or when the actor lacks confidence in its defense preparations, then publicity is less reasonable.

Capability

Capability is the second dimension that may be used for comparing deterrence, defense, and compellence. The actor's resources are essential to the success of each of these tactics. With defense, the actor needs a resource base that is sufficient for the task of countering such moves as the opponent might make. The requirements that this places on the actor depend upon the nature of the opponent. An adversary equipped with thermonuclear weapons and a ballistic missile delivery system creates defense problems that place demands on the actor's resource base far different from those that are presented by a more conventionally equipped adversary or by terrorists. In the thermonuclear case, an actor is confronted with the thus far unsolvable problem of how to stop an onrushing missile. The expensive Strategic Defense Initiative program inaugurated by the Reagan administration is an example of how untoward the problems of missile defense are. With a conventional adversary, capability issues center much more on creating and maintaining the troop strength and equipment necessary to take on and defeat an opponent and on being able to deliver those troops to the proper battlefield in a timely and efficient manner. Operation Desert Storm illustrated these problems very well. Terrorists and guerrillas create yet another sort of capabilities puzzle, for here above all else it becomes necessary to locate the opponent (see Chapter 4).

For the most part, the actor's primary problem in this kind of situation becomes one of policy. It is important to set priorities among these challenges and direct resources according to criteria based on where the perceived threat is potentially most damaging and at the same time most likely to occur. That is, policymakers must assess the nature of the threat, the potential destruction it may inflict, and the probability that an intangible threat may be converted to a tangible reality. In addition, decision makers must consider how effectively they might shift resources from safeguarding against more than one type of threat. Some dangers are very unlikely to happen, but would present problems beyond human comprehension if they occurred, as would thermonuclear warheads used against one's society. Other dangers might be relatively unlikely and, at the same time, might cause limited physical damage, as in the case of terrorism.[28] In each case, the most effective countermeasures are wholly irrelevant to the other case.[29] In the end, it must be realized that the modern world presents many potential dangers and that it is impossible to prepare an adequate defense against all of them.

Compellence presents capabilities issues that are in many ways a mirror image of those associated with defense. When a nation defends, it must seek to negate its opponent's moves. For sovereign actors, the essential capability problems of compellence involve overcoming the defense obstacles that the opponent creates and raising the costs for the target of noncompliance to an intolerable level. Among nonsovereign actors, such as international terrorist organizations, the greatest capabilities problems usually relate to avoiding detection by their opponents and to maintaining surprise as to when and where they might choose to exert pressure.[30] In both cases, as was true of defense, the actor's capabilities are action oriented in that it must prepare for the possibility that the antagonist will resist verbal warnings, necessitating the use of its resources in the effort to force compliance.

An example of this problem is the face-off between France, Britain, and Germany in May 1940. As has been mentioned previously, the basic German objective was to achieve a quick and decisive victory over their Western opponents in order to avoid the savage and costly trench warfare of the First World War. The basic problem confronting the Germans was the need to overcome what seemed to be formidable, but essentially static, French and British defenses. The Germans believed that if they could crush these defenses and in the process both destroy the Western capacity to resist and seize valued French territory, then they would be able to compel the French to surrender. When the moment of truth arrived, and when the Germans had indeed corralled the French armed forces and taken possession of Paris and most of northern France, it turned out that the Germans had calculated correctly. When confronted with the extent of the costs already incurred and of those that might yet be extracted, the French decided to give in. In this case, the key capability problem for compellence was the Germans' ability to neutralize the opponent's defenses and to present the possibility of even more unpleasant developments if the opponent did not succumb to their wishes.

As was just mentioned, the most important capabilities problems for contemporary terrorist groups lie in their need to avoid detection and to maintain surprise. The reason for this centers on the smaller overall pool of resources available to these actors in comparison with the sovereign states that they seek to compel. For terrorists, detection is the virtual equivalent of destruction because it allows the opponent to concentrate its greater capabilities for that purpose. Such actors therefore must rely on misdirection and the ability to hide. If they lack these capabilities, they will not last long. At the same time, their approach to compellence must vary from the one the Germans used in 1940, for their vulnerability to their opponent's superior resources means that they must operate by surprise. Thus, they seek to compel by creating such great uncertainty that the normal functioning of society is disrupted. Specifically, terrorists hope that bombings, assassinations, armed assaults, hostage taking, hijacking and piracy, and similar techniques can so damage the normal conduct of civil affairs as to force the target to give in to their demands.[31] The actual physical destruction they inflict is usually limited. The most important damage is to the target's confidence in its own abilities to respond effectively.

When an actor wishes to deter, the capabilities issue takes a somewhat different form. Here, the goal is to prevent, through verbal or other warnings, an opponent from taking action that is deemed inappropriate. However, the actor does not usually want to be placed in the position of actually using its capabilities. As already discussed, it may create this effect either by making it clear that it has the ability to punish misbehavior severely or by indicating that it has the capacity to deny the opponent its goals. In both cases, the actor seeks to force the opponent to engage in a form of cost-benefit analysis to calculate how much it stands to lose or gain from the forbidden behavior. As far as punishment is concerned, such calculations are simplified when an actor possesses an overwhelming array of strength, for it eliminates ambiguity and helps the target to have an accurate understanding of the risks involved. As George and Smoke state,

> deterrence has been theoretically most developed, and practically best applied, to acute bipolar conflict when great values are at stake and where there is a potential for great violence.[32]

The development hand in hand of nuclear weapons and advanced delivery systems is one of the fundamental reasons that the concept of deterrence moved to center stage for international theorists and diplomatic practitioners. The extremely destructive potential of these weapons, together with the absence of any practical compellent or defensive use for them, focused attention on deterrence. Suddenly, policymakers had at their disposal the means to raise to an exceptionally high level the costs that a would-be enemy could be forced to pay for misdeeds. When deterrence rests on finely tuned calculations pertaining to the relative capabilities of an actor and its target, it can (and does) fail on occasion (as before both world wars, when the Germans believed that they could triumph over their adversaries without paying too high a cost). When these calculations of cost and risk become so obvious that anyone can make them, then the practicality of deterrence, at least for some types of problems, is established. And the ability to inflict extreme casualties on one's enemy is the key to facilitating the calculation process.[33] Thus, the extreme magnification of an actor's capabilities that accompanies the possession of weapons of mass destruction makes it possible for the actor to conceive of pursuing a policy of deterrence.

When an actor seeks to deter through denial, the capabilities problem takes on a different complexion. Now the actor must have the capacity either to maintain military resources at such points as it wishes to protect, or to move resources to these locations with a great deal of speed.[34] When such capabilities are not present, the actor simply does not have the ability to convince the target that it is in a position to deny the target its goals. One of the key problems confronting the United States with regard both to the Iraqi attack on Kuwait and to the Carter Doctrine was the absence of adequate American military bases in the Persian Gulf region and the inability to move troops to the area quickly. These capabilities deficiencies undermined any thoughts the United States might have had about deterring a possible opponent by indicating that the adversary would be denied the benefits of any hostile acts.

Credibility

Credibility, the third dimension for comparing deterrence, defense, and compellence, refers to the actor's ability to convince the target that it will carry out the policy it has set for itself. When an actor contemplates the need for compellence, it faces credibility problems of a very different nature from those that confront it with deterrence and defense.

With deterrence, the actor wishes very much that the threat to take action will suffice and that the target will hesitate in the face of a warning. As mentioned in Chapter 4, comparisons between the actor's and target's capabilities and the actor's past and present behavior are important in establishing the credibility of the threat. An actor's credibility for deterrence is enhanced most when it is clear that it can either punish the target or deny it its goals with relatively little cost to itself. In addition, credibility is highest when it is known that the actor has engaged in similar actions in the past or that in the present situation the actor is attempting carefully to match the target move for move if the target becomes bellicose.[35]

When an actor adopts a defense posture, the credibility questions it confronts are not very different from those associated with deterrence. It wants the opponent to perceive that it is willing to do what it takes to engage in self-protection. An opponent who believes otherwise and who also covets something that another possesses may present a problem. A known capacity for defense, coupled with the clear willingness to use it, becomes potentially useful as a deterrent, thereby mixing the two approaches to safeguarding oneself.

The use of compellent tactics presents a very different situation. In this case, the actor often needs to hide its true intentions, particularly when it feels that action will be necessary and that surprise may be decisive in its attempt to force a target to go along with its demands. As described earlier, misdirection and confusing the potential enemy can be very important compellent tactics. Those who expect to take action have a strong incentive to cloud things and to create an air of false credibility for a policy that they have no intention of following. That is, they seek to convey the impression that they have decided on inaction, when in reality they are planning to make a move. Such was the behavior of the Iraqi government before it struck Kuwait: intermixed with its troop movements and verbal threats were professions of a sincere desire for peace.

There is a need for deception even when the actor banks on verbal threats as the sole means for compulsion. In this case, however, the actor tries to convince the target that it *will* take action that it in fact is not prepared to take. In this event, the actor is engaging in a variety of bluffing, for it wishes to create credibility for a policy of action when it actually has decided on inaction. This is precisely what Hitler sought to do when he confronted Chamberlain and Daladier at Munich with his demands that Czechoslovakia cede the Sudetenland to Germany (see Chapter 4). In this case, Germany was not yet prepared to fight and could attain its goals only through psychological intimidation. It achieved this intimidation by bluster and by its posture that war was a foregone conclusion unless the British and French caved in to the German demands. These tactics worked because Hitler convinced Chamberlain and Daladier not only that the Germans would go to war, but also that German capabilities were significantly greater than they actually were. Credibility was built for a policy option that Germany really did not possess.

Modern terrorist organizations seek to use a similar approach to compellence. For terrorists, the objective is to instill in the target the belief that they are prepared to strike ruthlessly anywhere and that they have the capacity to do so. Of course, the reality is that few terrorist organizations have the capabilities needed to mount such operations. As a result, they are forced to limit the scope of their activities considerably. Achieving a measure of success, however, requires that credibility be created for the idea that they can and will do almost whatever they wish. The possibility that violence can occur at almost any time and in any place is a very frightening prospect for most people. Consequently, they are likely to pressure authorities to give in to the demands that are made. If people believe that they confront a much more limited problem, they are much less likely to press for concessions. Credibility is in many ways at the heart of terrorist attempts to compel.

The Target's Reaction

The final dimension for comparing deterrence, defense, and compellence has to do with the target's reaction to the actor. Once again, we find a sharp distinction between compellence, deterrence, and defense. Military preparations of any sort, whether designed for defense, deterrence, or compellence, usually create or intensify animosity between actor and target. As observed at several places earlier in this book, a target's animosity toward an actor greatly reduces the target's willingness to go along with the actor's demands without a struggle. When the actor's requirements regarding the target's behavior are basically negative, however, and simply center on insisting that the target forgo behavior that it has not yet begun, then the chance for obtaining compliance is enhanced. Demands that the target initiate a new pattern of behavior that the target perceives as being against its best interests—and such perceptions almost always are present when military resources back up the demands—will meet with far greater resistance.

In other words, it is usually easier to get others to continue doing what they are already doing than to force them to adopt a new form of behavior that is less desirable.[36] With defense, and especially with deterrence, the actor seeks continuity of behavior. In such a situation, the only thing the target is being forced to give up is a plan for future action, if indeed such a plan exists at all. The target can achieve this kind of compliance without suffering too great a loss of dignity. Specifically, it can simply preserve the impression either that the actor is demanding something that the target never wished to do anyway, or it can claim that action is only being postponed and that in fact it has given up nothing permanently.

For example, in the recurrent crises over Western (British, French, and U.S.) access to West Berlin in the late 1950s, the West's basic problem was to prevent the Soviet Union and East Germany from cutting off their rail and highway access from West Germany to West Berlin, which was located deep inside Communist East Germany. On several occasions, the Soviets threatened to turn the administration of Western access over to the East German government, which the West, in deference to the West Germans, refused to recognize as legitimate. If administration were in the hands of the East Germans, the West would be forced to negotiate with East Germany, and this would be a form of tacit recognition.

To prevent this outcome, the Western powers indicated that they were not willing to bargain with the East Germans, that they held the Soviets accountable with regard to access to West Berlin, and that they were prepared to use force to guarantee their rights. In the face of this firm Western response, the Soviets announced that they would allow the access procedures currently used (which were acceptable to the West) to continue for the time being, but they claimed the right to make a change in the future. Basically, the West got its way in part because the Soviets could fall back on allowing the status quo to continue and reserving for themselves the right to do something new at a later date. Deterrence worked, and the status quo was preserved.

A compellent situation presents a very different set of circumstances because the target is being required to initiate a new form of behavior. Here, the demand is that the target do something that it probably regards as highly unacceptable. In addition, a greater burden is placed on the target because it is more difficult to disguise compliance in the manner described above. As a result, the target is far more likely to resist, and the actor faces a far more difficult task. Indeed, the application of violence in the attempt to force the target to comply may well lead only to more determined resistance from the target because it simply confirms the target's impression that the actor wishes it nothing but ill will. The German bombing campaign against Britain in the Second World War and the American bombing of North Vietnam are but two examples of the great difficulties a nation faces in seeking to compel through the use of violence. In neither case was the desired effect obtained.

Summary of Deterrence, Defense, and Compellence

Communications, capability, credibility, and the target's perception of the actor are useful dimensions for differentiating between deterrence, defense, and compellence. In order to deter effectively, communications between actor and target must be clear and precise, the actor's capabilities must be sufficient for carrying out the threats being made, and the actor's stated intentions must be highly believable. In addition, the target is given the opportunity to obscure whether it is actually complying or is only awaiting another opportunity to perform the forbidden deed. In defense situations, secrecy may require clouded communications, but the actor's capabilities should appear formidable, the actor must seem credible, and once again the target is not required to do anything new in order to appear to comply. Compellence presents a very different situation. Secrecy may demand obscure communications. In addition, the actor may have an incentive to hide its true capabilities and to create a degree of credibility for policies that it has little desire to pursue. Finally, it is very difficult to obtain compliance because the target must change its present conduct and conform to a new pattern of behavior. Those bent on a compellent approach may therefore find themselves forced to go beyond rhetoric and to employ coercion in their relations with others.

USING THE MILITARY IN THE CONTEMPORARY WORLD

Having discussed the characteristics of the three basic tactics for employing military resources as a means to exercise power in international politics, we can now consider the efficacy of the military in the contemporary world. Here it should be useful to focus on each of the already described tactics and to ponder their place in the world as it is presently evolving. A useful approach is to assess the problems that each tactic appears most suitable for handling, how these problems appear at present, and how the tactic in question relates to the sorts of military challenges that most often emerge in the current international arena.

The Changing Nature of Conflict

The nature of international conflict has shifted very dramatically over the last four to five decades. As was noted in Chapter 3, before the Second World War international clashes often involved violent confrontations between the largest, most industrially advanced, and most prestigious members of the international system. Since 1945, such conflicts have disappeared, and to the extent that countries have fought one another, the violence has taken place between the so-called less developed countries, or between a member of the Western world and a developing country.

For the most part, members of the Western world have intervened in less developed countries for one of three reasons. The first occurred during the cold war and had to do with preventing the spread of what was regarded as Soviet-sponsored communism. The American involvement in Vietnam and in many other locales provide examples. The second centered on the need to maintain stability in a country rich in important natural resources. Recurrent French and Belgian interventions in Zaire are illustrations. Finally, Western countries have moved to safeguard areas that they regard as strategically important, as the French and British sought to do in 1956 when they invaded Suez and the United States did when it deposed the Panamanian dictator Manuel Noriega early in the Bush administration.

Among developing countries, violence has resulted for entirely different reasons. In general, these countries have clashed over territorial, ethnic, and religious issues. Territorial clashes were at the center of the Sino-Indian encounters of the early 1960s, the ongoing Indian-Pakistani disputes, the Iran-Iraq Gulf War, the Iraqi invasion of Kuwait, and the Ethiopian-Somalian clash over the Ogaden, to name but a few examples. Among others, ethnicity and religion have played key roles in the Indian-Pakistani wars, the Arab-Israeli clashes, several intra-Arab disputes, and the Greek-Turkish encounters.

Thus, the analysis of the role of the military in the contemporary world must begin by taking into account both who is fighting and why. It is also important to consider the repertoire of resources being used by those who initiate international violence. As K. J. Holsti has noted, "there is some evidence that the world [now] faces not so much a problem of wars of the classical type—armies and navies arrayed against each other with the purpose of compelling surrender—but more an epidemic of limited military operations."[37] That is, international violence is increasingly nonconventional, both because sovereign actors find it more convenient to act in this way and because nonsovereign actors have no choice but to use such techniques. Hence, although states do continue on occasion to slug it out toe to toe in conventional wars, they are also more and more prone to resort to internal subversion and state-sponsored terrorism. With internal subversion, assistance is funneled to those within a country who oppose an antagonistic government, as when the United

States supported the Contras' attempt to undercut the Nicaraguan government. With state-sponsored terrorism, a government creates or supports organizations that seek to wreak havoc against targets that it opposes, as with Arab support for anti-Israeli terrorist groups, Iranian support for anti-American groups in the Middle East, and Libyan support for anti-American groups in Europe and in the Middle East.[38] Indeed, Bruce Russett and Harvey Starr point out that the use of nonconventional violence has become quite prevalent. While 80 percent of all international conflict before World War II involved traditional state-against-state action, since that time 80 percent of all clashes have been of the nonconventional variety.[39]

The Cost of the Military and the Availability of Arms

The changing nature of conflict is only part of the backdrop against which we must assess the use of the military. The use of this instrument has become increasingly expensive, and the international trade in armaments means that the world is far better armed today than it ever was in the past. The price associated with the military instrument can be depicted in several ways. Richard Rosecrance illustrates the escalating unit costs when he comments that

> in constant dollar terms, tanks went from less than $50,000 per unit in 1918 to more than $2,000,000 in 1980. Fighter planes that cost less than $100,000 in 1944 rose to at least $10,000,000 per copy forty years later.[40]

Table 5.1 Average Yearly Military Expenditures

	1965–69	1970–74	1975–79	1980–84	1985–87
United States	170.63	152.61	133.50	166.14	209.71
	857	732	614	714	868
Soviet Union	146.27	166.79	199.99	202.75	215.97
	620	674	772	748	767
NATO Europe	67.27	73.48	100.59	96.06	101.06
	226	236	312	291	300
Latin America	5.35	7.05	10.43	11.39	12.44
	21	24	31	42	42
Africa	3.20	4.94	10.41	11.65	10.77
	12	16	30	24	20
Middle East	6.15	15.99	41.95	68.19	57.75
	65	146	345	472	351
South Asia	4.42	5.41	6.02	6.48	8.55
	6	7	7	7	8
East Asia	29.29	45.71	68.61	46.07	50.55
	24	34	45	29	30
Oceania	3.63	3.43	3.50	3.49	4.11
	251	218	174	158	176

Note: All figures are in 1980 U.S. dollars. For each country, the top figure represents total expenditures and is in billions of dollars. The lower figure is per capita expenditures.
Source: U.S. Arms Control and Disarmament Agency, *World Military Expenditures and Arms Transfers*, various years; 1987 is the latest year for which data were available.

Geir Lundestad provides another indicator. In the post–World War II period, the world's leading military power, the United States, has consistently spent about 30 percent of its research and development funds on the military, as compared with 4 percent and 7 percent, respectively, for its two primary economic rivals, Japan and Germany.[41]

Yet another way of looking at the economic cost of the military is to examine total and per capita expenditures by the United States, the Soviet Union, and several developed and developing regions of the world (see Table 5.1). With the exception of a dip for the United States in the years after Vietnam, for Europe and East Asia in the early 1980s, and for Africa in the mid-1980s, total military spending for all parts of the world has gone from one height to another. Per capita expenditure figures follow a very similar trend. More money than ever before is being spent on the military, in both total and per capita terms, in almost every country and region of the world. Thus, the world is devoting far more resources to the military today than at any prior time in history.

Buttressing the effects of these increased expenditures is the widespread and growing availability of ever more sophisticated weapons on the international arms market. Weapons have always been available to those who were willing and able to pay for them. The major changes in the past four decades have had to do with the potency of the weapons that can be purchased, the availability of weapons as supplier countries seek to gain political influence and profits through arms sales, and the transfer of weapons technology from advanced to developing countries.[42] Weapons potency is the degree of damage that can be attained per unit of the device used. With the "forward" march of technology, potency has reached ever-higher plateaus. For example, it is now possible for guerrilla fighters with shoulder-launched rockets to worry even those with access to the most modern air support, as happened to the Soviets in Afghanistan. The availability of weapons can be illustrated by considering Table 5.2, which shows the constant dollar value of arms imported into several

Table 5.2 Average Yearly Arms Imports

	1965–69	1970–74	1975–79	1980–84	1985–87
Latin America	351	635	1,446	2,853	2,437
	1	2	4	8	6
Africa	397	628	4,558	6,217	3,691
	1	2	12	13	7
Middle East	1,243	4,081	8,682	15,267	11,792
	13	38	71	105	71
South Asia	694	579	939	2,007	3,098
	1	1	1	2	3
East Asia	4,415	4,556	2,452	4,255	4,280
	4	3	2	3	3

Note: All figures are in 1980 U.S. dollars. For each country, the top figure represents the total value of arms imports and is in millions. The lower figure is arms imports per capita.
Source: U.S. Arms Control and Disarmament Agency, World Military Expenditures and Arms Transfers, various years; 1987 was the latest year for which data were available.

regions in the developing world since the mid-1960s. The money spent on imports, in both total and per capita terms, has gone up steadily over time and fell somewhat only during the recessionary years of the 1980s. This pattern holds even among the world's poorest countries, which are located in Africa and South Asia. If money spent is regarded as a reasonable index of availability, then the world is increasingly awash in weapons.

The availability of technology from international suppliers also affects the military situation. Most industrial equipment can be used to produce any of several related products. Chemical equipment can be used to make insecticides or poison gas, biotechnology can make medicines or biological weapons, auto plants can make cars or tanks, and so on. The international market for international machinery is booming. As a result, the ability to produce deadly weapons is diffusing at a rapid rate from the Western to the developing world.[43] This is true whether the suppliers of the technology deliberately seek to assist the buyer in producing weapons or are ignorant of the buyer's true intentions. The Iraqi drive since the early 1980s to produce nuclear and chemical weapons serves as an example. Through their ability to produce many of the weapons they want and to purchase those they cannot make, many developing countries are becoming formidable opponents.

Contemporary Deterrence, Defense, and Compellence

Deterrence. When thinking about the value of deterrence, defense, and compellence in the contemporary world, one must consider the changing patterns of conflict and the availability of arms. To begin with deterrence: As stated earlier, most analysts and policymakers regard deterrence as most applicable to high-stakes conflicts where the use of extreme violence is possible. Such situations eliminate the ambiguity that often clouds communications and that makes the actor's and target's calculations of costs and benefits difficult. During the cold war, the confrontations between the United States and the Soviet Union and their respective allies almost always served as the basic conflict about which deterrence attempts revolved. These attempts centered both on protecting one's own homeland from assault and on guarding one's allies from attack either by the other superpower or by a client state.[44] In either case, the calculations by the superpowers, the fear of all-out nuclear war, and the ability of the strong to control their far weaker clients so that the behavior of the weak would not have unpleasant repercussions for the strong all figured prominently in the deterrent game.

The end of the cold war has changed this long-standing state of affairs. To the extent that deterrence is a game (at least in its military form) that can be played only under limited conditions, it may no longer be applicable to international politics, at least not in the dominant way that it once was. The context in which deterrence was applied is gone, and if it is to retain any applicability as a military concept, it must be found elsewhere. The most pressing present conflicts are not well suited to deterrence because of problems relating to communications, capability, and credibility.

With regard to communications, the value of deterrence is slipping because the nature of the threat posed to any particular actor has become less clear. As a result, actors simply do not know who to communicate their warnings to. At any particular moment, a threat could emerge in the Middle East that would pose the possibility of decreased oil shipments, in Central Africa that would put at risk the access to copper, or in Southeast Asia that would create uncertainty regarding tin or rubber supplies. These potential problems could result from the behavior of any of dozens of actors, sovereign and nonsovereign, and could be a product of either international violence or domestic turmoil. Actors no longer have any certainty regarding the identity of the cause of their problems, and this has a deleterious effect on the communications process needed to deter effectively. An actor cannot deter by simply communicating a broad message to all possible targets that they must respect the actor's needs. Such a communication is far too ambiguous to be of any value as a deterrent.

Capabilities problems also exist. The multiplication of threats, the increase in the potential targets that must be dealt with, and the widespread geographical scope of possible difficulties all point to a vast increase in the resources needed in order to deter. Resources can no longer be focused on a small group of adversaries; nuclear stockpiles cannot be used to overawe and thereby deter. With the wider scope of potential problems that now exist, a far greater range of resources is needed. Moreover, many of the threats that must be handled cannot be solved through resort to the extreme violence that makes deterrence calculations easiest to make. For example, nuclear weapons cannot be used in a hostage situation. Therefore, we are thrown back into a world in which targets are less able to discern exactly what risks they run in taking unacceptable behavior. In this situation, deterrence becomes difficult, for while the potential benefits may seem obvious, the possible costs may not be. In addition, the international trade in arms means that targets are better able to counterbalance an actor's capabilities than they ever have been in the past. Under these conditions, the basic calculations essential to deterrence simply cannot be made in the appropriate manner.

Difficulties exist with credibility as well. The effectiveness of deterrence relies largely on the target's belief that an actor is prepared to carry out its threats. When the question at hand appears to involve exceptionally high stakes for the actor, as was true of the U.S. desire to protect North America and Western Europe during the cold war, then the actor's threats are most likely to seem believable. In more marginal cases, threats tend to look suspect. The problem for those who would use deterrence in the world as it is presently evolving therefore boils down to the need to enhance the credence of the assertions they make regarding their intention to take action under any given set of circumstances. With the growth of the number of occasions, actors, and geographical arenas in which an actor may feel the need to respond, the ability to build this credibility becomes more difficult. The Persian Gulf War clearly illustrates this problem. Even though the United States had repeatedly stressed over the years the importance both of that region and of the free flow of oil, the Iraqi government apparently doubted that the United States would respond to an invasion of Kuwait. If deterrence is to work effectively, it requires a far greater degree of credibility. In a world where so many possible threats and so many potential antagonists exist, it is difficult to see how such credibility can be achieved.

Before turning to the discussion of defense, it is important to reiterate a point that was made earlier: deterrence works best when it is possible to put together an overwhelming array of strength and aim it at a limited number of targets over a relatively small number of issues. As the world is presently construed, these conditions are not as easily found as they were during the cold war. Still, they could exist, or they could be created. The key factor lies with the actor's ability to set priorities and to determine where and when it wants to respond, to signal this information clearly to the would-be opponent, and to back it up with the necessary resources. That is, any actor that wishes to use deterrence-based tactics in the post–cold war world must be able to rank its preferences and to act on that ranking. This is where the basis for deterrence will reside in the future.[45]

Defense.   The problems with defense in the post–cold war era parallel those connected with deterrence. It has become increasingly difficult for a country to identify its possible opponents and the areas it must try to protect. International interdependence, the multiplication of the numbers and types of organizations that use violence to attempt to achieve their purposes, and the increased availability of armaments to those with money have contributed to the greater complexity of defense. Interdependence makes defense more complex by increasing the international interests of actors. When an actor must rely on more and more entities from diverse regions all over the globe for the goods and services needed to maintain and increase its economic performance, there is an interest in defending those areas against changes that would disrupt this access. Hence, to the degree that interdependence grows, horizons may expand, thereby changing the definition of self-protection. Such an actor comes to the conclusion that it is safeguarded by taking action to protect others.[46] Thus, the bounds of defense needs expand.

The expansion of the number and types of actors that one must contend with is in part a product of interdependence. It is only natural that an increase in the scope of the actor's interests will lead to a larger *number* of targets that need to be handled. In addition, a greater scope of interests produces contact with more diverse cultures, tribal, national, and ethnic factions, and religious groups, thereby adding to the complexity of the defense problems to be faced. Moreover, a foreign presence is often the source of tension in any culture.[47] And at the same time, foreigners sometimes make convenient targets for expressing and dramatizing dissatisfactions. The seizure of the American embassy in Teheran and the hostage crisis that followed is but one example. When these factors are added together, as they increasingly have been in recent years, the result is a formula for defense-oriented issues that can take on nightmarish proportions. As was the case with deterrence, defense can no longer be easily focused on a single adversary or on a small group of opponents, as in the days when the great powers jostled with one another and constituted one another's only real defense threats.

Juxtaposed with the above is the ever-greater availability of sophisticated arms on international markets. These weapons may be acquired by almost anyone, ranging from sovereign states to guerrilla bands to terrorist groups. Consequently, the disgruntled have the means to inflict substantial penalties on those they blame for their plight. In these circumstances, it becomes very difficult for an actor to limit the potential damage to its interests.

Thus, defense tactics confront the same types of capability and credibility problems that face those who would try to deter. With interdependence there are now more areas to defend, a larger volume and greater diversity of actors means that the number of opponents and the ways in which they engage in violence has gone way up, and the availability of weapons increases the firepower that must be countered when defending. The consequent resource claims on any single actor can be phenomenal. Hence, the actor must be able to set the kind of priorities described above. In addition, collective efforts such as the one made in the Persian Gulf War must be emphasized, for they spread the costs of defense among several actors.

The basic difficulty with priority setting and with collective efforts is credibility. Priority setting is an extremely troublesome task, requiring that an actor carefully weigh the value of various entities and resources to its own well-being.[48] Much of the problem lies in the fact that, although almost any resource or market is valuable, virtually none is irreplaceable. Moreover, almost all resources have multiple sources. Therefore, the cost of defense, which can be very high, must be balanced with the cost of replacing either the resource or the source. When it is known that these types of calculations motivate an actor's behavior, then a potential aggressor may conclude that the decision to replace may tend to take precedence over the decision to defend. The rationale is that, while the costs associated with replacement are almost entirely monetary, those relating to defense also include the possible loss of human life. When defense involves a coalition of actors, these problems are multiplied. It then becomes necessary for several actors with diverse interests and attitudes to agree before a defense effort can take place.

When an actor's adversaries are confronted with these circumstances, the credibility of its defense commitments drops off considerably. The problem in today's world is that many aggressors feel they face exactly this situation. In the Persian Gulf, the Iraqis apparently felt that the United States would be unwilling to bear the burden of defending Kuwait and would simply pay a higher price for oil or would seek alternative sources of energy. Even after U.S. troops began arriving in Saudi Arabia, the Iraqis still felt action was unlikely. Part of this feeling stemmed from their belief that the coalition that was patched together to confront them would not hold.[49]

Thus, the cost of the capability to defend everything that is valued and needed has been increasing over the past several years. When these capabilities obstacles are coupled with the credibility problems just mentioned, such "defenses" as might be mounted might actually be liberations of areas, actors, or hostages that have already been seized, as happened in the case of Kuwait.

Compellence.   The problems associated with compellence have been discussed in the previous section. The most important of these relate to having the needed resources to overcome an opponent's defenses and being able to alter the adversary's perceptions so that the adversary is willing to conform to the actor's wishes. Prior to the twentieth century, the first of these considerations usually carried greater weight, and few analysts and world leaders thought about questions associated with the second. Indeed, Machiavelli expressed his lack of concern with altering adversaries' perceptions and his belief that compellence was a useful way to obtain what one wanted:

I maintain, then, contrary to the general opinion, that the sinews of war are not gold, but good soldiers; for gold alone will not procure good soldiers, but good soldiers will always procure gold.[50]

Such sentiments may have been reasonably accurate in centuries past, but they have a very hollow ring today. One reason, as mentioned elsewhere in this book, is the military's lack of a place in relations between members of the Western world. These countries cannot credibly threaten one another with military action, nor do they even try. At the most, those with greater military resources have at times tried to extract some political or economic concessions in exchange for the protection they give to others. Many claim the United States has done just that in the past in its relations with Western Europe and Japan. With the end of the cold war and the uncertainties surrounding how much protection is needed in the new world, it is not clear how much leverage behavior of this sort can provide in the future. As an example, consider the fleeting influence the United States obtained from its role in the Persian Gulf War.

Today military compellence is also limited by other considerations, many of which relate to capabilities. First, would-be targets are better able to defend themselves because of the international trade in arms. Second, many of today's opponents are not territorial actors, and therefore are not easily discovered and brought to battle. Third, many of the potentially explosive issues that exist are not easily handled with the use of military resources. Fourth, the use of force is somewhat less acceptable today than in the past, and aggressors are more likely to confront substantial international condemnation, perhaps even an armed coalition, as in the Gulf War. Finally, the needs of actors have become so extensive as a result of industrialization and interdependence that they simply cannot hope to fulfill them all, or even a reasonable proportion of them, through military conquest. Rosecrance provides an excellent illustration of this last point:

In the world economy of the 1990's, however, it would be much more difficult to conquer territories containing sufficient oil, natural resources, and grain supplies to emancipate their holder from the restraints of the interdependent economic system.... Such an aggressor would need the oil of the Middle East, the resources of Southern Africa, and the grain and iron of Australia, Canada, and the American Middle West. Too much dependence and too little strength make that list unachievable.[51]

This quotation applies best to the West. Western nations have such sophisticated economies and social structures that they would be hard pressed to make any appreciable gains through the use of physical compulsion. Among smaller and poorer countries, however, the benefits from seizing territory or resources from another actor may appear more worthwhile. After all, in the face of poverty, any increase in the ability to enhance income may seem valuable. Therefore, compellent tactics most probably will continue to appeal to at least some members of the developing world, thus increasing the burdens for those who would defend the attacked. The Iraqi attempt to secure a greater source of revenue by seizing Kuwait is a reminder of the ever-present tendency for some states to perceive the potential gains of aggression.

An actor bent on using compellence also faces problems pertaining to the will of the target. Of special significance are the rising desires of peoples everywhere for self-rule and the rejection of dominance by outside forces.[52] The collapse of the Soviet Union, of Yugoslavia, and perhaps even of Czechoslovakia in response to the demands of various nationalist groups for independence are European manifestations of this phenomenon. It is also found elsewhere: Kurds have rebelled against Iraq, Tamils against Sri Lanka, Palestinians against Israel, and Shabians against Zaire, to name only a few. Attempts at foreign conquest or control have also fared poorly in recent years. The Vietnamese ferociously resisted first a large U.S. presence and then a Chinese incursion into their territory, the Afghans forced the Soviets to withdraw, and the Chadians enjoyed considerable success in warding off the well-supplied Libyans. In each case, a fierce sense of nationalism was reinforced by capabilities provided by an external sponsor or purchased on the international arms market to create a formidable opponent that could not easily be brought to submission. This combination of willingness and ability to resist makes compellence very problematic in the present world.[53]

Thus, any actor's attempt to use military force to coerce other actors into doing what it wants is exceptionally difficult in the contemporary world. These difficulties do not, however, mean that such efforts will end. Nor does it mean that they will never succeed. The use of military compellence will continue as long as people believe either that "wealth and welfare are directly associated with territorial control"[54] or that violence is a useful means of promoting their programs and drawing attention to their goals. Success may be a greater problem. In cases related to territorial actions, success will be closely related to whether the attacker can convince the local populace that it is acting in their best interests (see Chapter 4 on theory and persuasion), as the United States did with some degree of effectiveness in its invasions of Grenada and Panama in the 1980s. The success of other forms of violence, such as terrorism, will also depend on persuasion. In these situations, the actor will have to demonstrate that it has a broader program of action for resolving the problems that motivate its actions and that it is not solely interested in violence for the sake of violence.

Summary of Contemporary Deterrence, Defense, and Compellence. The use of all military tactics has become far more costly in the contemporary world, and a greater degree of uncertainty is now associated with employing the military. Issues relating to an actor's capability and credibility plague both deterrence and defense. Compellence is undermined by the increased capabilities demands associated with the tactic and by the fact that possible targets are far more likely to resist than ever before. However, international actors will probably continue to rely on these tactics, in part because they have little choice in an armed and anarchic world.

COERCION WITH ECONOMIC RESOURCES

Attention will now turn to the use of economic resources for coercive purposes. In comparison to the military, which has played a major role in the use of force since antiquity, the use of economic resources for coercion is of relatively recent origin. Prior to the First World War, few political leaders and international analysts believed that economic moves had the same kind of coercive potential as political and military actions. To the degree that an actor's economic resources were seen as attached to the ability to force others to do as it wished, they were perceived as doing so by way of their contribution to the actor's military capabilities.

Economics and National Security

The connection between economics and the military has been especially prevalent since the mid-nineteenth century. Since that time, military weapons systems have become ever more sophisticated and expensive. As a result, actors require a sound economic infrastructure if they are to produce what they need in order to compete effectively in the area of military strength. As Morgenthau puts it, "the technology of modern warfare and communications has made the over-all development of heavy industries an indispensable element of national power."[55] E. H. Carr concurs, pointing to the "increasingly intimate association between military and economic power" and the fact that "only the most primitive kinds of warfare are altogether independent of the economic factor."[56] Indeed, William McNeill argues that a close relationship between the economic and military realms has been a fact of life for centuries. He maintains that the ancient Chinese found that "spending money proved a more effective way of mobilizing resources and manpower for war . . . than any alternative."[57]

The relationship between an actor's economic resources and its military capabilities has prompted many to promote autarky, or self-sufficiency, as an appropriate policy. Autarky is premised on the notion that it is not advisable to depend on others for the provision of goods and services in general, and most particularly for those products that the military establishment needs. Such a reliance supposedly leaves an actor at the mercy of possible opponents and increases the probability that its military efforts will fail. Thus, as Carr argues, "in modern conditions the artificial promotion of some degree of autarky is a necessary condition of social existence."[58] Furthermore, autarky "is primarily a form of preparedness for war."[59]

Over time, the pursuit of autarky has led in two directions.[60] The first has been the promotion of domestic production that is designed to meet an actor's needs. Included here are policies designed to encourage the development of, or to preserve, businesses that are perceived as contributing to a state's military needs. The U.S. government's efforts in the 1970s to bail out both the Lockheed Corporation and the Chrysler Corporation are examples of this type of behavior.

The second direction has included attempts to acquire control over territory that is seen either as possessing vital natural resources or as sitting astride important commercial routes. In both cases, the goal is to ensure access to the materials that a state needs to maintain its economic vitality. Seizing resources is meant to guarantee their availability when needed. Controlling trade routes is designed to guarantee the movement of products from their point of production to the locations where they are required for future use.

European colonial and imperial expansion was predicated on precisely such considerations.[61] For example, Spanish interest in the Americas was fueled by the desire to control a lucrative source of bullion, and British interest in Egypt and in Gibraltar was the product of the need to possess key commercial highways (Suez in Egypt and the Straits of Gibraltar). More recently, before and during World War II Japanese militarism was guided by the urgent need to gain access to raw materials, and German expansionism to the east was in part motivated by similar considerations. Even the recent Gulf War was a product of the wish to preserve unfettered Western access to a vital resource, oil.

Many scholars argue that multinational corporations now perform in a modern setting many of the functions of imperialism. The presence of these corporations in any society allows foreigners to control important resources and production facilities, which may then be used according to the preferences of foreigners and to suit foreign needs. In this way, foreigners secure a new and efficient means for ensuring their access to vital goods and services.[62]

Other Forms of Economic Pressure

In the years after World War I, international attention turned to another means by which economic resources might be used for coercive purposes. This was to direct economic embargoes, boycotts, and other sanctions against those who engaged in military aggression.[63] An embargo is the decision not to sell goods and services to a particular target. A boycott is a situation in which an actor refuses to purchase products from a target. For many the basic motivation for using such economic tactics was their near obsession with avoiding a repetition of the excessive slaughter of the First World War. It was hoped that economic resources would replace the military and that aggressors could be forced to back down by crippling of their economies. In turn this would both disrupt their war-fighting capacity and produce grumbling by civilians as they saw their standards of living decline. As Wolfers puts it, "after World War I . . . the threat and use of economic sanctions were hailed as substitutes for war."[64] With the creation of the League of Nations, it was expected that appropriate coordinating machinery would be in place to produce the greatest possibility of success for the new tactic.

The economic approach to coercion in the interwar years never worked as planned. The most celebrated use of economic sanctions fell flat in 1935 when the League was unable to employ this tactic effectively to counter Italian aggression against Ethiopia. Perhaps more than anything else, this incident colored the thinking of many analysts and policymakers about the value of using economic resources as a surrogate for the military. Other instances of failure, such as the United States' inability to use sanctions to halt Japanese aggression in the Far East in the late 1930s and the early 1940s, the Arab League's lack of success with sanctions in the 1940s and 1950s as a method for forcing Israel to create a Palestinian homeland, the Soviets' futile efforts in the early 1950s to force Yugoslavia to act as a satellite, and Spain's inability to employ sanctions effectively in the 1950s and 1960s to regain Gibraltar from the United Kingdom, have reinforced the impression that economic resources are not a very potent means of exercising power in international politics.

In fact, Baldwin states that at one time such fiascos so undercut analysts' confidence in economic tactics that "it would be difficult to find any proposition . . . more widely accepted than those belittling the utility of economic techniques of statecraft."[65] John Spanier reflects this attitude when he writes that "economic sanctions are ineffective in most circumstances unless backed up by the belief . . . that force may be used later."[66] Wolfers makes the same point, maintaining that "economic sanctions [are] insufficient unless supplemented by the willingness to move on to military action."[67]

Over the last two decades, many analysts have become less scornful about the efficacy of economic resources to regulate the behavior of others. Three developments may have relaxed their attitude. First, economic tactics have scored some successes in recent years. For example, the United States used these resources to compel the British and French to terminate their invasion of Suez in 1956. Economic sanctions were also prominent in convincing the white-supremacist governments first in Rhodesia and later in South Africa to relax minority rule and to begin respecting the will of their native African majorities. In addition, the temporary success of OPEC (the Organization of Petroleum Exporting Countries) in dominating international oil price structures and forcing their trading partners to pay exceptionally high prices highlighted the degree to which the ability to control a key natural resource could confer prestige and strength on an otherwise weak group of countries. In some cases, economic resources continued to prove far from valuable for exercising power, as was shown when the United States sought to use economic pressures to counter the Soviet invasion of Afghanistan and to force Manuel Noriega to yield the reins of power in Panama. Nevertheless, the success stories spurred a renewed interest in economic tactics.

Increased international interdependence is the second reason that economic instruments of coercion are receiving more attention. As mentioned elsewhere in this book, the economic linkages between many members of the international system have grown phenomenally and continue to multiply at a rapid rate. Interdependence means that two or more actors rely on one another for the provision of the goods and/or services they need and want. Such reliance creates the possibility that one of the partners in the relationship may seek to use the situation to exert influence over the others. The temptation to do so is especially great when the association between the partners is asymmetrical, with one party feeling that it is far more reliant on the relationship than are the others.[68] As one scholar states, "needs that cannot be fulfilled within national frontiers help create dependencies . . . [in these circumstances] possession of these resources can be transformed easily into political influence."[69] OPEC's apparent (but, as will be seen, dubious) success in the 1970s in converting its dominance in international petroleum markets into an ability to influence others served for many as the primary example of how economic resources might be used to attain power in an interdependent relationship.

The third reason for the increased interest in the connection between economic resources and power is found in the fact that the contemporary international arena presents few alternatives for seeking to pressure others. Violence is either too risky or inappropriate for many of the goals states now pursue. As Baldwin argues, in mixed motive games in which applying pressure and avoiding the evocation of a violent response are both important goals, economic tools are likely to be especially attractive. In such situations economic sanctions are not just "second-best" techniques, but rather techniques that promise to be effective in ways that military force could not be. They are not merely inferior substitutes for force but rather superior "first-best" policy alternatives.[70]

When the United States wished to express its displeasure with the Soviet Union's invasion of Afghanistan in a tangible way, but also wanted to avoid war, the grain embargo imposed by President Carter served a useful purpose. This move hardly affected whether the Soviets stayed or left, but it did allow the United States to counter the Soviet move without risking a war it could neither fight nor win.

In addition, in many cases the issue at hand cannot be handled effectively with violence. For instance, when the United States desired a change in India's agricultural policy in the mid-1960s, economic resources were more germane to the task than a military invasion would have been. Similarly, U.S. interest in pressuring South Korea, Chile, Paraguay, Guatemala, and Argentina into altering their human rights policies was better pursued with resources drawn from its economic reserves than from its military war chest.[71]

These changes in the presumptions of many policymakers and analysts regarding the value of economic assets as a means of influencing the behavior of others point to the need to consider economic tactics carefully. This is done in the next section, which concentrates on the use of economic resources for defensive, deterrent, and compellent purposes.

ECONOMIC DEFENSE, DETERRENCE, AND COMPELLENCE

As defined earlier in this chapter, defense tactics are used to protect one actor from the unwanted intrusions of other actors, with the focus on the ability to defeat an opponent's moves and to limit the damage inflicted by an adversary. Deterrence is also concerned with self-protection, but pursues it in a different way, attempting to prevent an opponent from ever initiating unacceptable behavior. This may be done either by threatening to punish the opponent severely, or by making it clear that the opponent can be denied whatever it seeks. Compellence is more positive, for it centers on an actor's attempts to force an opponent to change its behavior to conform to the actor's interests.

Economic resources may be used in any of these ways. For one thing, they may be included as part of an overall package that also involves use of the military. For instance, an actor's defense efforts during a war may have an economic component. The Allied blockade of Germany in both world wars is an example. In this case, the Allies sought to limit the damage that the German military could inflict by denying the German war machine important resources. Economic threats might also be included as an aspect of a deterrent strategy. An actor may state that its efforts to punish a would-be adversary would include economic as well as military penalties and responses. Finally, a government bent on militarily based compellence might feel that economic pressures would help to further its efforts, as was true during the Persian Gulf War.[72]

In each of these situations, the economic dimension of the actor's response is in many ways a "throw-in." If it is used, the military is usually expected to produce the desired result, and economic resources are often conceptualized as a way to enhance the efficacy of an actor's military instruments. In effect, when economic resources are tied to the use of the military, they become subservient to the armed forces. Moreover, their value is obscured by the overall atmosphere that prevails when life-and-death struggles are under way.

Economic resources may also be used independently. That is, an actor may decide that its goals preclude a violent approach, and, as Baldwin argued in the quotation above, may feel that an economic response is the best that is available. In defensive terms, these circumstances usually exist when the damage that the actor suffers is in the commercial realm. With economic deterrence and compellence, the situation is often mixed. In addition to aiming at economic objectives, the actor may try to use economic resources to accomplish politically or militarily oriented goals. As will be seen, the attempt to employ economic assets to accomplish too many different purposes is an important factor limiting their effectiveness. In addition, the discussion to follow illustrates the conceptual ambiguity that surrounds the use of economic resources.

Economic Defense

In its nonmilitary manifestations, economic defense includes an actor's efforts to protect its resources, productive capacities, and service sectors from harm at the hands of foreigners. Therefore, the actor usually seeks to construct some sort of barrier to foreign involvement in its economy. Such obstacles typically include restrictions on foreign imports that compete directly with goods produced locally and on investments whereby foreigners purchase local resources and facilities. Also included in this category are the efforts an actor might make to reduce its dependence on foreigners for important goods and/or services. Although they are not violent, these moves are coercive because they require that the target refrain from certain types of behavior or suffer the pain associated with such moves as the actor might make.

Examples of each of these defensive measures are easy to find. The quotas in the 1980s on automobiles exported by Japan to the United States (see Chapter 4) constitute an act designed to protect a local producer. Limitations on foreign investment are found in the policies of some countries, such as Mexico and India, that place restrictions on the proportions of local corporations that may be foreign owned. Limitations are also seen in the creation of governmental review boards such as those found in Canada which are charged with analyzing and approving (or disapproving) proposed foreign ventures. Reducing local dependence on foreign goods is exemplified by the creation in the United States of a strategic petroleum reserve that can be used in a time of emergency to lessen American exposure to the vicissitudes of the international oil market.

Many other like measures are employed to achieve the basic purpose of defending a society from the intrusions of foreign interests. These efforts are hardly new. Quite literally they have been around for centuries as countries have attempted to ensure their livelihoods in the face of foreign competition. The closely regulated trade of the mercantilist era,[73] the protective tariffs in the United States and in Germany in the nineteenth century,[74] and the imperial preference system favored by the British in the early part of the twentieth century[75] are all historical examples of the defensive use of economic instruments. The present purpose, however, is not to detail the many methods by which actors pursue economic defense.[76] Instead, it is to analyze the efficacy of such moves.

At first glance, we might presume that economic defense is relatively easy to achieve, especially when it is pursued by a sovereign actor. After all, sovereignty means that a government has absolute control over its territorial space and that it can make and enforce such laws as it deems appropriate. Thus, governments presumably are in a good position to enact effective policies to defend domestic economic interests against foreign intrusions. This, however, is far from true. In reality, economic defense is very difficult, and the results are usually far from those that are desired. We can determine why this is so by using the standards employed elsewhere in this book: that is, the communications process, the actor's capabilities, its credibility, and the target's reaction.

First, however, it is important to have a clear understanding of the goals actors seek when they engage in economic defense. In general, economic defense is motivated by the desire to promote a society's economic well-being and its autonomy.[77] Economic well-being refers to the ability to guarantee employment, a decent standard of living, and access to needed goods and services for the members of the society. Autonomy is the ability of a society's decision makers to create policy for that society without unwanted foreign interference. Economic defense is supposed to assure economic well-being by preventing foreigners from usurping local markets for domestically produced goods, which would harm local businesses and possibly force them to cut production and reduce employment. Under these circumstances, the society would become ever more reliant on foreign sources for goods and might be subject to foreign pressures, thereby reducing autonomy. When foreign ownership of local facilities is involved, local resources may be used to suit foreign interests, thus harming economic well-being. In addition, pressures may be put on local officials to create policy that benefits outsiders at the expense of local interests, undermining autonomy.[78] Economic defense is designed to avoid these untoward results by regulating the foreign presence. The idea is to save local jobs and industries and ameliorate the undue influence of foreigners on local policy-making.

Communications.   With economic defense, the communications process between actor and target functions best when the actor provides the target with a clear statement as to what it wants, how it plans to pursue the goal, and how it will react if the target does not cooperate. Obfuscating communications in order to achieve an element of surprise is far less useful for economic defense than it is when a military response is contemplated (see the discussion earlier in this chapter). In fact, a careful and forthright statement of concern over the injuries that foreign activities are creating, or are about to create, can be a useful first line of defense that may prompt an adversary to reconsider its behavior.

The value of such a warning is illustrated in the case of Japanese automobile import quotas described earlier in this book. An adequate defense was achieved in that situation when the U.S. government announced its concern over the harm being done to American manufacturers by Japanese activities and noted that congressional action might be in the offing. This communication was sufficient to prompt the Japanese government to organize an acceptable quota system among its automobile corporations. Defense was a result of a timely act of communication.[79]

Capabilities. Within the context of economic defense, two important questions touch on capabilities. The first is whether the defense tactics selected achieve the purpose for which they are designed. The second relates to the actor's ability to bear the costs associated with the tactics. As described earlier, the purposes pursued usually revolve around the society's economic well-being and its autonomy. Most often, economic well-being takes first place in policymakers' calculations because unfavorable economic circumstances can have a large impact on how much public support they will receive.[80] Moreover, it is often assumed that any moves to limit foreign influences on the local economy will almost automatically also curtail foreign threats to autonomy.

In promoting economic well-being, the usual goals center on maintaining locally controlled structures of production and preserving jobs. Problems with regard to these issues are usually perceived either when foreign trade competition threatens to overwhelm local businesses or when the competition from foreign investors who set up shop on the local scene undermines local firms. In the first situation barriers to trade, such as quotas or tariffs, are the usual response.[81] With foreign investments, the reaction often centers on local review boards, requirements for majority local ownership, and special tax or other provisions that favor local firms over foreign corporations.[82] In each case, the actor engaging in economic defense confronts three basic capabilities problems. The first is whether the defenses that are selected actually achieve their stated purpose. That is, are jobs saved, and is local control maintained over important industries? The second is the domestic costs of pursuing the defense policy and whether the actor has the capacity to bear those costs. Finally, one must consider a possibility raised in Chapter 4. This relates to shifts by the target from one form of unacceptable behavior to another and whether the actor has the ability to counter these shifts properly. As will be seen, there are no definitive answers to any of these questions, but the types of problems that actors confront can be sketched out.

Beginning with the first problem, Gary Hufbauer and Howard Rosen's examination of attempts by several countries to save jobs and preserve local industries in the face of trade competition casts severe doubt on economic defense as a long-term solution. As these authors state, "the experience of Japan, Australia, the United Kingdom, Germany, and the United States suggests that phoenix stories are rare. Successful industry adjustment usually means a smaller industry and . . . is usually aimed at downsizing, not expansion."[83] The same authors also note that "in terms of labor-force adjustment, the number of production jobs almost always dropped."[84]

Hence, research indicates that, in general, economic defense is not a very effective method for protecting either jobs or corporations, at least not as it is practiced by many of the Western industrialized countries. There probably are two basic reasons for its ineffectiveness. The first is that economic defense efforts almost always come only after local firms begin to suffer adverse consequences from foreign inroads. As a result, defense is oriented toward saving a patient that is already in dire straits, and this for the most part is a tough job. For example, the quotas on the Japanese exports of automobiles to the United States were not put in place when Japan first began sending cars to the United States in the late 1950s and early 1960s. At that time Japanese activities were too small to attract much attention. It was only two decades later, after U.S. automobile producers began to suffer substantial damage, that action was taken. By that time the domestic industry was considerably weaker. The same story has been played out in the United States in the steel industry, shoe manufacturing, and the electronics industry, to name but a few. In each case, timing problems complicated economic defense.[85]

Another complicating factor relates to the definition attached to success in an interdependent world. With interdependence, an industry usually is thought of as successful only if it is able to grow, prosper, and compete in an international environment. No matter how thorough an economic defense policy may be, it can protect an industry from foreigners only on its home turf. Economic defense has problems insulating an industry from competition when it seeks to market its wares abroad.[86] Thus, even if the industry is well shielded at home, it may still fall short of success if it cannot take on foreigners in the ferocious competition often found internationally. Naturally, as a result both the size and employment capacities of the industry in question will tend to be restricted.

The second capability problem associated with economic defense has to do with the cost of the policy. Whenever an actor restricts its access to international markets (either for trade or for capital), it raises the costs it must bear to secure goods and services. The only exception occurs if the actor is the world's most efficient producer of the products it is restricting. Restrictions, however, almost always are designed to make up for the actor's inefficiencies. Hence, protection means increased costs. Once again, Hufbauer and Rosen give us a picture of the problems involved. In an investigation of American protectionism, they concluded that

> protection is costly to consumers, both in total consumer costs and in consumer costs per production job "saved." Figures of $20,000 to $100,000 per job-year saved are common, and figures above $150,000 occur all too often . . . protection [also] diverts scarce resources to America's least promising industries . . . [moreover] protection is highly inequitable as between industries. Larger industries with political clout . . . are able to shake the US political system for massive benefits. Smaller industries with only regional influence . . . often get nothing.[87]

As this quotation shows, economic defense may mean higher costs to consumers, the diversion of resources from strong to weak sectors of the economy, and institutionalized favoritism among the various segments of society. Of particular concern in this regard is the fact that inefficiencies in the protected industry may create problems for other parts of the economy that use the protected goods in their own production process. Thus, a mushrooming effect may be created whereby protectionism weakens the international competitive abilities of these industries as well. For example, defending inefficient computer chip companies may undermine those who produce excellent personal computers by forcing them to pay more for the basic equpment they use in making their product. When this happens, political turmoil may be another of the prices paid. That is, those who do not benefit from some form of protection may feel some resentment that leads them to engage in political protest and obstructionism.[88] These costs are troublesome in immediate terms, and over time they can lead to a declining standard of living for the members of the society that practices a high degree of economic defense. Smaller and poorer countries are especially prone to these types of problems.[89]

The third capability problem is associated with changed behavior within the target of economic defense. An example was provided in Chapter 4 when the Japanese automobile quotas were discussed. As may be recalled, the American goal was to safeguard its hard-hit automobile manufacturers. The initial behavior prompting American defense measures was the export to the United States of low-cost, fuel-efficient cars. When protection was instituted, the Japanese shifted to the export of upscale cars and to the location of production facilities in the United States. The threat detected and countered early on was replaced by a new type of problem.

Such behavior is not uncommon in the economic realm.[90] It is difficult to handle, however, unless an actor is prepared to sever external economic linkages altogether, for an imaginative opponent will seek new methods for circumventing any barriers that are erected. And the reactive nature of defense virtually guarantees that responses to the new behavior will tend to come only after damage has been inflicted. Moreover, foreigners usually have local allies who prosper from external linkages and who will resist too many restrictions on the source of their livelihood. A further complication is that economic defense almost always must be directed not only at the behavior of other states, but at multinational corporations as well.

Credibility. Economic defense may also include credibility problems. Questions about an actor's credibility may stem from many sources, but two are particularly important. The first is the degree to which the actor has committed itself to international norms and procedures that are designed to eliminate economic protectionism. The second is whether the actor depends so heavily on its international ties that it would suffer substantially if other actors retaliated for its act of protection.

Beginning with the commitment to international norms and procedures, we should note that many international actors have pursued international codes, such as those embodied in the General Agreement on Tariffs and Trade (GATT), that guard against discriminatory trade practices. Generally, the protection afforded by economic defense policy is diametrically opposed to these principles. Nondiscrimination means that favors may not be granted to one actor without granting them to all and that penalties may not be applied to one without applying them to all.[91] By its very nature, however, protection means discrimination, for the rules created to save any single industry would not be likely to have equal implications for all members of the international arena. This is especially true when a quota system (a particularly popular form of economic defense) is employed. Quotas usually vary from country to country and, as a result, automatically discriminate against some but not others.[92]

Thus, if an actor has displayed a strong attachment in the past to freer and nondiscriminatory trade, then its willingness to pursue economic defense policies at present may be doubtful. The United States has consistently found itself in just this position. As mentioned earlier, the United States was the leading figure in creating and promoting the post–World War II system of freer trade. In addition, every president since World War II has publicly favored free trade. As a result, American threats about protectionism do not have the same force as the same comments from a less committed actor. Moreover, the commitment by some of an actor's key decision makers to free trade principles might bring into doubt whether such protectionist policies as might be enacted would be enforced with any vigor.[93]

A heavy dependence on foreign commerce also affects an actor's credibility. The reason is that an act of economic defense by one actor may lead to retaliatory defense actions by other actors. Retaliation occurs because protection usually restricts the access of others to the actor's markets. Such limitations cost them money. When this happens, those that feel harmed generally seek to get even for the damage they have suffered. The method they normally employ for this purpose is to effect counterrestrictions. Countermoves may then redound on the actor who first implemented the restrictions, affecting its income as well. If the initiator of this move and countermove sequence has little trade to begin with and if few sectors of its economy rely on foreign sales, it will not be particularly hurt by this series of developments. However, if the initiator is heavily dependent on international commerce and if some key sectors of its economy need foreign sales to sustain themselves, then these types of developments may be devastating.[94] Looking just at North America, we may recall from Tables 3.1 and 3.2 that the United States is far less dependent on international commerce than is Canada. Thus, while selected U.S. corporations would suffer from a trade conflict of this sort, as a whole the Canadian economy is in greater jeopardy. Given that the degree of reliance on international commerce is well known for almost all actors, this factor can have a strong bearing on the credibility of their assertions about their economic defense policy intentions.[95]

The Target's Will.   A basic concern with regard to the will of the target is whether the target will try to overcome the actor's defenses through a change in its behavior and whether the target will engage in retaliatory measures. As has been noted previously, changes in the target's behavior occur frequently and should be expected when economic defense policies are initiated. On the other hand, retaliation is not so automatic, but depends on whether the target is denied access to the actor's market altogether, whether the target is singled out for discrimination, and how dependent the target is on the market that is being closed (at least partially) to it. Targets are most likely to accept restrictions when the actor's defense simply freezes their access at a given level instead of rolling it back substantially, when the restrictions are applied in a nondiscriminatory manner, and when it does not rely on the market in question.

As Hufbauer and Rosen note, the first of these factors is often the most important. The reason is that targets may accept limitations on their access to a market even when it is discriminatory, and, when a lot of income is involved, if they believe they can maintain a reasonable share that will generate a decent, if not optimal, income.[96] The previously mentioned Japanese automobile quotas is an example of successfully negotiated limitations, even though high stakes were involved for both actor and target. For the United States the stakes were seen as involving nothing less than the preservation of its automobile industry. For Japan, hundreds of millions of dollars in profits from the American market were at risk. Success was achieved without any substantial retaliation in part because the quotas that were arrived at left the Japanese with a good hold on the American market. The Japanese also saw that they could at least partially sidestep the restrictions by changing their own tactics.

This relatively successful outcome can be contrasted with the rancor that accompanied the bargaining pertaining to the sale of American beef in Europe in the mid-1980s. The European Community objected to the Americans' use of hormones to promote the growth of cattle, claiming that this practice posed health risks to those who ate the beef.[97] As a result, the Europeans refused to allow the United States to export its beef to Europe. This action denied American producers any access to the European market and appeared to be discriminatory.[98] Even though the amount of money involved was far smaller than in the case of automobiles, the twin facts that Americans felt they were being treated unfairly and that Europe was completely closed to American beef led to a full-scale political dispute. The United States retaliated against selected European agricultural goods sent to the United States. In the end, the key to retaliation was not the amount of money at stake but the perception that the restrictions were unreasonable.

Summary of Economic Defense.   Economic defense policies are a common response when foreign economic penetration threatens an actor's economic well-being or autonomy. On the surface, such policies may appear effective and fairly easy to put in place and to enforce since most actors can close themselves off from the outside world, if they so choose. In practice, however, economic defense is not always as useful as might be presumed. Three types of problems stand out. The first pertains to capabilities. Protectionist policies generally lead to higher costs for consumers, save far fewer jobs than might be supposed, and foster the funneling of resources into the weakest segments of the economy. Each of these developments tends to weaken society as a whole. The second problem is associated with credibility. Both a strong commitment to freer trade and a high degree of exposure to retaliation can bring into question an actor's desire to pursue economic defense vigorously. Finally, economic defense may lead to a counterresponse from the target. In one type of response the target may change its behavior to allow it to bypass the defense mechanisms. Another is a policy of retaliation, wherein the target imposes its own commercial restrictions in an effort to pay the actor back for the limitations it imposed. Each of these considerations makes the reality of economic defense far less attractive than the appearance.

Economic Deterrence and Compellence

Economic deterrence may be defined as a situation in which an actor seeks to prevent a target from engaging in unwanted behavior by threatening to employ its economic resources either to punish the target or to deny the target its goals. Economic compellence occurs when an actor seeks to force a target to alter its behavior in a way that the target finds unacceptable by threatening to use or by using its economic resources. Two of the most common forms of economic compellence are a state's employment of economic sanctions[99] and multinational corporations' use of their vast capital, technological, and entre-preneurial capabilities to get what they want.[100]

Using Economic Deterrence and Compellence. Explicit international acts of economic deterrence are rare for two reasons.[101] One is that governmen-tal and other officials tend to think defensively, reacting only when they per-ceive that damage is already under way, instead of attempting to avert the conditions that might lead to damage through the use of deterrence. Another is that no economic resources parallel the horribly destructive role that nuclear weapons play in the military arena. As noted earlier in this chapter, the evolu-tion of deterrence theory has been intimately connected to the rise to promi-nence of nuclear weapons. In the absence of a comparably harsh deterrent role for economic resources, international theorists and practitioners have had little need to explain the importance of tools that can be used only to threaten and intimidate, which is precisely the part that nuclear weapons have played in the military realm.[102]

Economic deterrence does indeed play a role in the international arena, but for the most part, such deterrence as exists is implicit. Actors refrain from behavior that they perceive others would find intolerable because they are sensi-tive to the reactions that they believe would accompany this behavior. In effect, they are deterred by their own conceptions of what might happen, and not by explicit statements from other actors about how they would react to unaccept-able behavior. Implicit deterrence plays an especially important role in the highly interdependent setting found in the Western world. Actors in the West are linked so tightly to one another that they must be wary of provoking each other lest the reactions of their partners to such provocations destroy their own welfare.[103]

When economic deterrence and compellence are used, they very frequently are conceptualized as tactics for securing a particular international political or military objective, as opposed to the economically oriented goals that are gener-ally sought with economic defense.[104] This notion is illustrated in Table 5.3, which presents data on the frequency with which economic sanctions have been used to pursue political and military objectives on a decade-to-decade basis from 1914 to 1990. Clearly, political and military goals have been a basic objective throughout the entire time period examined. As might be expected, the decades since the end of the Second World War have witnessed a substantial increase in the use of economic sanctions as a means of securing political and military objectives.

Apparently, most of those who use economic sanctions envision them as a substitute for military resources. Indeed, they are now employed to accomplish many of the same objectives that military displays, if not outright fighting, were once used for. Among the political/military objectives now sought with economic sanctions are forcing a government to leave territory that it has invaded, compelling a government to change its domestic social and human rights policies, destabilizing a government, and encouraging a government to adhere to nuclear safeguards.

Table 5.3 Number of Economic Sanctions
Initiated That Had Political or Military Goals

	Frequency of Sanctions Used for Political or Military Objectives
1914–1919	3
1920–1929	2
1930–1939	5
1940–1949	9
1950–1959	15
1960–1969	24
1970–1979	42
1980–1990	26

Source: Gary Clyde Hufbauer, Jeffrey J. Schott, and Kimberly Ann Elliott, Economic Sanctions Reconsidered: History and Current Policy (Washington, D.C.: Institute for International Economics, 1990), 16–27.

This tendency to use economic resources in the same way that the military was once used may help explain why many analysts label economic coercion as ineffective (see the discussion earlier in this chapter). As mentioned elsewhere in this book, it is not possible simply to use any resource at hand to accomplish a certain purpose. Economic pressures cannot automatically be applied effectively to do what the military does best.

Judgments regarding the efficacy of economic pressures may be clouded by two other considerations. First, an actor often employs an economic response as a display of displeasure when it is upset by a target's behavior but can do little else.[105] For example, the Carter administration decided to impose an embargo on grain sales to the Soviet Union in 1979 after the Soviet invasion of Afghanistan. The United States did so because it had almost no prospect of forcing the Soviets out of Afghanistan, but felt that it had to do something to express its disapproval and to organize international opposition.[106] The grain embargo was expressly designed to accomplish this purpose and at the same time to raise the cost to the Soviets of their misdeed by disrupting their agricultural network of suppliers.

The embargo worked reasonably well as an indicator of displeasure and as a disrupting agent. It failed to dislodge the Soviets from Afghanistan, however, and so many people regarded it as a flop. When we view the embargo in this way, it fails to take into account the actor's actual purposes in imposing it. We must be careful to consider what the actor was trying to accomplish when we judge the results achieved. Unfortunately, economic pressures all too often are not judged in this way and thus are treated as an ineffective means of exercising power.

A second factor that clouds the evaluation of the use of economic resources is that they are often employed to intervene in the target's domestic affairs. As mentioned in Chapter 2, international conventions guarantee sovereign states against such interventions, which are regarded as anathema by all

Table 5.4 Economic Sanctions Classified According to Whether the Goal Is to Affect the Target's Foreign or Domestic Policy

	Foreign Policy Goal	Domestic Policy Goal
1914–1919	3	1
1920–1929	2	0
1930–1939	4	1
1940–1949	8	2
1950–1959	11	3
1960–1969	14	13
1970–1979	23	24
1980–1990	16	16

Source: Gary Clyde Hufbauer, Jeffrey J. Schott, and Kimberly Ann Elliott, *Economic Sanctions Reconsidered: History and Current Policy* (Washington, D.C.: Institute for International Economics, 1990), 16–27.

actors, both sovereign and nonsovereign. Nonetheless, in recent years economic pressures have been increasingly used to try to force others to make domestic changes that conform with the actor's wishes. The increased use of economic sanctions is illustrated in Table 5.4, which classifies the economic sanctions that were initiated between 1914 and 1990 according to whether they were designed to obtain a change in the target's foreign or domestic policy behavior. Since 1960, sanctions have been increasingly envisioned as a method to force a target's government to adjust the way it manages its society. One half of all sanctions initiated in the last three decades were oriented toward this purpose. Since targets might be expected to resist such attempts as much as possible, using sanctions to this end should ultimately lower their rate of success. Spanier makes just this point when he writes that

> no power, and certainly not a great power, will admit publicly that it has mistreated its own citizens; none will promise to improve its behavior under pressure and in return for certain material goods. Domestic affairs are considered the business of the national government and no one else.[107]

The Efficacy of Economic Deterrence and Compellence.   In assessing the efficacy of using economic resources to pressure others, in either a compellent or a deterrent manner, the nature of the phenomena being analyzed must be taken into account. Both economic deterrence and compellence are based on influencing others through the threat or use of economic deprivation. That is, an actor tries to impose its will on others by denying them (or threatening to deny them) the access they need to such economic goods as raw materials, finished goods, services, technology, and entrepreneurial expertise. With deterrence, the purpose is to prevent the target from doing something the actor would find unacceptable. With compellence, the objective is to force the target to alter its present behavior to conform to the actor's preferences. In either case, deprivation is supposed to be the key to success.[108]

The attempt to use denial tactics as a means of exercising power requires meeting several conditions pertaining to communications, capability, credibility, and the target's resolve.[109] With regard to communications, three basic considerations are important. First, the target must know what the actor wants and how it is (or will be) penalized for noncompliance. Such information is important if the target is to make the cost/benefit calculations necessary in a deterrent or compellent situation. And, as previously mentioned, when demands are smaller and penalties higher, the probability of success is enhanced.

The second requirement has to do with the manner in which the communications process may interact with the target's capabilities. Essentially, here we are dealing with something akin to the surprise element that was described as important to military compellence. With the use of economic resources, this translates into the actor timing its announcement of sanctions (or the threat of sanctions) so that the target does not have the opportunity to stockpile the items the actor plans to deny it, to develop substitutes, or to create an alternative network of suppliers. Finally, with economic pressures the communications process works best when it does not involve public confrontations. As Spanier argues, when highly publicized demands are made, it becomes difficult for an actor to go along because "compliance [will be] considered a surrender of an [actor's] dignity and independence to decide its own fate."[110]

Study of the relative capabilities of actor and target shows that the resources being denied to the target must be of such great importance to the target that it will suffer without them.[111] In addition, the target must be unable to replace or substitute for the resources being denied, either from its own resource base or by turning to alternative international suppliers.[112] Replacing resources means locating other ways to secure whatever has been denied, and substituting resources means using something else in place of the item that has been denied. When a target is able to do either, then economic pressures lose a lot of their "bite." It is much easier to prevent the target from securing alternative suppliers if the item needed is available from very few sources.[113]

The credibility of an actor's attempt to use economic resources to exert pressure is enhanced when two requirements are met. The first is that the target must not have the ability to retaliate against the actor to such an extent that the actor suffers severely and is forced to loosen its hold on the target. When a target can retaliate, the same credibility problems are encountered that the United States faced when it tried to use the threat of a massive nuclear attack on the Soviet Union to safeguard Europe (see Chapter 4). Basically, credibility is lost because the target will question the actor's seriousness when it is clear that any move by the actor would result in the actor's own destruction (or at least substantial damage, in the case of economic retaliation). Thus, credibility is greatest when the target has little chance of striking back. This situation is most likely to occur when a great discrepancy exists between the actor's and target's resources. Such a discrepancy in resources means that the actor is better positioned to handle retaliation by the target.[114]

The second factor relating to credibility is whether the actor has any domestic groups within its population that are closely tied to the target and that may as a result suffer if contacts with the target are lost. When the actor has such groups, they may pressure the actor's decision makers to end or modify the use of sanctions so that the groups will not be forced to bear any burdens. Of course, the more politically potent the affected groups, the more difficult it may be to ignore their demands. When a target sees that an actor confronts these problems, it quite naturally tends to question the actor's resolve to pursue its policy and to "stay the course" in applying economic pressure.

One example occurred when the Carter administration attempted to embargo grain to the Soviet Union after the invasion of Afghanistan. In this situation, numerous American farmers and grain merchants relied for a good portion of their income on grain sales to the Soviet Union. These groups protested the embargo vociferously and played an important role in the 1980 presidential election, which Carter lost. A short while later, President Reagan lifted the embargo. The initial protests undermined the credibility of the American policy. Moreover, the later defeat of Carter and the lifting of the embargo confirmed the judgment of those who thought that the United States did not have the ability to stand by a policy that "hurt" domestically.

The final set of conditions affecting the success of economic pressures is the way the target responds to the actor's behavior. One significant factor in this regard is the manner in which the actor communicates its demands to the target. A highly public communication process is likely to make the target bristle. Another key to the target's reaction is the severity of the demands that are made. The more that is demanded of the target, the greater the chance that it will choose to suffer the consequences associated with economic deprivation or with seeking replacements or substitutes rather than yield.[115]

Economic Deterrence by Punishment.   The manner in which these factors complicate the attempt to use economic pressures may be illustrated by looking at three examples: deterrence by punishment, deterrence by denial, and economic compellence. Deterrence by punishment is exemplified by the League of Nations declaration in the years between World Wars I and II that international acts of aggression would be penalized through the use of economic sanctions. Deterrence by denial is found in the trade restrictions that the Coordinating Committee on Export Controls (COCOM), an association that included the United States and its principal cold war allies, imposed on the Communist bloc in 1948. Economic compellence is represented by the attempts by the Organization of Petroleum Exporting Countries (OPEC) to force other members of the international system to pay OPEC-determined prices for the petroleum they consumed.

In the first example, the primary goal of the League of Nations was to prevent acts of international aggression. It was hoped that this objective could be achieved through the threat to use economic sanctions to paralyze the economy of any state that engaged in unacceptable behavior. Article 16 of the League Covenant stated that international aggressors would be "subject . . . to the severance of all trade or financial relations [and] the prohibition of all [commercial] intercourse."[116] The idea was that potential aggressors would so fear the loss of their international economic linkages that they would shrink from acting out any nefarious designs they might have. The intent clearly was to deter by threatening to punish, for the League issued its warning out of a desire to stop conflict from ever happening. The last thing the League members wanted was to confront the need to react to an attack by one state on another. The threat of severe economic punishment was supposed to ensure that members could avoid just this situation.

The League's efforts presented some fundamental problems, however.

One set of difficulties had to do with the communications process. Since the League meant to deter anyone who might act aggressively, and since the identity of the aggressor was unknown beforehand, the League's warnings were of necessity obscure as to exactly what penalties would be imposed, the target they would be imposed against, and the actors that would participate in administering the punishment. Though unavoidable, such vagueness meant that potential targets had no idea as to what costs they would incur if they acted unacceptably. Thus, no target could possibly make the essential cost/benefit calculations that are at the heart of deterrence. It was noted earlier that deterrence by punishment works best (and perhaps only works at all) when targets clearly understand that they face overwhelming costs if they engage in the unwanted behavior. This condition was not met in this example.

Another communications problem involved the highly public nature of the League's enforcement mechanisms. Thus, the aggressor would be threatened with a highly visible confrontation that it could not easily back away from. Moreover, the League's plan was to use sanctions to deter "big" problems, such as invasions of other countries, not "small" ones, such as trade disputes. As noted, these are precisely the kinds of problems that economic deterrence is ill suited to handle.

The League's efforts also entailed some basic capability and credibility problems. If economic deterrence was to function effectively, it required that actors cooperate to create airtight sanctions that would truly hurt the target by denying it the goods and/or services that it desperately needed. The requirement that many others must cooperate meant that any would-be aggressor might wonder about the possibility of defection. In addition, any potential target would naturally be inclined to question the League's ability to organize sanctions that would deprive the target of what it vitally needed. This was especially applicable if the target offered potential suppliers substantial inducements, such as a higher price or political support on issues that a supplier might value greatly.

In the end, the League's efforts failed to deter Italy from invading Ethiopia, and each of the problems mentioned here arose when the League tried to use economic sanctions to punish Italy. From the beginning, the Italian government never took the League sanctions seriously. It expected that it could induce some League members to defect from the application of sanctions and that it would be able to frighten others into watering down such sanctions as were imposed so that they would create little problem for Italy. The Italians were correct. The League never was able to isolate Italy completely, in part because many members expected to reap commercial benefits from supplying the Italian war effort. In addition, Italy was able to take advantage of the fact that the two most important members of the League, the United Kingdom and France, felt they needed Italian cooperation in the face of the rise of Nazism in Germany.

Thus, the League's attempts at economic deterrence fell flat. It simply was not possible to communicate a warning effectively, the necessary capabilities were lacking and therefore posed no terror for potential targets, the League's efforts had no credibility because would-be targets could expect to crack such coalitions as might be formed, and targets could be expected to resist demands both because they were well publicized and because they demanded that targets renounce highly cherished goals.

Economic Deterrence by Denial.   An example of economic deterrence by denial is found in COCOM's attempt to prevent Communist countries from developing weapons systems that would allow them to compete effectively and to pose a threat to the West. Through trade restrictions these countries were denied strategic materials and technology that they could use to upgrade their military establishments. Without access to the technology and other goods produced in the West, it was hoped that the Eastern bloc would be stymied in its continuing effort to produce sophisticated weapons systems.

COCOM's designs ran into problems on several fronts. For one, the highly publicized sanctions upset the Soviets and were one more bit of evidence convincing the Soviet leadership that the West wished to isolate them. Therefore, their already heightened suspicions about Western intentions were confirmed. Instead of inclining the Soviets to tone down their challenges, the trade sanctions encouraged the Soviets to become more belligerent. Moreover, the sanctions appeared to contain an implicit demand that the Soviets forgo the modernization of their armed forces even as the West attempted to race ahead. This was too much, for it appeared to pose a direct threat to Soviet security, something no Soviet government could ignore. Thus, the sanctions involved both communications problems and difficulties pertaining to the target's reaction to the sanctions.

The COCOM program also fell far short of what is needed for success in terms of capabilities. Capabilities problems existed at two levels. One was a continuing Soviet ability either to find Western corporations that were willing to sell militarily related technology to the Soviet Union in violation of the trade restrictions or to acquire needed information through the use of espionage. The other was the Soviets' ability to develop technology of their own. This meant that the Soviets were able to evade the full force of the West's denial strategy. They found alternative international suppliers, and they used their own resource base to supply their own needs (although at extremely great expense to themselves).

The West's credibility was also questionable. For one thing, the Soviets consistently believed that the Western corporations' quest for profits would incline them to sell to the Eastern bloc. They were not disappointed in this expectation. For another, Western governments hardly presented a united front in interpreting COCOM rules: the Western Europeans consistently pressed for more liberal interpretations, while the United States demanded more restrictions. Even within the United States itself, various corporations and bureaucratic agencies favored differing views of COCOM regulations. For instance, the U.S. Department of Commerce took a more relaxed approach, whereas the Department of Defense favored more restraints. As a result, the Soviets tended to feel that the Western allies were not committed to tight enforcement of COCOM rules.

Hence, in both examples of economic deterrence, the actor ran into a considerable amount of trouble in its effort to prevent the target from pursuing an unacceptable course of action. Economic sanctions apparently failed in the interwar years because of difficulties associated with making the costs of unacceptable action clear to the target and because of fundamental capability and credibility problems. For their part, the COCOM trade restrictions did not work well because they merely reinforced the Soviets' determination to engage in the very action the West sought to prevent. In addition, the West could not stop the Soviets from finding international suppliers or producing the needed goods for themselves. These are typical of the problems that actors confront when seeking to use economic resources for deterrent purposes.

Economic Compellence.   The problems associated with economic compellence may be illustrated by examining the behavior of OPEC. At first glance, the outcome in this case appears quite different from those just described.[117] OPEC was created in 1960 in order to give oil-producing countries a greater voice in international petroleum markets. The cartel's basic goal was to secure higher prices for oil so that member governments could promote domestic economic growth and development. During the organization's first decade of existence, it relied almost entirely on persuasion as a means of obtaining the agreement of others to pay more for oil. These tactics were only marginally successful. For example, throughout the 1960s oil was sold internationally for just under $2.00 per barrel. In 1971 OPEC was able to negotiate a new agreement that would raise the price of Persian Gulf oil over a five-year period from $1.80 to $2.29 per barrel.[118] Although these price increases fell far short of what OPEC members wanted, they seemed the best that could be achieved.

In 1973, however, the October War between Israel and several Arab neighbors broke out. This war prompted several Arab members of OPEC (which also included six non-Arab states as members) to try to use their roles as suppliers of a key commodity, oil, as an economic weapon. In an attempt at economic compellence, these Arab suppliers announced their decision to embargo oil to all countries that supported Israel in the war. While the purpose of the embargo was political (denying Israel allies), the immediate effects were economic. The embargo set the stage for very dramatic and rapid increases in the price of oil. Within a fortnight, oil more than doubled in price from $2.50 per barrel to $5.12. In another three months the price rose again to $11.65 per barrel.

These price increases occurred because many Western nations had become heavy users of oil to meet their energy needs. In the early 1970s 60 percent of the energy consumed in Europe was derived from oil. In Japan, the comparable figure was 73 percent. In the United States, oil accounted for 46 percent of the energy used. At the same time, all the oil used in Europe and in Japan was imported and one third of American oil needs were met through imports, with substantial portions of this oil coming from the Middle East in each case. Thus, when the Arab embargo drove the international supply of oil down, prices went up quickly. OPEC's control of 85 percent of the oil available on world markets put its members in a commanding position.[119]

The end of the October War and the heady price increases of 1973 and 1974 brought OPEC back to its original purpose—to control the international oil market. The diversity of the cartel's members, however, made it difficult to agree on a common political agenda. Indeed, the varying levels of development and sizes of the states that made up OPEC meant that cooperation was not easily achieved even on the economic issues that were central to the cartel's very existence. Larger and poorer countries favored rapid price increases, whereas smaller and wealthier members pushed for conservation of oil resources and stability.[120] Still, the general thrust of the thinking of most members revolved around the need to dominate the international pricing structure for petroleum and to obtain the maximum profits available.

The unique nature of the product that they sold allowed OPEC members to gain a good measure of success in pursuing their goals, at least initially. As has been mentioned, OPEC dominated the international supply of oil. Substitutes were few and costly. Alternative suppliers were almost nonexistent in the mid-1970s, and it would take years to locate and develop new sources of oil and to build the needed distribution networks. Most advanced industrialized countries were very dependent on oil to maintain their industrial infrastructures and to fuel their economies. And very few of the members of OPEC were so highly dependent on their customers that any meaningful acts of retaliation were possible in the short run. In fact, OPEC's customers were largely divided among themselves, and thus were unable to develop a useful united response to OPEC's dominance.[121] Hence, initially OPEC was in an enviable position with regard to capability and credibility factors.

This state of affairs did not last, however. The announcements regarding pricing policy that accompanied the frequent meetings of OPEC ministers were always well publicized and as such served as challenges to many in the Western world. In addition, the rapid increases in the price of oil disrupted Western economies, leading to stagflation, a condition in which economic stagnation and unemployment were joined by high rates of inflation. These problems became especially acute after events in the Persian Gulf in 1979 created new oil shortages that allowed OPEC to push the price of oil above the $30 per barrel level by early 1981.

Such developments stiffened the resolve of governments and corporations around the world and provided new opportunities for investors to take advantage of new international conditions. Conservation and greater efficiency in the use of fuel characterized the reactions of many to OPEC's attempt to dominate prices. In addition, substitutes for petroleum and alternative suppliers were sought. Coal, nuclear power, synthetic fuels, natural gas, and solar and wood energy sources were tapped. The North Slope, the North Sea, Mexico, and the Soviet Union, none of which was under OPEC control, began to produce more oil. Beginning in the late 1970s and continuing throughout the 1980s, OPEC's share of the international oil market and the demand for petroleum both declined. By 1985 OPEC was producing and selling only about one half of what it had produced and sold a decade earlier. OPEC fell from a dominant to a marginal role almost as quickly as it had scaled the heights in the early 1970s.[122]

This brief account of the rise and decline of OPEC as a controlling force in international petroleum markets illustrates the problems associated with economic compellence even under the best of conditions (from the actor's point of view). OPEC's goal was to set the price structure for oil and to force other members of the international system to pay whatever OPEC decided on. The result was supposed to be an international shift of wealth favoring OPEC members. In pursuing this goal, OPEC had advantages relating to capabilities and credibility that few international actors ever attain, particularly when they operate in the economic arena. Had the members of OPEC been more judicious in their exploitation of these advantages, they might have been able to maintain their dominance.

The problem for OPEC was that all too often its messages to its customers were communicated in a very public and seemingly uncaring and belligerent manner, causing many political leaders in purchasing countries to react negatively. Moreover, the extreme price increases that customers were forced to accept (albeit temporarily) created a sense of resolve among targets that led them to search for ways to evade OPEC's grip. Through conservation, substitution policies, and the location of new suppliers, it was possible to break OPEC's strong grasp on international energy markets. In failing to ensure that they did not offend their targets' sensitivities, the members of the cartel produced the very circumstances that made their customers determined to undo the conditions that allowed OPEC to experience a measure of success early on. Too blunt an application of force tends simply to redound to one's own disadvantage, whether the resources used are from the military or the economic arena.

In conclusion, economic deterrence and compellence are difficult to apply in international politics. Both require that the actor have a near monopoly on a vital resource (or resources) that cannot easily be replaced or substituted for. Few resources fall into this category. Moreover, the target must be incapable of effective retaliation. Even when these conditions are met, the actor is well advised to keep its demands to a minimum in order to avoid either offending the target or appearing too threatening. To do either will merely prompt the target to bear the pain instead of giving in to the actor's demands. Thus, economic pressures work best when applied quietly either (1) to affect policies that the target is not particularly committed to or (2) to alter conditions that the target is not attached to or that it does not value highly.[123]

CHAPTER SUMMARY

International actors typically use three broad tactics when they employ force. Two, defense and deterrence, are used to prevent others from imposing their will on the actor. Defense involves an actor's efforts to limit the damage that an opponent inflicts on it once the opponent has begun to take action against the actor. Deterrence is designed to prevent an opponent from initiating unacceptable behavior. The third tactic, compellence, involves an actor's attempt to force others to conform to its wishes.

Each of these tactics may be pursued with either military or economic resources. Whichever resource is employed, the use of each tactic presents a unique combination of requirements as far as communications, capabilities, credibility, and the target's reactions are concerned.

With deterrence, an actor seeks to threaten a target to such a degree that the target refrains from engaging in unacceptable behavior either because it fears the punishment it will receive or because it believes it has no prospect for success. In general, these impressions in a target's mind are most easily created when the actor has at its disposal exceptionally powerful weapons that can inflict very severe penalties on the target. In addition, the actor must communicate a clear threat to a specific target in order to prevent any ambiguity in the target's mind as to what the actor intends to do about misbehavior. It is also important that the target have little or no capacity for retaliation and that the actor have a reputation for carrying out precisely the sorts of threats it is making. Finally, with deterrence, the target is given an "out," for it simply may act as though it has no plans for engaging in the forbidden behavior. Alternatively, the target may maintain that it is postponing its plans.

These conditions for optimal deterrence are easily summarized, but they are far more difficult to put into practice. Indeed, only since the introduction of nuclear weapons has deterrence become a centerpiece of military planning. Before that, actors had only a limited ability to make the kind of horrible threats that give deterrence its greatest prospects for success. In the economic realm, where there is nothing remotely similar to nuclear weapons, deterrence is largely unknown, at least in any explicit form.

Defense is premised on a different set of requirements. Here one finds some variation in what one must do, depending on whether military or economic resources are employed. In the military arena, actors often find that they must shroud their preparations in secrecy, lest they provide their opponents with the opportunity to develop an effective counter. While secrecy is often important, the actor must be certain that it maintains its credibility that it *will* react to unacceptable behavior.

The capabilities that an actor needs for defense depend heavily on the types of opponents it faces. Suffice it to say that the actor requires a resource base that is sufficient to blunt and defeat whatever moves its adversaries may make. When many possible adversaries pose a variety of threats, the actor must also have the ability to develop a policy that determines how its resources may be used most effectively. Finally, since it is a reactive policy, defense again leaves the opponent an opportunity to conform to the actor's wishes without appearing to give up something. All the target must do is refrain from or postpone the behavior that the actor finds objectionable.

Economic defense operates differently. A key reason for the difference is that, although military defense seeks to avoid any damage at the hands of the opponent, economic defense usually begins only after damage, such as the loss of jobs or declining profits, has begun. As a result, the tactical requirements vary somewhat from one realm to the other. Since damage is under way, an actor's economic defense plans must be communicated clearly to the opponent. Without such communications, compliance becomes difficult. Capabilities requirements center on the actor's ability to absorb the costs of the defense strategy, whether it is able to rescue the affected industry, and how well it can handle tactical shifts by its opponent. Each of these requirements is very hard to meet.

As far as credibility is concerned, the key problems are associated with the international values espoused by the actor and with the degree to which the actor is exposed to retaliation by the target. Finally, the target's willingness to accept the actor's economic defense restrictions rests to a large extent on whether it is singled out for discrimination and on how much the target stands to lose. When the effects of each of these factors are added, economic defense is seen to be no easy task.

Compellence was the last tactic examined in this chapter. When plans are made to use the military for this purpose, secrecy is almost always vital, for it allows an actor to strike at an unprepared opponent. Thus, communications must be vague. Moreover, actors have a strong incentive to act as though they have no serious grievances and even to build an air of credibility for false policies. As was true for defense, the actor's capabilities needs are determined by the would-be opponent. Essentially, the actor must have sufficient resources to overcome the opponent's defenses. Even overcoming these defenses may not be enough, however, for international actors tend to be obstinate and uncooperative when subjected to acts of aggression. Hence, the final, and perhaps most daunting, problem is the actor's ability to bend the target to its will.

In the economic arena, an actor tries to compel by denying the target much-needed goods and services. This requires that the actor communicate carefully to the target the action that is taken. The actor must not, however, announce its intentions too far in advance, for it would allow the target to stockpile the restricted goods or to locate new suppliers.

Economic compellence also requires that the actor must be capable of depriving the target of items that it must have if it is to avoid economic disaster. Beyond this, the target should be unable to substitute for or to replace the goods that are denied, and it should have little capacity for retaliation. Finally, economic compellence works best when the actor keeps its demands to a minimum. Otherwise, the target may be tempted to suffer rather than give in to the actor's requests.

In conclusion, an examination of international coercion leads to the observation that an important part of success is found in the degree to which actors are able to moderate their demands so that targets feel they can comply without too great a loss of dignity. Unless this is done, coercion is a difficult road to travel, no matter how many resources the actor possesses and how much resolve it has.

Notes

1. In considering defense, deterrence, and compellence, the operational specifics associated with these broad approaches to the use of force are not examined. Thus, such things as nuclear war fighting and blitzkrieg operations are beyond the scope of the current discussion.

2. For a definition of economic sanctions, see Chapter 3. For an in-depth discussion of this type of coercion, see Gary Clyde Hufbauer, Jeffrey J. Schott, and Kimberly Ann Elliott, *Economic Sanctions Reconsidered: History and Current Policy* (Washington, D.C.: Institute for International Economics, 1990), chap. 1. Also see Chapter 3, Table 3.7, in this book.

3. See Bruce Russett and Harvey Starr, *World Politics: The Menu for Choice* (New York: W. H. Freeman, 1989), 128.

4. Glenn H. Snyder, "Deterrence and Defense: A Theoretical Introduction," in *American Defense Policy*, eds. Mark E. Smith III and Claude J. Jones, Jr. (Baltimore: Johns Hopkins University Press, 1968), 55.

5. Thomas C. Schelling, *The Strategy of Conflict* (New York: Oxford University Press, 1963), 195. The emphasis was in the original.

6. Alexander L. George and Richard Smoke, *Deterrence in American Foreign Policy: Theory and Practice* (New York: Columbia University Press, 1974), 11.

7. Snyder, "Deterrence and Defense," 33.

8. The similarities between deterrence and compellence are discussed in some detail in David Baldwin, "Power Analysis and World Politics: New Trends vs. Old Tendencies," *World Politics* 31, no. 2 (January 1979): 161–94.

9. Schelling, *The Strategy of Conflict*, 195.

10. See Frank C. Zagare, *The Dynamics of Deterrence* (Chicago: University of Chicago Press, 1987), 7.

11. These concepts are discussed in Snyder, "Deterrence and Defense," 40–41; George and Smoke, *Deterrence in American Foreign Policy*, 48; and Paul K. Huth, "Extended Deterrence and the Outbreak of War," *American Political Science Review* 82, no. 2 (June 1988): 424.

12. Robert J. Art and Kenneth N. Waltz, "Technology, Strategy, and the Use of Force," in *The Use of Force: International Politics and Foreign Policy*, eds. Robert J. Art and Kenneth N. Waltz (Boston: Little, Brown, 1971), 6.

13. In this book Zagare's definition of rationality is used. Someone is judged rational when he or she behaves in a goal-oriented fashion. That is, a rational person evaluates the alternatives open to him or her according to how they contribute to the goal that the person seeks to attain, choosing the alternative that allows for the attainment of the goal at the lowest possible perceived cost. See Zagare, *The Dynamics of Deterrence*, 8–9.

14. In the case of both denial and punishment, one is assuming that one's opponent wants to engage in unacceptable behavior. If this is not true, then there is nothing to prevent, and one is posturing for naught.

15. Snyder, "Defense and Deterrence," 33.

16. R. Harrison Wagner, "The Theory of Games and International Cooperation," *American Political Science Review* 77, no. 2 (June 1983): 336.

17. Robert Jervis, "Cooperation under the Security Dilemma," *World Politics* 30, no. 2 (January 1978): 203.

18. The Western strategy was based on the assumption that the Soviets wanted to seize Western Europe. If the Soviets had no such desire, then deterrence would be irrelevant because there would be nothing to prevent.

19. Neither the United Kingdom nor France thought explicitly in terms of deterrence when making their preparations to help Poland. Apparently, both countries were only vaguely aware of the exclusively deterrent nature of their actions. The upshot was a considerable degree of confusion in their policy planning. See Alistair Horne, *To Lose a Battle: France 1940* (New York: Penguin Books, 1979), chaps. 4–5.

20. Art and Waltz, "Technology, Strategy, and the Use of Force," 6.

21. See Hedley Bull, *The Anarchical Society* (New York: Columbia University Press, 1977), 118. In a creative effort designed to test indirectly the validity of deterrence theory during the cold war, Jacek Kugler makes the same point. See Jacek Kugler, "Terror without Deterrence: Reassessing the Role of Nuclear Weapons," *Journal of Conflict Resolution* 28, no. 3 (September 1984): 472.

22. See George and Smoke, *Deterrence in American Foreign Policy*, 15–16; and Harold Sprout and Margaret Sprout, *Toward a Politics of the Planet Earth* (New York: D. Van Nostrand, 1971), 158.

23. See George and Smoke, *Deterrence in American Foreign Policy*, chap. 6; and John W. Spanier, *The Truman-MacArthur Controversy and the Korean War* (New York: W. W. Norton, 1965), 15–23.

24. See Elaine Sciolino, "Deskbound in U.S., the Envoy to Iraq Is Called Scapegoat for a Failed Policy," *New York Times*, September 12, 1990, A19; and Elaine Sciolino and Michael R.

Gordon, "U.S. Gave Iraq Little Reason Not to Mount Kuwait Assault," *New York Times,* September 23, 1990, A1.

25. See Jervis, "Cooperation under the Security Dilemma," 189–90; and Sprout and Sprout, *Toward a Politics of the Planet Earth,* 158.

26. Stephen Van Evera, "Why Cooperation Failed in 1914," *World Politics* 38, no. 1 (October 1985): 105.

27. For a discussion of surprise and deception as factors affecting defense planning, see Edward N. Luttwak, "The Operational Level of War," *International Security* 5, no. 3 (Winter 1980/81): 61–79.

28. For a discussion of the cost and characteristics of international terrorism, see Charles W. Kegley, Jr., ed., *International Terrorism: Characteristics, Causes, Controls* (New York: St. Martin's, 1990), part 1.

29. For a discussion of how the capabilities for fighting a conventional war are not very applicable to guerrilla warfare, see Andrew F. Krepinevich, Jr., *The Army and Vietnam* (Baltimore: Johns Hopkins University Press, 1986).

30. It should be noted that while there are many other types of international actors, only a limited group of these actors employ violence when they attempt to compel.

31. For a discussion of terrorist tactics, see Brian M. Jenkins, "International Terrorism: The Other World War," in *International Terrorism: Characteristics, Causes, Controls,* ed. Charles W. Kegley, Jr. (New York: St. Martin's, 1990), 36.

32. George and Smoke, *Deterrence in American Foreign Policy,* 32.

33. For further elaboration on these points, see Bull, *The Anarchical Society,* 119; and George and Smoke, *Deterrence in American Foreign Policy,* 21–26.

34. Research by Paul Huth shows that capabilities factors of this sort are vital to this type of deterrence. See Huth, "Extended Deterrence and the Outbreak of War," 435.

35. Recent research shows that a diplomatic strategy in which the actor carefully matches the target's moves toward higher degrees of confrontation is important for building the actor's credibility. See Huth, "Extended Deterrence and the Outbreak of War," 435.

36. See David A. Baldwin, "Inter-nation Influence Revisited," *Journal of Conflict Resolution* 15, no. 4 (1971): 471–86.

37. K. J. Holsti, "The Horsemen of the Apocalypse: At the Gate, Detoured, or Retreating?" *International Studies Quarterly* 30, no. 4 (December 1986): 368.

38. For brief discussions of state-sponsored terrorism and internal subversion, see K. J. Holsti, *International Politics: A Framework for Analysis* (Englewood Cliffs, N.J.: Prentice-Hall, 1983), 241–66; and Russett and Starr, *World Politics,* 174.

39. Russett and Starr, *World Politics,* 171.

40. Richard Rosecrance, *The Rise of the Trading State: Commerce and Conquest in the Modern World* (New York: Basic Books, 1986), 157.

41. Geir Lundestad, "Empire by Invitation? The United States and Western Europe, 1945–1952," *Journal of Peace Research* 23, no. 3 (September 1986): 275. It should be noted that extensive research and development expenditures in the military arena draw money away from product development in the civilian sector, thereby reducing a country's ability to compete with its rivals in the commercial realm. The only clear exception to this occurs when military technologies can be readily transferred to civilian uses.

42. For a discussion of the evolution of the international arms market, see Andrew J. Pierre, *The Global Politics of Arms Sales* (Princeton: Princeton University Press, 1982), part 1. A description of technology transfer is available from Janne E. Nolan, *Trappings of Power: Ballistic Missiles in the Third World* (Washington, D.C.: The Brookings Institution, 1991).

43. See Nolan, *Trappings of Power.*

44. For a discussion of how useful deterrence was for protecting client states, see Paul K. Huth, "Extended Deterrence and the Outbreak of War"; Paul K. Huth, "The Extended Deterrent Value of Nuclear Weapons," *Journal of Conflict Resolution* 34, no. 2 (June 1990): 270–90;

Kugler, "Terror without Deterrence"; and James Lee Ray, "The Abolition of Slavery and the End of International War," *International Organization* 43, no. 3 (Summer 1989): 405–39.

45. It is not inaccurate to note that this has always been the key to deterrence. The fact that not everyone has understood this clearly is due to the cold war, where the identity of the opponent one wished to deter and the nature of the threat always were obvious.

46. The protection given under these conditions is not altruistic and may involve preserving repressive regimes that appear to be prepared to ensure one's access to what one needs.

47. For a discussion of the relationship between interdependence and domestic political tensions, see John M. Rothgeb, Jr., "The Effects of Foreign Investment upon Political Protest and Violence in Underdeveloped Societies," *Western Political Quarterly* 44, no. 1 (March 1991): 9–38.

48. John Lewis Gaddis describes how difficult this task is in his discussion of the development of the American strategy of containment after the Second World War. See John Lewis Gaddis, *Strategies of Containment: A Critical Appraisal of Postwar National Security Policy* (New York: Oxford University Press, 1982).

49. See Martin Walker, "Victory and Delusion," *Foreign Policy* 83 (Summer 1991): 168.

50. Niccolò Machiavelli, *The Prince and the Discourses* (New York: Modern Library, 1950), 310.

51. Rosecrance, *Rise of the Trading State*, 123–24.

52. See John Lewis Gaddis, "Toward the Post–Cold War World," in *The Future of American Foreign Policy*, eds. Charles W. Kegley, Jr., and Eugene Wittkopf (New York: St. Martin's, 1992), 16–32; Joseph S. Nye, Jr., *Bound to Lead: The Changing Nature of American Power* (New York: Basic Books, 1990), 30; Joseph S. Nye, Jr., "Soft Power," *Foreign Policy* 80 (Fall 1990): 162–63; and Rosecrance, *Rise of the Trading State*, 32.

53. These are the factors that have brought Carl Kaysen to observe that compellence has become a very risky business. Indeed, he has observed that "nations that have initiated wars in this century have generally come out the loser." See Carl Kaysen, "Is War Obsolete? A Review Essay," *International Security* 14, no. 4 (Spring 1990): 59.

54. Barry Buzan, "Economic Structure and International Security: The Limits of the Liberal Case," *International Organization* 38, no. 4 (Autumn 1984): 603.

55. Hans Morgenthau, *Politics among Nations: The Struggle for Power and Peace* (New York: Alfred A. Knopf, 1948), 119.

56. E. H. Carr, *The Twenty Years Crisis, 1919–1939* (New York: St. Martin's, 1939), 113.

57. William H. McNeill, *The Pursuit of Power: Technology, Armed Force, and Society Since A.D. 1000* (Chicago: University of Chicago Press, 1982), 25.

58. Carr, *The Twenty Years Crisis*, 121.

59. Carr, *The Twenty Years Crisis*, 121.

60. Barry Buzan, "Economic Structure and International Security," 597–624.

61. For a discussion of the economic motivations for European colonialism and imperialism, see Nazli Choucri and Robert C. North, *Nations in Conflict: National Growth and International Violence* (San Francisco: W. H. Freeman, 1975); and Benjamin J. Cohen, *The Question of Imperialism: The Political Economy of Dominance and Dependence* (New York: Basic Books, 1973).

62. For a critical summary and evaluation of these arguments and for a useful bibliography of those who write in this vein, see John M. Rothgeb, Jr., *The Myths and Realities of Foreign Investment in Poor Countries* (New York: Praeger, 1989).

63. See Inis L. Claude, Jr., *Swords into Plowshares: The Problems and Progress of International Organization* (New York: Random House, 1971), chap. 12.

64. Arnold Wolfers, *Discord and Collaboration* (Baltimore: Johns Hopkins University Press, 1962), 109.

65. David A. Baldwin, *Economic Statecraft* (Princeton: Princeton University Press, 1985), 57.

66. John Spanier, *Games Nations Play* (Washington, D.C.: Congressional Quarterly Press, 1987), 286.

67. Wolfers, *Discord and Collaboration,* 109.

68. See Robert O. Keohane and Joseph S. Nye, Jr., *Power and Interdependence* (Boston: Little, Brown, 1977), 10–11.

69. Holsti, *International Politics,* 214.

70. Baldwin, *Economic Statecraft,* 110.

71. These examples are drawn from Gary Clyde Hufbauer, Jeffrey J. Schott, and Kimberly Ann Elliott, *Economic Sanctions Reconsidered: History and Current Policy* (Washington, D.C.: Institute for International Economics, 1990); and Gary Clyde Hufbauer, Jeffrey J. Schott, and Kimberly Ann Elliott, *Economic Sanctions Reconsidered: Supplemental Case Histories* (Washington, D.C.: Institute for International Economics, 1990).

72. In the Gulf War, economic sanctions were instituted before the war and were included as an adjunct to the military when fighting began.

73. See Cohen, *The Question of Imperialism,* 20–23.

74. See Edward L. Morse, *Modernization and the Transformation of International Relations* (New York: Free Press, 1976), 70–72.

75. See Carr, *The Twenty Years Crisis,* 80–82; and Richard N. Gardner, *Sterling-Dollar Diplomacy in Current Perspective* (New York: Columbia University Press, 1980), 12–22.

76. For a discussion of some of these techniques, see Holsti, *International Politics,* 215–16; and Walter S. Jones, *The Logic of International Relations* (New York: HarperCollins, 1991), 346–47.

77. See Michael Dolan, Brian W. Tomlin, H. Von Riekhoff, and M. A. Molot, "Asymmetrical Dyads and Foreign Policy: Canada-U.S. Relations, 1963–1972," *Journal of Conflict Resolution* 26, no. 3 (September 1982): 391–92.

78. For a discussion of arguments regarding the threat that foreign investments pose to local autonomy, see Rothgeb, *Myths and Realities,* chap. 3.

79. It should be noted that this constitutes an example of defense and not of deterrence because the warning came *after* the Japanese had already taken actions that were damaging to American corporations. As should be recalled, deterrence is action designed to prevent one's opponent from initiating undesired behavior. Since in this case the unwanted behavior was in progress, the situation involves defense.

80. See Gary Clyde Hufbauer and Howard F. Rosen, *Trade Policy for Troubled Industries* (Washington, D.C.: Institute for International Economics, 1986), 73.

81. A quota is a limit on the quantity of goods that other countries may export to the society in question. A tariff is a tax on goods and services as they enter a society. Quotas limit foreign competition by restricting the absolute numbers of goods that may enter a society. Tariffs do so by raising the price of foreign goods relative to domestically produced goods, thereby making their purchase less attractive. See Hufbauer and Rosen, *Trade Policy for Troubled Industries,* chap. 2.

82. For a discussion of some of the techniques for regulating foreign investments, see David H. Blake and Robert S. Walters, *The Politics of Global Economic Relations* (Englewood Cliffs, N.J.: Prentice-Hall, 1987), 129–37; and Joan Edelman Spero, *The Politics of International Economic Relations* (New York: St. Martin's, 1990), 245–50.

83. Hufbauer and Rosen, *Trade Policy for Troubled Industries,* 72.

84. Hufbauer and Rosen, *Trade Policy for Troubled Industries,* 19.

85. Military defense is designed to avoid these problems, for it almost always involves a near instantaneous reaction to foreign incursions.

86. Of course, many governments try to extend their protection to international competition. This may be done by providing the industry in question with some sort of subsidy for the goods that it exports, thus allowing it to sell its products for less money on the international market. Such policies can be very expensive, and may carry with them substantial costs for taxpayers and for other corporations in the country that chooses to pursue this course.

87. Hufbauer and Rosen, *Trade Policy for Troubled Industries,* 27.

88. For a discussion of the connection between trade and domestic political conflict, see

Ronald Rogowski, "Political Cleavages and Changing Exposure to Trade," *American Political Science Review* 81, no. 4 (December 1987): 1121–38.

89. The particularly exposed positions of smaller and poorer countries to trade and to protectionism is discussed in Stephen D. Krasner, "State Power and the Structure of International Trade," *World Politics* 28, no. 3 (April 1976): 317–47; and in Rosecrance, *Rise of the Trading State*, 137–38.

90. Another variation is for a country to shift production to a third site in order to give the appearance that it is not exporting too high a volume of goods to a particular location. For example, one method that Japanese corporations have used to avoid pushing the Japanese imbalance of trade with the United States to an intolerably high level is to locate production facilities in Southeast Asia. Goods may then be sent from these plants to the United States without affecting the balance of trade between Japan and the United States. See David E. Sanger, "Power of the Yen Winning Asia," *New York Times*, December 5, 1991, C5.

91. The purpose of nondiscrimination is to avoid having actors use trade as a weapon against one another, which could increase the probability of warfare.

92. See Hufbauer and Rosen, *Trade Policy for Troubled Industries*, chap. 2.

93. There is a basic difference between enacting and enforcing policy decisions. Even when a policy is enacted, it may not have the intended effect if those who are charged with its enforcement are not prepared to do so vigorously. In the American context, presidents are the key enforcement agents. Thus, a lack of presidential commitment to protection may rob such a policy of much of its credibility. For a discussion of how the American political system handles trade policy, see I. M. Destler, *American Trade Politics: System under Stress* (Washington, D.C.: Institute for International Economics, 1986).

94. These effects are not unlike those that undermine the credibility of a military policy based upon the use of nuclear weapons to respond to the unacceptable moves of others. In each case, an actor's credibility is damaged by the fact that any move on its part would bring substantial harm down upon itself.

95. Even actors who are most exposed to damage from the moves just described still may institute protectionist policies. Usually, such policies are found when an industry that is important to the military, such as steel, is threatened, or when the industry that is harmed by foreign competition is a major source of employment, as is the case with the automobile industry in the United States.

96. Hufbauer and Rosen, *Trade Policy for Troubled Industries*, 15.

97. American producers suspected that the European health complaints were a ruse and that the actual goal was to protect European beef producers from American competition.

98. In fact, the European move was not discriminatory because anyone using hormones was banned.

99. As discussed in Chapter 3 (see note 77), economic sanctions are government-inspired alterations in normal commercial relations that are designed to induce another actor (usually a state) to change its behavior. See Gary Clyde Hufbauer and Jeffrey J. Schott with Kimberly Ann Elliott, *Economic Sanctions in Support of Foreign Policy Goals* (Washington, D.C.: Institute for International Economics, 1983), 2.

100. Multinational corporations tend to behave as exceptionally well-endowed domestic interest groups, using their ability to withhold their wholehearted cooperation from the governments of the states in which they do business to influence governmental policy-making. Such corporate cooperation is often essential to governmental policy, for corporate investments may play a key role in the creation of jobs, the development of new industry and technology, and the training of the elite business managers who help guide the commercial performance and development of society as a whole. For an extensive examination of the role played by multinational corporations in social, economic, and foreign policy–making, see Rothgeb, *Myths and Realities*.

101. The reference here is to *international* acts of economic deterrence and not to those that occur domestically. In the domestic arena, economic deterrence is common. For example, almost

all governments threaten to levy fines or otherwise deprive people of resources in order to deter them from engaging in unwanted behavior.

102. Of course, as Robert Jervis argues, there is no inherent reason why deterrence cannot be applied to international political economy. He states that "the deterring of exploitation may be as relevant to the stability of monetary systems as to arms control." See Robert Jervis, "Realism, Game Theory, and Cooperation," *World Politics* 40, no. 3 (April 1988): 319.

103. It must be pointed out that this investigation is concerned only with the examination of explicit acts of deterrence and that the sorts of implicit behavior just described fall beyond the scope of this analysis.

104. It should be recognized that economic defense still has powerful political repercussions and usually leads to a considerable amount of political conflict. The political distinction between economic deterrence and compellence, on the one hand, and economic defense, on the other, is that for the former, political and military considerations often are the basic reason for action, while with the latter, economic matters usually are the reason for action, and politics emerges as the implications of the policy become apparent.

105. Baldwin, *Economic Statecraft*, 109.

106. See Jimmy Carter, *Keeping Faith: Memoirs of a President* (New York: Bantam Books, 1982), 472.

107. Spanier, *Games Nations Play*, 304.

108. This is quite unlike the situation found when the military is used. In the military arena, the ability to seize and hold and to destroy are central to the actor's tactics and considerations revolving around the denial of resources tend to be relegated to the periphery.

109. For more complete discussions of the conditions that are needed for an actor to apply economic pressures effectively, see Baldwin, *Economic Statecraft;* James A. Caporaso, "Dependence, Dependency, and Power in the Global System: A Structural and Behavioral Analysis," *International Organization* 32, no. 1 (Winter 1978): 13–44; Karl Deutsch, *The Analysis of International Politics* (Englewood Cliffs, N.J.: Prentice-Hall, 1978), 27; Dolan, Tomlin, Von Riekhoff, and Molot, "Asymmetrical Dyads and Foreign Policy"; Hufbauer and Schott with Elliott, *Economic Sanctions in Support of Foreign Policy Goals;* Robert O. Keohane and Joseph S. Nye, Jr., *Power and Interdependence* (Boston: Little, Brown, 1977); and Karen Mingst, "Cooperation or Illusion: An Examination of the Intergovernmental Council of Copper Exporting Countries," *International Organization* 30, no. 2 (Spring 1976): 263–87.

110. Spanier, *Games Nations Play*, 303–4.

111. Keohane and Nye refer to this as the target's sensitivity to economic pressures. See Keohane and Nye, *Power and Interdependence*, 12.

112. Keohane and Nye call this the target's vulnerability. See Keohane and Nye, *Power and Interdependence*, 12–16.

113. See Mingst, "Cooperation or Illusion," 265.

114. See Hufbauer and Schott with Elliott, *Economic Sanctions in Support of Foreign Policy Goals,* 77.

115. See Hufbauer and Schott with Elliott, *Economic Sanctions in Support of Foreign Policy Goals,* 76.

116. Quoted in Claude, *Swords into Plowshares,* 459.

117. The following discussion is based on Paul Jabber, "Conflict and Cooperation in OPEC: Prospects for the Next Decade," *International Organization* 32, no. 2 (Spring 1978): 377–99; Mingst, "Cooperation or Illusion"; Theodore H. Moran, "Modeling OPEC Behavior: Economic and Policy Alternatives," *International Organization* 35, no. 2 (Spring 1981): 241–72; Theodore H. Moran, "Why Oil Prices Go Up, The Future: OPEC Wants Them," *Foreign Policy* 25 (Winter 1976–77): 58–77; Bijan Mossavar-Rahmani, "The OPEC Multiplier," *Foreign Policy* 52 (Fall 1983): 136–48; Robert S. Pindyck, "OPEC's Threat to the West," *Foreign Policy* 30 (Spring 1978): 36–52; and Spero, *The Politics of International Economic Relations*, chap. 9.

118. Spero, *The Politics of International Economic Relations*, 266.

119. These figures are from Spero, *The Politics of International Economic Relations*, chap. 9; and Blake and Walters, *The Politics of Global Economic Relations*, 179–93.

120. See Jabber, "Conflict and Cooperation in OPEC."

121. See Blake and Walters, *The Politics of Global Economic Relations*, 190–92.

122. See Mossavar-Rahmani, "The OPEC Multiplier."

123. See Hufbauer and Schott with Elliott, *Economic Sanctions in Support of Foreign Policy Goals*, 76–85.

6

Some Final Thoughts

Power is one of the most important and often-used concepts in the analysis of international relations. Consequently, it is essential to understand what power is, the distinguishing features of the international actors who wield power, the nature of the international system in which power is used, the types of violent and nonviolent resources that are typically employed to exercise power, and how some of these issues are changing in the contemporary world. This book has grappled with each of these aspects of power. It is now time to reflect on a few of the basic points that have been presented and to offer some final observations.

THE VALUE OF RESOURCES

When the definition of power was considered in Chapter 2, we described several problems that result when we rely on a conception of power as the sum total of the resources available to an actor for conducting its foreign relations. Although a resource-based approach to defining power may have its shortcomings, we must realize that an actor's pool of resources retains substantial importance for the analysis of power. As the discussion throughout this book has illustrated again and again, although an actor's resources in themselves do not necessarily confer power on it, resources are closely related to the ability to influence others.

The range of material rewards and punishments available to an actor and the efficiency with which they are used were found to play a major role in shaping the relationships between actors and targets. For one thing, resources are a key determinant of the perceptions that actors and targets have of one another. As noted elsewhere, one is strong if others believe that one has power. To the extent that an actor controls large amounts and many types of resources, others tend to regard it as an imposing entity that must be obeyed. Resources are also vital to an actor's capabilities, which in turn are fundamental to the use of coercion and threats, bribes, and persuasion. Moreover, an actor's credibility rests largely on its ability to withstand retaliation and to provide the benefits that it asserts will accompany the acceptance of its offers of assistance and the values it espouses. In addition, an actor's communications are often attended to only when it has sufficient resources that others feel it cannot be ignored.

Thus, although resources alone do not spell power, they are a basic part of the overall equation that leads to influence. And this situation is not likely to change in the future. Indeed, one of the largest sources of international uncertainty in the years ahead most probably will center on determining which resources are most appropriate for affecting the behavior of others. Military capabilities seem to be playing a less vital role in the competition between many international actors; instead, economic and intellectual resources seem to be in the ascendance. In the years immediately ahead, one of the most important challenges to all international actors will be the need to shift their attention from one resource arena to another.

POWER AND INTERDEPENDENCE

We defined power as an international actor's ability to get others to conform to its preferences when they do not want to do so and to prevent others from making it do what it does not wish to do. This relatively simple definition carries with it two particularly interesting implications: (1) Power requires a degree of interdependence, or mutual reliance, between actor and target; and (2) power exists only when actor and target are in conflict with each other.

Traditionally, the interdependence and conflict at the heart of international power relationships have revolved around security matters. Given the anarchy of the international system, each member of that system had to protect itself from the possible aggression of other members. This aggression consisted mostly of attempts at territorial conquest, and the threats came from other sovereign actors. The closer states were to one another in terms of physical proximity and the more they interacted, the greater the potential for disputes and conflict. Interdependence was related to security, for the safety of each actor depended very much on the behavior of others, and protecting oneself depended in part on the ability to control one's fellow actors. The frequent trouble in the compact European system served as the classic example.

In the years after the Second World War this picture changed. As Chapter 3 showed, the nature of both interdependence and conflict has been altered, particularly for some actors. Commercial matters have become the centerpiece of attention for many. With these changes, some observers might now presume that power has become less important for the study of international relations. Such views, however, confuse power itself with one type of conflict and with one technique for exercising power—military conflicts involving the use of armed forces. The analysis in this book argues that interdependence as such is fundamental to power because there is little point in expending one's efforts and resources to control a target if the target's behavior is of little, if any, relevance to the actor's welfare, whatever form it may take, whether territorial or economic. Actors seek to regulate those they depend on, and, presumably, as the degree of mutual dependence among entities grows, then so too does the need to manage others.

Therefore, in an increasingly interdependent world we might expect the power relationships among international actors to become a subject of more, rather than less, concern. The basic reason has to do with the greater contacts between actors and the inevitable collisions of interests that lead to a desire to manipulate another's behavior in order to protect one's own interests.

As a result, the end product of the interdependence in the contemporary international arena, and most especially among the members of the Western world, is most likely to be their increased attention to their power positions in relation to one another. Although the basic resources and techniques used in the drive to acquire influence may change, the need to control the behavior of others will remain constant. The key factor to remember is that the attempt to exercise power occurs because actors and targets are in frequent contact with each other and believe that they affect one another. With fewer interactions and mutual effects, there is less need to worry about how another behaves, and power is not as useful for conceptualizing how actors relate to each other. As interactions and impacts on one another increase, for whatever reason, exercising power becomes more vital.

THE TARGET'S ATTITUDE

One key determinant of the power relationships between actors and targets is the way in which targets react to the actor's attempts at control. When targets are reasonably willing to give in to an actor's demands, then actors face a far easier task than when targets behave stubbornly. Indeed, truly recalcitrant targets often leave the actor with the choice between giving up and exercising fate control (see Chapter 2). Giving up means abandoning the goal in a passive way. Exercising fate control, which may involve attempts to destroy or severely punish the target, means that the goal is abandoned in a much more vengeful way. Neither choice leaves the actor any closer to its objectives.

Hence, the target's attitude is a particularly significant part of exercising power. In the contemporary world the target's reactions to attempts at control are becoming a more prominent part of the power game because more and more entities are organizing for international activities and are refusing to accept restrictions on their behavior.

Under these circumstances, actors must do several things if they are to influence the behavior of others. The first is to moderate their demands. Extreme demands are usually perceived as threatening the target's autonomy. More moderate demands leave the target with the feeling that it may retain control of its ability to choose for itself. The second is to convince the target that the actor's requests are legitimate. To the degree that this is possible, a sense of obligation is created within the target. A third is to ensure that the target benefits from compliance. This may be done through some sort of economic or political payment, or bribe. Or it may be done through a reciprocal arrangement wherein the actor agrees to behave according to the target's preferences in one arena in exchange for the target's cooperation in another. Whatever course is chosen, one thing has become clear: the simple and brutal application of force as a means of getting one's way has less and less value as time passes.

ACTORS AND ALLIANCES

Chapter 2 noted that international relations is no longer the exclusive province of the state. Many new actors have emerged. The basic characteristics that make an entity an international actor are an ability to set its own goals and to make its own policy, the conduct of business (of whatever type) across international borders, and the refusal to recognize any organization as possessing the authority to overrule its policy preferences. In today's global system an array of diverse entities now plays the role of actors. These include international organizations, multinational corporations, nationalist, terrorist, religious, and criminal groups, international financial organizations, and resource cartels. These actors come from and represent exceptionally disparate cultural backgrounds. They often have very different views of such elements as morality, the proper behavior that should be displayed when conducting foreign policy, and the appropriate goals and ways of acting when pursuing those goals.

The multifaceted nature of the actors in the contemporary world, together with the problems of identifying exactly which entities are responsible for the problems one confronts, has rendered the exercise of power far more complex than it was in earlier eras when the state dominated the international scene. When territorially based actors were the primary source of concern, it was far simpler to determine what targets to focus on. Today it is not nearly as easy. We might take as examples the comments made in earlier chapters about the difficulties in locating terrorist groups and controlling multinational corporations.

A further complication is the changing nature of the alliances that actors form with one another. In the past, international alliances involved formal arrangements between states that were designed to augment their territorial security. The emergence of new actors means that alliances have taken on new characteristics. They now tend to be more informal, and they often include non-state actors as members. Today, states ally themselves with such non-state entities as terrorist organizations, multinational corporations, and resource cartels as they pursue their international designs. When this happens, the non-state actor may obtain considerable advantages over similar non-state actors that are unable to form such associations. Examples include the benefits that accrue to corporations backed by state subsidies and protected by trade barriers, and terrorist organizations that are shielded from reprisals. States also gain in that in some cases they are able to improve the positions of key segments of their economies in an increasingly competitive international environment and to harass their antagonists without running the full risks associated with armed encounters. If the events of the past decade provide any indication of the future, we can expect alignments of this sort to play an ever-greater role in world politics.

THE END OF DETERRENCE

It was pointed out in Chapter 5 that the concept of deterrence emerged as the centerpiece of superpower military security arrangements in the years after World War II. Prior to that time, deterrence did not enjoy the level of conceptual clarity and acceptance that it acquired in those years. It also was stated that deterrence may be achieved either through denial or through punishment. In either case, it is essential that the actor communicate clearly and precisely with the target, that the actor have the capacity to carry out whatever threats it makes, that the consequences for the target be very severe, and that the actor have a high degree of credibility.

In a nuclear world populated by two conservative and essentially status-quo-oriented superpowers, deterrence could appear to work quite effectively. Both superpowers were able to focus their attention and communications on a clear-cut rival, both valued survival more than territorial or other gains at one another's expense, both realized how horribly destructive nuclear weapons could be, and neither envisioned nuclear weapons as devices that could be used in a compellent way to gain an advantage over a rival. All of this meant that the primary antagonists in the deterrence game would be wary of threatening each other's interests, whether directly by menacing the rival's home territory or indirectly by challenging one of its opponent's allies too boldly. As a result, deterrence appeared to function well during the cold war years, and many came to see it as a basic element in a major power's security policy framework.

Many of the conditions necessary for effective deterrence do not appear to be in place any longer. Issues have become prominent that are not well suited to deterrence. Economic, cultural, and nationalist problems do not fit the deterrence mold. Neither do the activities of such actors as multinational corporations and international terrorist groups. The excessively threatening posture that deterrence demands an actor take is counterproductive when used with corporations, and it is very hard to pinpoint and punish international terrorists. Thus, for some issues and actors, deterrence is irrelevant, and to the extent that they play an important role in world politics, deterrence will be relegated to conceptual obscurity.

Deterrence has even become more problematic in the military arena. It is unlikely that dominant military actors will be able in the future to protect far-flung interests either through threats to punish or promises to deny. An important part of this ability always revolved around the antagonist's fear that unacceptable moves might escalate into all-out nuclear war. In addition, the credibility of deterrence for protecting these types of interests always seemed to rest with the belief that nuclear powers might be prepared to use their nuclear weapons against one another. There has always been a suspicion, however, that nuclear powers would be hesitant to use their vast capabilities against smaller opponents. In other words, if Goliath fought Goliath, nuclear weapons might be used, but if Goliath fought David, no nuclear weapons would be used.

With the end of the cold war, Goliath/Goliath confrontations have become very unlikely. Hence, an important part of the credibility needed for deterrence as it applied to something besides one's own home territory has been lost. The end result is that deterrence may continue to have applicability in the limited sense that actors with substantial military capabilities, especially nuclear, can frighten others into respecting their territorial integrity. It is unlikely, however, that deterrence will function in any other military sense or in any other issue areas.

ECONOMIC DEFENSE

Perhaps it is fitting that the final observations in this book should relate to economic defense, for this is the power-related issue that more than any other may be a subject of controversy over the next decade. As was stated in Chapter

5, economic defense originated in the state's attempts to guarantee self-sufficiency and to promote internal economic development by protecting domestic industries from international competition. With the rise of interdependence, where the acceptance of mutual reliance replaces the attachment to autarky and where economic efficiency supposedly determines who produces what, economic defense should be a concept on its way out.

Such, however, has hardly been the case. Instead of eliminating the desire to defend, interdependence has in many ways magnified it. The basic reason is that freer commercial exchanges between differing societies almost always result in discomfort for someone. When actors engage in high levels of trade and investment with one another, competition intensifies. Those who are not as capable or who do not enjoy the advantages that may be derived from alliances with corporate and governmental actors are bound to suffer. Such suffering frequently leads to losses in profits and in employment in key industries and to calls for governmental policies designed to forestall these problems. To put it differently, international practices built on a free trade and investment foundation almost inevitably lead to problems for weaker and less advantaged corporate actors and for the workers associated with them. If these difficulties manifest themselves in large employment losses and in the bankruptcy or near bankruptcy of well-established domestic actors, as they sometimes do, then pressures for economic defense are bound to arise.

In other words, interdependence often leads to political pressures on governments from corporate actors and labor unions to create barriers designed to slow or reverse the consequences that flow from increased international commercial transactions. Pressures of this sort have long been a part of the post–World War II European climate. They have also been at work in the United States, but in the past they were in part overshadowed by the drama associated with the cold war. The end of the cold war means greater prominence for this issue.

Hence, we can expect economic defense measures to become a focal point for political debate both within and between international actors. The advocates of defense may be expected to maintain that it is necessary if one is to avoid significant losses in income, investment, employment, and local political control to foreign interests. The opponents of defense most probably will point to the loss in efficiency and to the high costs that usually accompany defense. Each argument is correct, at least in part. As was observed in Chapter 5, additional factors that must be included in any assessment of economic defense are the degree to which one's opponent can simply alter its tactics and the extent to which one's restrictions are regarded as evenhanded and fair. The first is commonly found and tends to undermine defense. The second may lead to animosity and to the sort of retaliation that can work to the detriment of all those involved in the dispute. When these considerations are included, the economic defense formula becomes very complex and one must move carefully to avoid incurring damage that exceeds the benefits gained.

In conclusion, this book has examined the role of power in a changing international environment. Change is common in all political activities. The years since World War II, however, have witnessed very significant alterations in the international arena. During the last decade events have moved with even more exceptional speed. We may now expect that a process of settling down will begin and that a new pattern of international interactions will develop. One characteristic that is certain to be prominent in that pattern will be the give-and-take among international actors and their attempts at influence as they seek to control the behavior of those that affect the things they hold dear. Recent years show that specific actors, issues, and patterns of influence are ephemeral, but that power is eternal.

Index